CUSTOMER SERVICE

S/NVQ

Allan Woods

Lesley Hebron

Sally Bradley

Candidate Handbook

Heinemann Educational Publishers,
Halley Court, Jordan Hill, Oxford OX2 8EJ
A division of Reed Educational & Professional Publishing Ltd

Heinemann is a registered trademark of Reed Educational & Professional Publishing
Limited

OXFORD MELBOURNE AUCKLAND JOHANNESBURG BLANTYRE GABORONE
IBADAN PORTSMOUTH NH (USA) CHICAGO

First published 2001
2005 2004
10 9 8 7 6 5 4 3 2

A catalogue record for this book is available from the British Library on request.

ISBN 0 435 45227 4

Typeset by ⊼ Tek-Art, Croydon, Surrey

Printed and bound in Great Britain by Scotprint, East Lothian

Acknowledgements

The authors and publisher would like to thank the following individuals and
organisations for permission to reproduce photographs and other copyright
material:

ACE Photo Agency/Alexis Sofianopoulos page 219; Corbis page 134;
Haddon Davies pages 30, 75, 176, 271; Sally & Richard Greenhill pages 189, 287;
The Photographers Library page 101; Pictor International pages 329, 353;
Thomas Cook page 7; Tropical Places page 89.

Tel: 01865 888058 www.heinemann.co.uk

Contents

Introduction

Knowing how to deliver high standards of customer service is a major challenge facing all organisations, whether in the private, public or voluntary sectors. Customers are much more demanding than they were even five years ago; they are less likely to tolerate poor service and more likely to take their custom elsewhere if they get poor service. Research by the Institute of Customer Service indicates that this trend will continue.

Successful organisations in the future will be those which build and sustain a reputation for excellent service. A key element of success will be the competence of those people employed in customer-facing roles within organisations, **customer service professionals.** There will be a steady increase in the demand from employers for customer service professionals with the right mix of skills and the ability to deliver customer service to the right standards. As a result, their status and profile will continue to rise.

The National Occupational Standards in Customer Service at Level 3 are detailed statements of what individuals must be able to do to deliver customer service effectively at that level. They have been written by the Institute in response to what employers have told us they need from customer-facing staff. The Standards are designed to challenge individuals to raise their customer service performance by thinking reflectively about **what** they do to deliver customer service and, just as important, **how** they do it.

If you can demonstrate that you can work to these Standards you can obtain a Scottish or National Vocational Qualification in Customer Service at Level 3. Over 75,000 people have already achieved one of these qualifications, placing them among the most highly used vocational qualifications in the UK.

This Handbook has been written by three people who are themselves customer service professionals and who played a significant role in helping the Institute of Customer Service write the Standards. The Handbook is designed to help you work with the Standards and give you support and guidance in preparing for assessment for the SVQ or NVQ.

Delivering customer service to a high standard is important and challenging work. But it is also very satisfying and can be lots of fun! Good luck with your journey towards becoming a customer service professional.

David Parsons
Chief Executive, Institute of Customer Service

The **Institute of Customer Service** is the professional body for people working in customer service and also the National Training Organisation for Customer Service. Individuals working towards or holding an SVQ or NVQ in Customer Service can join the Institute at different levels of membership.

2 Castle Court
St. Peter's Street
COLCHESTER
Essex
CO1 1EW

Telephone: 01206 571716
Fax: 01206 546688
Email: *enquiries@instcustserv.com*
Web: *www.ics-nto.com*

Unit CL 1

Organise, deliver and maintain reliable customer service

Achieving this unit will show you are able not only to give great customer service on a day-to-day basis but also that you consistently look to maintain and improve the service you give. The unit includes what you need to do to make sure something is done about the comments customers make to you. You need to show you use this customer feedback to improve customer service, not just for today but for tomorrow as well.

Maintaining the service you give will also involve you keeping records relating to customer service information. You will need to do this both to give information to customers and to record information they give to you. The recording systems you use should be whichever system your organisation uses, and these can be manually based, computer based or electronically based. You do not have to be a manager or a supervisor to achieve this unit but you are expected to show you take responsibility for the resources and systems you use which support the service you give.

You will need to show you can organise, deliver and maintain reliable customer service with a variety of customers over a period of time, including:

• easy-going and demanding customers

• customers who are familiar with your products or services as well as those who are not.

Customers can be internal or external to your organisation or a combination of the two.

You must also show you meet the requirements of this unit in both busy and quiet periods and when systems, people or resources have let you down. The elements for this unit are:

1.1 Plan and organise the delivery of reliable customer service.
1.2 Review and maintain customer service delivery.
1.3 Use recording systems to maintain reliable customer service.

Getting started

You are one of many thousands of people working in a rich variety of customer service environments. You may work in a restaurant or at an airport or perhaps you are a care worker or a bus driver. What about meter readers, shop workers and doctors' receptionists? Are you working in a call centre, a bank, the local library or in web design?

You may consider customer service to be the prime function of your role. Alternatively, you may see customer service as taking second place to the key purpose of your job but, nevertheless, you recognise the importance of providing great customer service.

Whoever and wherever you are, what you have in common with all the other people reading this book is that you have *customers*.

What you will need to consider (as for all the units in this book) when working through this unit is how what you are learning relates to your own customer service environment and the types of customers you deal with. You will also need to remember what your colleagues and your organisation expect from you and what you expect from them.

Keep these three points in mind

1 'What am I required to demonstrate?'

2 'What am I required to know and understand?'

3 'How do I relate this to what I do and the way in which I do it?'

The key word in this unit is *reliable*.

Think it over

Picture yourself in a situation where you are buying something from somebody else – perhaps your daily newspaper or the weekly food shop or perhaps a ticket for the cinema.

You are the customer and you want to be dealt with in a *reliable* manner.

• But, what does *reliable* mean to you?

• What do you expect from the person serving you in terms of reliability?

• What about the shop or the cinema – the organisation itself – what do you expect from them in terms of reliability?

What is *reliable* customer service?

The following are some thoughts about what the word reliable could mean to different people:

✓ being dependable

✓ being trustworthy

This customer buys her newspaper from the same newsagent every day. In what way is this newsagent delivering *reliable* customer service?

✓ being professional
✓ keeping promises
✓ doing things on time
✓ being efficient
✓ doing what is expected (although it's nice to be surprised with customer service that is even better or different from what is expected!).

Can you add to this list?

Now write down your *own* definition:

Reliable customer service is . . . .

Element CL1.1 Plan and organise the delivery of reliable customer service

- How to plan and prepare.
- How to organise the resources available to you.
- The products and services of your organisation that are relevant to your role.
- Your customers' rights and the specific legislation and regulations that affect your customer service role.
- How to cope with the unexpected.

How to plan and prepare

The amount of planning and preparation you need to do to deal with customers effectively and efficiently will vary according to the nature of the service you are providing and your role within your organisation's structure. Day-to-day customer service, where you are dealing with customers on a routine basis, may not involve you with much formal preparatory or planning work.

However, if you are involved with a customer service project that involves you working with many different people, having access to resources or preparing for contingencies or the unexpected, you may need to use planning techniques to assist you.

Let's look first at some key points to consider when planning and preparing for both routine work – i.e. *informal planning* – as well as more detailed customer service projects – *formal planning*.

How planning helps you to use your time effectively

Most people value their time immensely and resent it when someone or something 'steals' their time. But in order to use your time effectively, you must first know what it is you should be focusing on. Many people work very hard all day doing unimportant tasks they enjoy doing but that do not actually contribute to the quality of their work or to what they are supposed to be achieving. You are more likely to be effective and efficient if you enjoy your work than if you loathe it. But make sure you are enjoying doing things that actually help you provide great customer service!

Keys to good practice

Working out your priorities

✓ Break up everything you do into categories:

- urgent and important – must be done now
- important – must be done soon
- urgent but unimportant – must be done eventually
- neither urgent nor important – can wait.

✓ Estimate how much time you spend on each category on a daily basis.

✓ Look closely at how much time you are spending on each category – is everything you do urgent and important? If so, do you have enough time to do them all?

✓ Are you spending too much time doing things that are not urgent and not important?

✓ Be flexible – learn to fit things in!

✓ Use the four 'D' system:

- *dump* anything that does not need to be done
- *delay* what you cannot dump
- *designate* a time for what you cannot delay.

And then **do it!**

Once you have worked out your priorities, the next stage is to learn how to plan and prepare to achieve the results you and your organisation require. Planning is the process by which you work out what you want to achieve and then think through the who, what, why, where, when and how of achieving that goal in the most effective and efficient way possible.

If you plan well, you can ensure you concentrate only on those tasks that will enable you to achieve your aims in the most effective way possible and without being distracted by other things.

Organisational skills

How well organised are you?

Active knowledge

Answer yes or no to the following questions:

1 I always know who to refer to if I cannot help the customer.
2 My work area is tidy and gives the correct impression to customers and/or colleagues.

3 I find information quickly and easily, such as literature about my organisation's products and services.

4 My work is accurate.

5 I know what I should have achieved by the end of the day.

6 Any equipment I use is in good working order.

7 I create a good first impression with customers.

8 I know what I need to achieve by the end of the year.

9 People I work with ask me for help.

10 I make it easy for the customer.

Now, find someone whom you trust to give you open and honest feedback – perhaps a colleague, a friend or a customer who knows you well. Ask him or her to complete the same checklist about you.

Keys to good practice

How to be well organised

✓ A regular check of any equipment you use will help to ensure everything is in good working order by the time you come to deal with customers.

✓ Check any signage or instructions on display to customers are accurate.

✓ A tidy working environment means you will know where to lay your hands on information quickly.

✓ Keep any stocks of your organisation's literature up to date and in adequate supply.

✓ Know whom to refer to for help when you are unable to help yourself.

✓ When learning to be well organised, try reviewing your actions at the end of each day – assess where anything went wrong and where mistakes were made.

✓ One-seventh of your life is spent on Monday! Being organised wherever possible a day ahead of time will help to stop that Monday morning feeling happening on Tuesday, Wednesday . . .

A tidy working environment shows you are well organised

Case study

Jilly works in the customer service department of a stationery store. One day, a regular customer who does a lot of business with her organisation phoned to chase up an order for ring binders he had given to Jilly some time ago. Jilly looked on her screen and found no record, but her customer insisted the order was placed and that it was her he spoke to.

1 What should be Jilly's first priority?
2 What steps might Jilly then take?
3 What could the consequences be if the steps you identify that Jilly should take still leave the customer dissatisfied?

Checking equipment

We mentioned earlier that having your equipment in good working order will help you to maintain reliable customer service. As part of your planning to 'be reliable', you may find it useful to play a part in the maintenance of the equipment you deal with. Indeed, not doing so may actually pose a potential safety risk, so take some responsibility for your equipment. It will be to everyone's advantage you do so. However, a word of warning! Getting it fixed does not mean *you* should reach for the screwdriver – find out your organisation's procedures for repairing equipment.

There are all sorts of equipment you might use, from the phone to a computer system, to the till or the credit card sales machine, to kitchen equipment or a photocopier.

Active knowledge

Make a list of the different types of equipment you deal with.

• How often do you check it is working *before* you start to deal with customers?

• What is the effect on customer service if it breaks down?

• How do you go about reporting equipment faults?

• How do you deal with customers when it is not possible to 'fix' equipment on the spot?

Your organisation's procedures for maintaining equipment

Your organisation has a responsibility for ensuring the proper maintenance and upkeep of equipment. On 5 December 1998, the Provision and Use of Equipment Regulations 1998 came into force. These regulations require that equipment for use at work is:

• suitable for the intended use

• safe for use, maintained in a safe condition and, in certain circumstances, inspected to ensure this remains the case

• used only by people who have received adequate information, instruction and training

• accompanied by suitable safety measures (e.g. protective devices, markings, warnings, etc.).

Generally, any equipment used by an employee at work is covered (e.g. knives, ladders, photocopiers, motor vehicles, etc.). The regulations do not apply to equipment used by the public (e.g. compressed air equipment on a garage forecourt).

Active knowledge

Check a piece of equipment you use regularly at work. Were you satisfied all the points in the Provision and Use of Equipment Regulations 1998 had been (and are being) followed for this piece of equipment?

Informal planning

On how many occasions have *you* been a customer and have been kept waiting because someone had not put enough thought into what he or she needed to do by way of preparation and planning before dealing with you? Frustrating, isn't it!

Much of what you need to do to plan and prepare everything you might need to deal with your customers efficiently and effectively

Dealing with customers efficiently requires planning

could be compared with getting ready to go on holiday. Unless you are a very impulsive person, most people would take the time to plan what they need to do (perhaps by using a tick-list or a 'to-do' list). Using one of these tools simply ensures you have thought about every eventuality before embarking on your holiday. It is just the same when you are dealing with customers.

To-do lists

To-do lists are lists of tasks you need to do to achieve your goals. For instance, you might have goals relating to specific targets set to improve customer service, or you might have a list of things to do that may simply be related to the effective administration of your day. You should prioritise your to-do list in order of importance of the tasks/things you need to do to ensure you do not waste time doing unimportant and non-urgent things.

To-do lists are a very simple informal planning tool you can quickly put together yourself. They are an extremely effective way of organising yourself efficiently to motivate yourself towards providing reliable customer service.

Active knowledge

Refer back to your definition of *reliable*. Now write down a to-do list of what you need to do at the start of each day in order to plan and organise the delivery of reliable customer service.

It's a good idea to prepare to-do lists at a time that suits *you*. You may care to do one on a daily basis – either at the beginning of each day or at the end of the day in readiness for tomorrow. These will include things for you to do that are non-routine. However, it is also likely you have drawn up a list of things to do that will help you give a reliable service on a consistent basis and that do not change very much from day to day.

If you have not used to-do lists before, try them – they are one of the key ways to being really efficient and reliable. Figure 1.1 is a specimen to-do list Jilly might have written. As you can see, Jilly has also used her to-do list to help with her personal life. Getting a balance between what you do at work and what you do socially or at home helps to ensure a more well rounded approach to life. You are likely to perform better at work if you are able to do this, and be happier at home too.

To do

✓ Send letter of apology to customer re lost ring binders.

✓ Find out why order was not placed on system.

✓ Phone customer on Thursday to check binders have arrived.

✓ Put warning message on computer to signal he has complained.

✓ Book date in diary with Mahmood for appraisal.

✓ Review new stationery items due out at the end of the month.

✓ Check with Sue date for Christmas night out.

✓ Get birthday card for Gran.

Figure 1.1 An example of a to-do list

Formal planning

What about more complex customer service projects – perhaps those that involve you taking responsibility for the resources and systems available to you? In these instances, a more formal approach will help with planning and preparation.

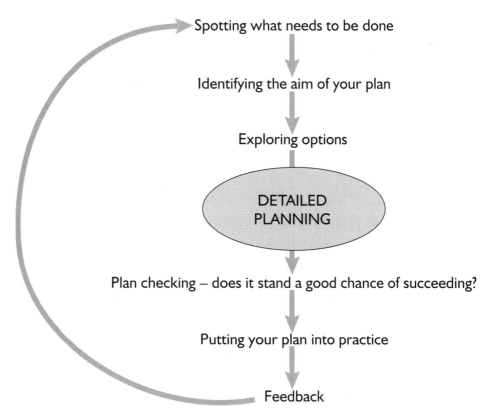

Figure 1.2 The planning cycle

The planning cycle

Planning is best thought of as a circular journey – it is not enough to identify your aims without also putting in place various 'stops' along the way to check what you are doing is right (see Figure 1.2).

Case study

So, what might a formal plan look like? Take a look at the one shown in Figure 1.3 that was prepared by Pam, who has been asked to arrange a small stand in the shop in which she works to publicise local produce in the run-up to Christmas. This plan covers Pam's thoughts when organising what needed to be done.

Outcome

On 13 December Pam had received all the goods from the local suppliers and set about putting up the stand. Unfortunately, when she found it, it was in a rather tatty state and it took a lot of time to make it look presentable. Customers didn't seem to take much notice of it although she knew the local produce on display usually sold well in the run-up to Christmas. At times, there was a member of staff on the stall but, at other times when the shop was busy, staff had to open the second till, leaving the stand unmanned. Some customers complained there was either no one on the stand to help or that there was someone on the stand but not enough tills open. Two customers complained they had not been advised there were nuts in some of the chocolates they had purchased from the stand.

Looking at the outcome of Pam's attempt at running this publicity stand, how effective was her planning?

- Did Pam involve anyone else to generate ideas?
- Did Pam establish the aim of having a publicity stand in the shop?
- Pam identified some things to sort out. What did she miss out?
- Why did customers complain?

To be done	Help needed	Action required	Notes
Identify dates		Speak with Neil	14 Dec-24 Dec
Decide where in shop stand should be	Ask Neil to get everyone to help me put stand up that was used last year	Speak with Neil	Near the tills Put up on 13 Dec
Advertise event		Produce leaflets and posters	Have on display during first two weeks of Dec
Identify local produce and suppliers		Speak to our existing suppliers	
Decide on quantity needed	Speak to others about number of customers coming in last year		
Budget		Speak with Neil	

Figure 1.3 Pam's plan for the run-up to Christmas

How to organise the resources available to you

What Pam needed to do was *organise the resources* available to her. Adopting the following points would have helped her stand be a success.

Keys to good practice

Organising resources

To make your plans effective, follow these points:

✓ Use KISS – **K**eep **I**t **S**hort and **S**imple.

✓ Involve other people affected by your plans to gain their support.

✓ Explain why the plan is needed.

✓ Emphasise the benefits to everyone involved, stressing how customers, colleagues and your organisation will benefit.

✓ Ensure the required resources are available and will remain so.

✓ Try not to reinvent the wheel!

✓ Build in milestones – dates – to review progress.

✓ Keep your plan flexible to allow you to reschedule priorities or tasks in the light of the unexpected happening.

✓ Develop a contingency plan so that problems or changes do not impact on the achievement of your aims.

✓ Take corrective action as a result of monitoring and reviewing the progress of your plan.

Managing time as a resource

One of the key resources available to you is *time*. We have already discussed how working out your priorities, effective planning and using a to-do list could help you to become more organised. Clearly, all this will also save you time. Figure 1.4 shows some more ways in which you can make the best use of your time.

Building on what you have learnt in this element, try the following activity to help you understand how well you manage your time.

Active knowledge

Think back over the last day you were at work. Analyse what you did and break the tasks down into things that were:

- urgent and important
- important
- urgent but unimportant
- neither urgent nor important.

Have you been left with things you have not achieved but are, nevertheless, important and urgent? Was this because you spent too much time doing things you enjoy doing but which were not particularly important to your customer service role?

Make a note in whatever system you use (electronic or paper) of all your appointments – don't be late!

Keep a daily to-do list (preferably prioritised)

Improve your work environment – give yourself space to work, remove any clutter and cut down on unwanted noise wherever possible

Don't be a paper shuffler – action paper: put it in pending, file it or throw it away!

Managing Time

Allow yourself more time to do things you are not too familiar with

Organise any filing system(s) you have

Sort out your paperwork

Try to allow for emergencies

Set goals and plans that will lead to your success

Control distractions – unwanted visitors, handling phone calls efficiently, etc.

Use travelling time effectively

Figure 1.4 Managing time

Save time and energy by prioritising your work

Remember

Only you can answer these questions – save yourself time and energy by prioritising your actions – everyone will benefit!

Did you know?

Peter Drucker, a management writer, said a person was efficient if he or she did the task right, but only became effective if he or she did the right task!

Similarly, the Pareto Principle states that 80% of a job is completed in 20% of the time. If you are *not* organised, the Pareto Principle states that 80% of the effort tends to achieve just 20% of the results.

By managing resources in an effective manner, by being organised and by planning things out, you can reverse this to 20% of your effort achieving 80% of the results.

Managing other resources

We have looked at organising your time and equipment, but there are other resources you may be involved with (i.e. people and budgets).

Remember

You do not have to be a 'manager' of these resources in the traditional sense, but you may have responsibility for them.

Taking responsibility for people

For the purposes of achieving Unit 1 and the S/NVQ Customer Service as a whole, you need to know the basic people skills involved in working with others. You will read more about this as you work your way through this book. In the mean time, the following are some ideas to start you thinking about taking responsibility for other people when providing reliable customer service.

Above all, *be a customer service role model* (see page 260) to others through the way you deal with customers and their links to your organisation's needs and the needs of the people you work with. (For more details on working with other people, see Unit 3.)

Remember

You will need to ensure you get the most from everything and everybody you are responsible for in order to deliver and maintain reliable customer service.

The products and services of your organisation that are relevant to your role

- How many products or services does your organisation offer its customers?
- Are they suitable for every customer?
- How will you know which customer a particular product or service is designed for?
- What are the features of each product or service?
- What are their benefits?
- How will customers find out about your organisation's products and services?

How will *you* find out about your organisation's products and services?

You can be sure that, as fast as you learn about what your organisation has to offer its customers, there will be new products or services that become available, as well as some that are withdrawn or are amended. It is vital to the delivery of a reliable customer service that you are not telling your customers about out-of-date products and services.

There are many reasons why you need to keep yourself properly informed. Not only is it important for your organisation's reputation but also there are legal and safety reasons. Look at the following case study.

Case study

Sheena visited her travel agent to book a holiday for herself and her elderly mother. The holiday arrangements were discussed to her satisfaction and the travel agent asked her about insurance cover. The travel agent's own insurance was discussed, together with the amount of the premium. The discussion took into account destination and duration but did not disclose that the premium would be doubled on account of the age of Sheena's mother. Forms were signed to take the premium by direct debit from Sheena's bank account.

Is there cause for concern? Explain your reasons.

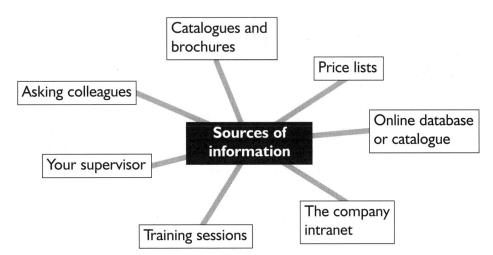

Figure 1.5 How to find out about your organisation's products and services

You can find out about your organisation's products and services from a number of places (see Figure 1.5). If you are in any doubt about the accuracy or validity of the information you are giving a customer, it is much better to check first and then get back to the customer rather than giving misleading information.

Keys to good practice

✓ Make sure you know where to find information about products and services and about their features and benefits, or whom to go to for help when necessary.

✓ Make sure you have this information readily available or easily accessible.

✓ Take the time to check regularly that the information you have has not been changed.

✓ Take any action necessary to alert others you are responsible for about any changes to products and services or their features and benefits.

✓ Always look for ways to improve your knowledge of products and services.

Active knowledge

Write down the ways you can find out about your own organisation's products and services. Give the advantages of each.

Make sure the information you give customers is 100% accurate

Your customers' rights and the specific legislation and regulations that affect your customer service role

This section discusses the major pieces of legislation that *might* affect your customer service role. It is possible you work in an area that might be covered by other regulations or legislation not included here. You are therefore advised to take steps to identify any other areas that are specifically concerned with your work role.

Clearly, everyone has the right to be treated fairly and courteously and to be given correct information – this is just basic common-sense and a best practice to stick to when dealing with other people. After all, it is probably the very least you would expect when you are a customer.

Unfortunately, it is not always the case that people treat each other in a proper manner, and so there is legislation in place aimed at preventing people being treated unfairly and discourteously.

Equal opportunities legislation aims to prevent people being discriminated against on the grounds of their:

- race, ethnic origin, nationality and skin colour
- gender or sexual orientation
- disability, sensory impairment or learning difficulty
- physical characteristics
- age
- personal beliefs.

Health and safety legislation covers things like dealing with equipment and the health and safety responsibilities you and your organisation have to each other.

Legislation that covers transactions involving goods and services where you *supply information* is dealt with in Element 1.3. There you will learn about copyright and the Data Protection Act. Element 1.3 also covers *consumer legislation*, such as the Sale of Goods Act and the Trades Description Act. In this element we will look at equal opportunities and health and safety legislation.

The Disability Discrimination Act 1995

Did you know there are more than 6.2 million disabled adults in the UK? This Act seeks to end discrimination against people with disabilities. It sets out the rights of disabled people in relation to:

- employment
- access to goods and services
- buying or renting land or property.

The Act has been described as the 'most significant piece of consumer legislation to hit Britain in 50 years' and became law on 1 October 1999. It is likely it will affect you no matter where you work.

The Act:

- makes it unlawful for service providers to refuse to offer a service they offer other people to anyone with a disability

- makes it unlawful to offer disabled people a lower standard of service than anyone else

- requires service providers to make 'reasonable adjustments' to ensure people with disabilities can use or access a service. This does not include installing ramps, etc., although this will be necessary when the next section of the Act becomes law in 2004.

'Service providers' is simply a catch-all term to encompass organisations involved with providing goods and services. The Act defines disability as 'a physical or mental impairment which has a substantial and long-term adverse effect on a person's ability to carry out normal day-to-day activities'.

Research indicates that people tend to focus too much on making physical adjustments and expensive adaptations to premises when what is really required is a change of attitude. Since 95% of disabled people are not wheelchair users, it would be of so much help to the disabled community if customer service people would simply have the confidence to give them the same treatment and level of service (providing it is good!) as they would to any non-disabled customer.

Giving people with disabilities excellent service can often mean *not* making assumptions about them such as 'they won't want what I sell' or 'they will want me to choose for them'.

Helping visually impaired people

Raising your voice will not make it any easier for a visually impaired person to understand you. So speak in your usual voice. If you are offering to help someone walk around, say, a shop, ask the person if he or she would like to take your arm; this enables the person to follow where you are going.

Do you know in what format your organisation sends out information – is it available in large print, Braille, audiocassette, computer disk and e-mail for those with 'talking' computers? What can you do to help?

Remember that colour and typeface can make a big difference as to whether a poster or notice can be read by a partially sighted person. Black on yellow works best.

Helping people who are wheelchair users

Always treat someone in a wheelchair as having the same personal space as anyone else – respect it! Don't talk down to someone who is in a wheelchair as if he or she were a child. If your customer is in a wheelchair and is accompanied by someone, don't talk to the companion as if your customer isn't there.

Helping people with a hearing or speech impairment

When talking to a hearing impaired person who lip-reads, make sure your face is well lit and don't try to exaggerate your lip movements; this makes it harder to lip-read.

When listening to someone with a speech impediment, don't try to make out every word. If you wait until the end of the sentence, the meaning will often become clear.

Don't shout at people just because they have a speech impediment – they can usually hear perfectly well.

As a general rule of thumb, never assume anything – ask if and how you might help. Some people may decline your offer, but the next might be delighted to receive assistance.

Case study

Mrs Simpson is an elderly lady who loves shopping in the ground-floor food hall of her local store. Because she is unsteady on her feet at times, she uses a walking stick and avoids using stairs and escalators.

One day, Mrs Simpson left her walking stick behind in the store. When she returned to collect it, Trudy, the sales assistant, told her it had been taken upstairs to the customer services help-point. Trudy offered to accompany Mrs Simpson upstairs in the lift and duly escorted her to the help-point, which was quite busy when they got there. Trudy said her goodbyes to Mrs Simpson and left her there in the queue.

When Mrs Simpson finally got to the front of the queue she was told that the staff at the help-point, in realising the lost property was a walking stick, had sent it back downstairs to avoid the owner having to come up to the first floor. Mrs Simpson understood their motives and made her way alone back to the lift. After waiting for what seemed ages for the lift to arrive, she decided to try the stairs as she was starting to feel uncomfortable from standing up for too long. She made her way to the stairs, started to go down unsteadily, slipped and fell, breaking her arm badly.

When Trudy heard what had happened, she was both horrified and upset and cried: 'But I thought I did the right thing.'

1 What went wrong?
2 What should Trudy have done differently?
3 How could the help-point staff have assisted?
4 How might Mrs Simpson's family react?
5 What might be the consequences for the store?

The Human Rights Act 1998

This Act introduced the European Convention on Human Rights into British law in the autumn of 2000. This means that people can pursue cases through the British courts if they believe their rights have been violated, rather than going through the European Court of Human Rights.

The Act deals mainly with the individual's rights in relation to the *state*. So, the Act applies to public sector bodies (e.g. government departments, the NHS and the police). It also applies to organisations that carry out a public role, such as the utilities and Railtrack.

The Act makes it unlawful for any 'public authority' to act in such a way that it is 'incompatible' with a right under the Convention. There is currently a degree of uncertainty about the impact of the Human Rights Act. It is likely that British society will never be the same again as individuals learn how to challenge the state in their own courts. The Act includes people's fundamental rights, such as to life, and their procedural rights, such as to have a fair trial.

There are three areas that might have a significant impact on customer service. These are people's rights to:

- privacy in relation to their private and family life, their home and their correspondence
- freedom of conscience. This means people have the right to freedom of thought, conscience and religion and beliefs
- freedom of expression. This includes the freedom to hold opinions.

Some experts are currently arguing it would be unlawful to ask people if they would mind wearing a uniform or to ask them not to wear jewellery or to tie long hair back. This is because it takes away the individual's right to freedom of expression.

At the time of writing, the Act is so new that test cases are currently going through the courts. We recommend you keep an eye on the press to keep up to date with developments.

Sex and race discrimination

Discrimination on the grounds of sex or race is covered by the Sex Discrimination Act 1975 (as amended by the Sex Discrimination Act 1980) and the Race Relations Act 1976 (as amended by the Race Relations [Remedies] Act 1994).

Sex discrimination means being treated unfairly because of your sex or marital status or because you are pregnant. Discrimination also exists where there is a requirement (a rule, policy, practice or procedure) that is the same for everyone, but which has an unfair effect on particular groups.

Racial discrimination occurs when a person is treated less favourably than someone else in a similar situation because of his or her race, colour, nationality or ethnic or racial origin.

The law is there to protect people from being discriminated against because of their race or sex. Think about any possible implications for you and your line of work.

What health and safety law requires

The basis of British health and safety law is the Health and Safety at Work Act 1974. The Act sets out the general duties employers have towards employees and members of the public, and that employees have to themselves and to each other. These duties are qualified in the Act by the principle of 'so far as is reasonably practicable'. In other words, the degree of risk in a particular job or workplace needs to be balanced against the time, trouble, cost and physical difficulty of taking measures to avoid or reduce the risk.

The Act applies to all work premises. Anyone on the premises is covered by and has responsibilities under this Act (i.e. employees, employers and visitors to the premises).

Employers are required 'as far as is reasonably practicable' to ensure the health, safety and welfare at work of their employees (see Figure 1.6). If you work for an organisation that employs five or more people, your organisation is required to prepare a written statement of its general policy, organisation and arrangements for health and safety at work. This policy must be kept up to date and be brought to the attention of employees. You will often find such a policy pinned to noticeboards in the workplace.

Employees are required to take reasonable care of their own health and safety and that of others who may be affected by their activities. It is this point that is of particular importance to you when dealing with customers. You are also expected to co-operate with your employer in meeting the statutory requirements.

Figure 1.6 The employer's responsibilities for the health and safety of employees

For example:

- Do you read any information that is passed to you by your employer on health and safety issues, or do you simply get it off your desk by passing it to the next person?
- Do you make changes to any protective clothing you are required to wear to make it more comfortable?
- Do you take part in any health and safety training or say 'I'm too busy to watch that video'?
- Do you leave chairs or other bits of equipment in awkward places so as to make access by customers difficult?
- Have you placed something over a tear in a carpet to hide it?
- Will customers trip over any electrical cabling?

Active knowledge

- Is your organisation's health and safety policy on display?
- Where is it displayed?
- What guidance or training have you had in health and safety issues?
- How does what you do affect customer service?
- What changes have you made (if any) to what you do to ensure the health and safety of those around you?

Don't forget all the other pieces of legislation that you will read about elsewhere in this book. Whilst it may seem a lot to digest, much of it is common-sense and about treating others as you would wish to be treated yourself.

How to cope with the unexpected

You are organised, you know all about the products and services of your organisation and you feel confident about the way in which you work. But what about coping with the unexpected – with all those irritating things that sometimes get in the way of you doing your job effectively? Some will be a total surprise to you and outside your control, such as when the weather becomes awkward or when there is a newspaper article customers read that affects your work. Other unexpected situations may put you and others at risk (e.g. transport problems, lift and equipment breakdowns, fire, flood, etc.).

However, coping with some unexpected situations can be planned for – i.e. you should know what to do in the event of the unexpected happening. This is called *contingency planning*. Contingency planning involves you knowing and understanding the part you play in your organisation's procedures for dealing with emergency situations. Never get caught out when the fire alarm rings – finding yourself unable to help customers, those you work with and, of course, yourself, reach a place of safety.

Active knowledge

Find out *now* about dealing with emergency situations where you work. What are your responsibilities during these times?

A common situation you may find yourself in is maintaining customer service during periods of staff sickness or during holiday periods. During these times, your customers will not wish to be told you cannot deal with them in your usual efficient manner because Darren is off sick or because three members of your team are enjoying a sunshine break.

Active knowledge

• What plans do you need to make to ensure the service you and your team give customers is not affected?

• How will you cope with additional workloads because there are fewer pairs of hands around?

Draw up a checklist covering all the points you need to consider during times when you are short-staffed.

Figure 1.7 (overleaf) is an example of a contingency checklist that could be used by someone working in an office environment on first notification of sickness. It sets out to ensure customer service is maintained, not to deal with the sick person him or herself. That is another issue entirely!

Active knowledge

Spend some time thinking about your customer service nightmares.

• What crises have you had to cope with?

• What unexpected happenings would fill you with dread if they were to occur?

Make a note of some of the unexpected situations you may or do have to deal with.

Now write down some key actions you will need to take to maintain reliable customer service.

```
CONTINGENCY PLANNING – ABSENT STAFF

Date and time of notification: ..................................................................

Enough people left to maintain reliable customer service? Yes/No

Job positions affected: ........................................................................

Is cover required all day? Yes/No

Is peak-time cover only required? Yes/No

Is the operation of any equipment affected? Yes/No
────────────────────────────────────────────────────────────
List here (or know where to find) contact details for staff who can move
job positions to cover for absent staff or details about casual staff who can
be brought in temporarily



────────────────────────────────────────────────────────────
Contacted by: (you)  ......................  Date/time:  ...............................

Outcome (i.e. able to help or not. If a positive answer, list here when
help will arrive!)



────────────────────────────────────────────────────────────
Advise ABC department of situation.

Monitor progress.
```

Figure 1.7 Contingency planning for absent staff

Consolidation

If you were working with a colleague new to a customer service role,
what would be the four key points you would ensure he or she learns
about in order to maintain reliable customer service?

WHAT YOU NEED TO LEARN

- Methods for ensuring all your customers receive appropriate attention.
- How to use customer feedback.
- How to communicate customer feedback to others.
- How to act upon customer feedback and improve your performance as a result.
- Ways of monitoring your own customer service performance.

Methods for ensuring all your customers receive appropriate attention

Element 1.2 looks at your need to provide a reliable service to customers during times when you are very busy or when other people, resources or systems let you down. You will already have learnt something about this (e.g. dealing with the unexpected) when you worked through Element 1.1. So check your evidence now!

Just how much time *do* I give to each customer?

There can't be many people who haven't found themselves lining up in the shortest queue at the supermarket, post office or bank only to find other customers arriving after them who join different queues that are served faster than the one they are in. Even more frustrating is waiting to be served by someone who is discussing what he or she watched on TV last night with the customer in front of you!

Remember

As an absolute minimum, customers have the right to expect a friendly and efficient service.

Despite various queuing systems, express checkouts, cash-only service points and telephone systems technology, it is inevitable that, sometimes, customers will have to wait for your attention. Even if there is only one customer being served in front of the next one, what do you do if the person you are with wants a lot of your time? Just how do you balance the need to be friendly and efficient with your immediate customer – the person who you are dealing with now – with the needs of the person who is waiting for your attention?

You know customers don't like to wait any more than you do. So you need to find ways of ensuring you make life easier for yourself by not antagonising customers who have to wait by means of balancing out the time you take with each of them.

Strategies for when the customer has to wait for help
Telling the next customer you are ready

- If the system where you work involves you in 'calling' the next person, think about how you are going to signal to that person you are ready to help.

- Don't call out 'next' – this is not a particularly friendly way to start a conversation! Try saying something like 'How can I help?' or 'What can I do for you today?'

- Whatever words you choose to use, they should demonstrate your willingness to help.

Dealing with customers who know you well

- Never act as if you are catching up on lost time with a friend or relative.

- During especially busy periods, don't give your favourite customers or 'the regulars' priority treatment over others. It is tempting to spend too much time with people whom you enjoy serving or even to let them jump the queue! This is likely to upset other customers. During busy periods, simply acknowledge those you know well when you see them, and treat everyone equally.

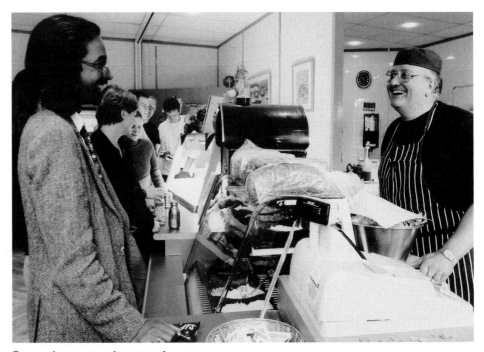

Be enthusiastic despite the queues

Be enthusiastic despite the queues

Your customers have been queuing for a while and you can see some are disgruntled at having to wait – some are checking their watches every few seconds. When they do reach the front of the queue, make sure you greet them with enthusiasm and with a warm smile, however tired you may be feeling. A warm greeting will often disarm even the most annoyed customer who may find it hard to be unpleasant when faced with your positive energy.

You should also do this when dealing with customers on the phone whom you know have been held in a queuing system. You may not be able to see how they have reacted to the wait but they will certainly be able to tell whether or not you are willing to help them – talk to them with a smile on your face!

Apologise for the wait

Recognise the fact that your customer has been delayed and apologise for the wait. Be quick with this acknowledgement without going into unnecessary detail about the cause of the queue – this may bring up issues that are best avoided and may prolong the wait even further. Just say 'Sorry you had to wait. How can I help you?' Then get down to the business of helping your customer.

Call the customer by name

Most customers like to be called by their name so, if you do know a customer's name, use it at the beginning, during and end of your conversation. However, sometimes you may not know the name until you are ready to say goodbye (e.g. from looking at a credit card at the end of a transaction) – so use it then.

Using a customer's name helps to confirm that customer's status as an important person who is valued by you and your organisation.

What is your organisation's policy on using customer names during conversations?

Make the wait worth their while

Waiting in a queue can make people feel anxious. They may be thinking it is better to leave. Was it worth the time spent? Will you be able to help? If you can't help, will they have to wait again for somebody else?

All customers need to feel they made a good decision in using your organisation but those who have to wait need to feel it even more. So, confirm to them they have made a good choice – give them great service.

If you are personally unable to help, make sure you give your customer:

Customer feedback can help organisations to improve service, not just to solve problems

Case study

Kalwant was due to attend a celebratory event in London to mark the end of a long project she had been involved with. Arriving at her local small railway station 10 minutes early, she was sure she had allowed plenty of time to buy a ticket. There was just the one ticket desk open but only one customer in front of her. This customer seemed to be asking lots of questions about a journey he wished to undertake two days later. To her horror, the time quickly passed and she was very aware that, with only two trains per hour, it was vital she caught the next train. Being an honest sort, Kalwant didn't feel she could travel without a ticket and, despite trying to catch the attention of the ticket clerk and also to alert the other customer to her predicament, nothing happened. The train pulled out.

When Kalwant eventually reached the ticket clerk, identified by his name badge as Victor, she expected some sort of apology. What she received was very different.

Victor didn't say anything. He merely sat there waiting for his customer to speak. Kalwant explained what had happened and expressed her dismay that Victor hadn't responded to her frantic waves that she needed to catch the train that was about to leave. Victor simply said he dealt only with the person in front of him, and why didn't she ask the other customer to move away? So, it was Kalwant's fault!

Similar situations occurred when Kalwant used this station again over the next three months. She wrote to the train company to complain and to offer suggestions about what should happen in the future.

1 What feedback do you think Kalwant gave to Victor?
2 Having experienced repeated problems when travelling again, what feedback did Kalwant give when she wrote to the company?
3 What would you have done?
4 What should Victor and his employers learn from this feedback?

This case study illustrates how spontaneous feedback given to a ticket clerk at a railway station was ignored. Let's consider this situation in more detail – and you may have already come up with some of the following points when reflecting on Kalwant's dilemma.

It should come as no surprise that Victor had heard many complaints from customers (given that he works at a small railway station, can see the trains from his desk and is often the only person serving). But he should be more alert to the time of day and recognise that some queries could be dealt with differently.

Victor had failed to:

- recognise the increasing trend in the number of people making similar complaints
- tell his colleagues or his supervisor that people with queries were blocking access to the ticket desk when he was on his own, and that this meant the internal policy about concentrating on the person at the front of the queue and no one else was causing problems for other customers
- balance the time spent with one customer with the needs of others
- respond appropriately to Kalwant's frustration.

If only he had reacted to the feedback he had been consistently receiving, Kalwant may not have had cause to write to the train company.

Of course, not all feedback is negative. It's just that people appear to be more prepared to spend time discussing things that have gone wrong than they are to saying 'thank you'.

Did you know?

Twice as many customers feel like complaining as those who actually register a complaint.

You must make use of the feedback given to you. It is just as critical to make good service even better – to improve it – as it is to make poor service better. By using feedback you should look to change dissatisfied customers into satisfied customers and satisfied customers into very satisfied customers.

'Type' of feedback	To use or not to use
Over time, several comments have been made about the same thing.	Clearly, a number of people are bringing the same thing to your attention. This trend probably means something should be done.
Only a few people have mentioned this	What is the *significance* of this feedback? Is it important? If so, to whom?
Comments about your own behaviour and skills.	If a trend appears or if you are surprised by what you have been told, try asking a trusted colleague, a line manager or a friend for his or her honest opinion. Take action where necessary and always approach feedback given to you as an opportunity to learn and develop.
Comments about something no one has control over.	Are you sure no one has control? What about contingency planning? Would that help you to assist customers when the unexpected happens?
The comments you have heard and read are not true.	Who says they are not true? Check it out!
The comments are unreasonable.	It meant enough to your customer to tell you. What will be the impact of doing nothing?
I am not able to change anything concerning the feedback I have been given.	If a customer is suggesting you make radical changes to a product you are selling or that the terms and conditions of a service you deal with are altered, it may be the decision to do so is not within your power. However, if a number of people are saying the same thing, it is probably best not to keep quiet – you should consider telling someone who can make the decision about the way forward.
Taking notice of the feedback you have been given would cost too much money/involve too many people/take too long.	Is it worth looking for a compromise? How about looking at the possibility of putting into action a part of what is being suggested?

Figure 1.11 To use or not to use customer feedback – a quick guide

Find the best option/solution

- Is it possible to put into effect?
- Is it workable?
- Is it the best for the customer, for the organisation, for colleagues and for you?
- Is it the best for the combination of people concerned?
- Who will benefit and at what cost?

Implement the decision

Taking action

You have now reached the stage where you have decided the feedback you have received is useful and that you will take action on it. In other words, you are converting information into action. As soon as you take action, you are closing the feedback loop and implementing your decision.

In some cases, you will need to gather support for the decision you have made. In others, particularly where your own behavioural skills are concerned, you could take action without reference to others.

Your decision to act on feedback may simply be that you want to tell colleagues about the comments you have received rather than keep quiet. You have decided to do this because you feel the issues raised are of sufficient value to make a positive difference to customer service, if acted upon. You may also have developed a solution, although this might not always be the case.

Alternatively, you may have decided to act upon feedback that relates solely to your own way of working. For instance, customers may have remarked that you don't appear to be able to find the information they want very quickly. You know this is because you work in an untidy environment and cannot find literature easily. You can easily put that right and can act on this on your own, without the need to involve others.

Feedback that relates to organisational procedures will nearly always involve you seeking the support of the people you work with. This is because you may not have the necessary authority to act on your own.

When telling others about feedback make sure you:

- *don't leave out the bad bits* and only talk about the good! – be honest

- *time the giving of your information appropriately* – if the feedback is not urgent and there are no risks involved in not passing on the information immediately, wait for a convenient time. However, this should be within a reasonable timescale as, if you wait too long, things may have been overtaken by events

- *choose the most appropriate method* for advising others. Don't use e-mail to pass on bad news – this can be very impersonal. Decide on which method of communication is most suitable for the feedback you have (i.e. face to face, telephone, meetings, e-mails, newsletters)

- *are ready to respond to questions* others may have about the feedback, and always make sure you are able to say where it has come from

- if you have acted alone, say in improving your own interpersonal skills, remember to *let your supervisor or line manager* (if you have one) *know* you have taken action on feedback given to you

- *find ways of celebrating* the good news with others

- don't forget you also need to consider whether it is appropriate to tell those who have given you the feedback of the action you are taking. If you do not, you run the risk of them thinking nothing has happened and that they have wasted their time and energy. *Keep relevant people informed of progress.*

Ways of monitoring your own customer service performance

Clearly, there is not much point in taking action if you don't then check if what you have done has made a positive difference. This is sometimes called *evaluating* or *monitoring* your actions. If you do not do this you will never know if you have achieved your desired results.

This means actively seeking feedback or using existing processes to enable you to monitor the effectiveness of your actions.

You could consider:

- asking people (customers or colleagues) about the changes you have made and their effects

- devising a questionnaire

- analysing feedback obtained using existing organisational procedures (these may, of course, be the same procedures you originally used to make any changes)

- discussing changes with your line manager or supervisor (if you have one) during review meetings or performance appraisals.

Go back to Figure 1.9 (page 34) to see if any of the other methods listed will help you monitor the effect of your actions.

Case study

Monica works as a receptionist at a doctor's surgery. Last year there was negative feedback concerning the running of the flu clinic for elderly patients, so Monica decided she would change the way things were done for this year. With the agreement of the practice manager and her colleagues, she put in place various changes that she thought would help make things run more smoothly. In order to monitor the effects of these changes, each patient (client) was asked to complete a short form before leaving the clinic. These are the areas Monica decided to cover.

Making an appointment

- Length of time from first contact to appointment date.
- Ease of contacting clinic.
- Availability of information about flu jabs.
- Manner in which calls are dealt with.

Service statistics

- Number of new clients.
- Number of revisits for flu jabs.
- Number of referrals to the clinic by friends, relatives or other sources.
- Number of 'no-shows'.
- Number of clients who visited for a flu jab but left without having had one.

Client feedback

- Number and types of compliments.
- Number and types of complaints.

Staff procedures – procedures established for

- Responding to a client who has a complaint.
- Knowing to whom to refer a client who has non-flu jab-related issues.
- Reporting a difficult situation.
- Handling client suggestions.
- Keeping the clinic clean and tidy.
- Providing comfortable and sufficient seating for waiting clients.

Clinic environment

- Correct signage suitably positioned to direct flu clients to waiting area.
- Appropriate privacy provided in consulting area.

Consolidation

Looking at the areas selected by Monica, turn each statement into a question or questions that could be used by her on a feedback questionnaire.

What you have done in working through this element will help to promote continuous improvement in the customer service you and those around you give. Unit 5 develops this theme by looking at planning, implementing and reviewing the changes that are made.

WHAT YOU NEED TO LEARN

- Methods of recording and storing customer service information.
- How to identify and select the right information, at the right time and in the right format.
- Ways of passing customer service information to others.
- The impact of legislation on recording and supplying customer service information.

Methods of recording and storing customer service information

Note-taking and note-making hints

It is unlikely you will be able to remember everything a customer has to say to you as you will probably be moving on to deal with the next person very quickly after 'saying goodbye'. So, in order to remember the key points of your conversation, you need to be able to take notes effectively. Sometimes this can help when reading customer correspondence as well.

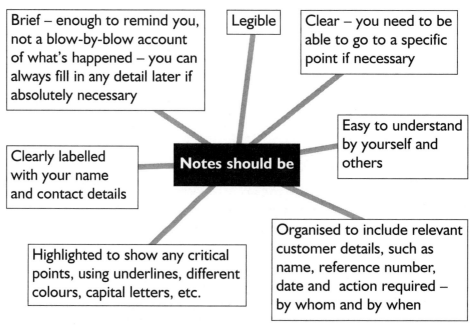

Figure 1.12 The qualities of good notes

Notes help you to remember what has been agreed with the customer, what action is required or simply form the basis of recording a conversation that has occurred between customers and your organisation. Done effectively, they also enable you to highlight, summarise and plan for the action required so you can maintain reliable customer service.

Remember, the notes you take are not a word-for-word copy of what has been said; they simply help you, or someone else, to help your customer (see Figure 1.12). They may also help you to satisfy your organisation's requirements.

Use the tips in the figure to help you record the information the customer has given you or you have given the customer when you are unable to make a record or note whilst you are actually dealing with your customer.

Message forms

It may help if you have a pre-prepared stock of message forms. They could be either paper-based or electronic. Figure 1.13 is an example.

Message for: .... Message taken by: ....

Date: . ... Extension/contact details: ....

Time: ....

Customer name: .... Account no./reference no.: ....

Customer query/feedback

....

....

....

....

....

....

Action required:

....

....

....

....

....

....

Figure 1.13 A sample message form

Think about coding the form (for example, by colour) so that when you need to pass it on to someone else it is instantly recognisable as being urgent or non-urgent.

How to identify and select the right information, at the right time and in the right format

When you are a customer you know all too well that it is irritating to be given out-of-date, inaccurate or incomplete information. Even worse are the situations where you have waited ages for this information only to find you cannot trust it. The 'wrong' information not only displays a lack of care for customers but can also, in some instances, be dangerous. Imagine what would happen if you worked in a situation where the safety of customers was an important issue and you worked from an out-of-date safety manual.

Working in customer service, you will also know that if you do not take steps to make sure your information sources are up to date, it is very easy for you unknowingly to give out the wrong information to customers.

Identifying the right information

Before you can take steps to help customers and other people by finding the information they need, you must first make sure you have understood what information they require. Once again, your ability to communicate with others comes into play. When dealing with people face to face, you need to be able to listen, confirm your understanding and summarise key points back to the customer in order to check your understanding is correct.

Never be afraid to go back over any areas of misunderstanding, as you must always be in a position where you supply information that is *trusted* by others. This also applies to written requests for information – make sure your time is not wasted (as well as that of your customers) by searching for the wrong information.

What's in a word?

When clarifying the information needs of others, watch your language! Just one wrong word or the use of jargon can send people down the wrong track.

Case study

Freda opened a savings account last year and, in order to prepare her income tax return, needed to know the amount of interest credited to her account. She thought it would be quicker to get these details over the phone. Freda got through and was asked for her name and account number, the first line of her address and her date of birth. She was then asked for her password. Freda couldn't remember ever having established a password with her building society and told the customer service operator this. He replied he was unable to speak any further over the phone without this password. Freda searched her mind and thought of a few words it might be. The customer service operator told her she could have as many tries as she liked! However, there was no success until Freda wondered whether her place of birth was what was required. 'Redhill,' she said in desperation. 'That's it!' came the reply. Freda said that 'Redhill' wasn't her password – it was simply her place of birth and that she had supplied this information when opening the account.

1 Why did asking for a password cause such confusion?

2 What would you do to improve the processes at this building society?

3 What impression do you think Freda has of the service she has received?

Be specific

For whatever reason you are identifying the information, it will help all concerned if attention to detail has been paid to the original request. This is true for situations where you are dealing with information *about* customers as well as *for* customers.

For information searches that involve an element of research, you need to have a *specific objective* (see Figure 1.14).

Notice how this request for information includes *why* it is needed, *when* it is needed and *which period* it covers. Can you think of

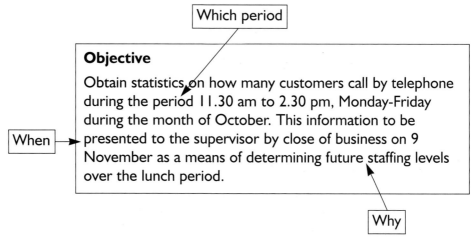

Figure 1.14 Setting an objective

anything that is missing that would help you compile the statistics for the supervisor?

Sources of information

Having established what customer service information is required, where are you going to get it from? Much will depend on the nature of your information search. Figure 1.15 suggests some sources of information which you may need access to in order to maintain reliable customer service.

Perhaps the most important, but often forgotten, information source is *you* – never underestimate the value of your own knowledge.

When dealing with information you are obtaining *for* customers, it is vital your own filing systems (if these are appropriate to your role) are comprehensive, up to date and readily accessible. If you have not done your filing recently (whether manually or electronically), how

Source of information	Type of information
Books and the Internet	Anything you ever wanted to know about customer service – just find the right book or website (e.g. customer tastes, how to deal with difficult people, keeping customers loyal, etc.)
Newspapers/magazines	Sharing best practices, latest customer trends/statistics/competitor activities
Manuals	Guidance on systems and processes
Newsletters	In-company information or external newsletters sharing best practices in customer service and latest developments
People	Colleagues – advice and guidance; customers – feedback
Video/audiotapes/CD-ROMs	Customer service knowledge and skills training
Internal records and the intranet	Specific customer records/progress with a particular transaction; latest developments

Figure 1.15 Sources of information

can you possibly expect to answer queries quickly? If you have not kept manuals and contact lists up to date, how can the information you provide be trusted?

Keeping on top of routine tasks such as filing and ensuring you keep abreast of your organisation's customer service initiatives, product and service developments and other activities will help you to maintain reliable customer service.

When dealing with information *about* customers, it may be that your organisation has its own *management information system* (MIS). This is increasingly done by computer systems that capture information about customers, their activities, wants and desires. Clearly, any MIS that is going to help you and your organisation deliver reliable customer service needs to record feedback in order to maintain reliable service and to improve the way in which things are done. However, it will only be effective if the person inputting the data into the system does so accurately.

Active knowledge

Find out what your organisation does to record information obtained from customers and about customers. How is it used to benefit customer service? What part do you play in using this management information?

Ways of passing customer service information to others

Just as there are many ways people receive customer service information (e.g. through hearing, seeing, touching, tasting and smelling) so there are also many different ways of telling others about it. This is sometimes known as *presenting information*. For the information to have the right impact, you need to be sure you are presenting it in a format that will make it easy for the receiver to understand it and, if appropriate, to take the right action.

Remember, there are two types of information you may deal with:

1 information **about** customers
2 information **for** customers.

In both cases, you should be aiming to communicate this information in a clear, polite and confident way, all the time recognising this information (or feedback) from customers can be used by yourself and others to maintain reliable customer service. You should also be looking to select the most appropriate method to pass the type of information on, depending on the nature of the request, the costs involved and the speed with which the information is required.

Presenting customer service information

An effective customer service practitioner will know that one of the major ways he or she can help customers is to give them the information they need in a manner which suits the customer and in a timely fashion. Not only must you pass information on but also you must ensure you do so in a way that ensures it is *understood.*

You will find yourself in the position of needing to do this via all manner of routes: you may be responding to a specific customer request; you may be dealing with feedback a customer has given you; or perhaps you are wanting to advise customers about a change to a product or service you offer.

Active knowledge

Think about the situations you find yourself in where you pass on information to others:

- What methods do you use?
- How do you pull all the facts and figures together?
- Does it take you a long time?
- What impact does your communication have?

You should now be thinking about the manner in which you pass on information to others and the decisions you will need to make for it to be effective:

- What *types* of information do you present?
- How *much* information should you present?
- In what *order* should you present the information?
- What *methods* should you use?
- What *words* and *style* should you use?

Selecting the right format

There are two key methods available to you to pass information on to others (i.e. the written or the spoken word). Figure 1.16 should help you choose the most appropriate method.

Another factor you should consider when passing on information to customers is to look at the manner and style in which *they* contacted you:

- look at the manner in which the customer told you about *his or her* needs and mirror the language the customer used
- make sure you cover all the points that have been raised
- how much do you know about your customer – is it someone who prefers to listen to you or does he or she prefer to see something in writing?

Method of communication	Examples	When to use
Written word	Letters, memos, reports, faxes, minutes of meetings, interview notes, plans, discussion documents, e-mails, leaflets, posters, Internet, intranet.	When a relatively permanent or formal record is needed. Take care about the speed with which you need the recipient to see the information. If you are sending something by post, will it take too long and would a phone call therefore be better? E-mails are fast becoming a key method of communication. When sending an e-mail, are you sure only the intended reader will see it? Is what you are writing about too sensitive to be dealt with by e-mail? E-mails have the speed and informality of a verbal conversation. You may wish to adopt the rule that states you should never write something in an e-mail that you would not be prepared to *say* to someone.
Spoken word	Conversations, face to face or on the phone, interviews, meetings, briefings and debriefings.	Useful if people are available to talk with you and there is an immediate need to pass on information. This is probably the main method you would select when passing on information internally within your organisation. However, e-mails have become popular as a way of communicating with others. But, is it really the most effective means of communication? If everyone is sending e-mails, will your message 'get lost' amongst all the others? Would a quick phone call be better? But remember, if you pass on a message verbally there may also be a need to keep a record of what has been said. You need to establish for yourself the degree of importance the information has and whether it would be best passed on verbally or in a written format.

Figure 1.16 Methods you could use to pass on information to others

Finally, you need to give some thought to the purpose of passing on the information, as this may dictate which method you choose. So decide on what you need to pass on first, then select the best method to convey it.

Writing skills – how to communicate detailed information quickly and effectively

Whichever written method of communication you select, what you are writing needs to make an impact. Following these steps will help you to do this for those occasions where you have several facts, opinions or ideas to pass on.

1 Who is/are your reader(s)?

You are passing on customer service information to others for a reason. You should establish why they need to read it or why you wish to pass the information on if others have not specifically requested it. So, why you are sending it, where and when should it be read, and what will the reader want to get out of it?

2 Preparing an outline

Try jotting down all the key issues you need to raise. This will help you organise your information into a logical structure. Once you have done this, you should look at what you want to put in the introduction and what you want to put in the conclusion or summary. An introduction helps the reader to understand why you are writing to him or her and the summary pulls together all the things you have written about in the middle of your piece. The summary may also include any action that needs to be taken by the reader.

3 Style

The style in which you write needs to be focused on the needs of the reader, not on your own needs. So it should be written using language appropriate to the reader and without jargon unless you are sure that jargon or abbreviations will be understood. This may be the case where you are passing on information to others within your organisation, but jargon is less likely to be understood by your customers and should be avoided.

Try using short sentences and paragraphs, and stick to the point! You are aiming to communicate information in a clear and concise manner, and this does not necessarily mean using long words and sentences!

4 Specifically for e-mails – top tips for effective messages

1 Think before you write! Just because you have an e-mail facility, is it the best method of communication to use?
2 Keep your message concise and think about the merits of including a summary or action list at the end.

3 Give your e-mail an effective title in the subject line that makes the reader want to open it.
4 Remember that e-mails are not necessarily confidential.
5 DON'T TYPE IN CAPITALS – it appears you are shouting!
6 Don't type in all lower case – the rules of English grammar apply.
7 Read through your message and don't rely on the spellchecker. Sloppiness in an e-mail is just as bad as in a letter, and you will quickly lose your credibility with a customer.
8 Remember steps 1–3 above apply as well!

Active knowledge

Make a note of the five most important or most frequently collected types of customer service information you have collected and recorded in the past two weeks. Include how you received the information (e.g. verbally, by e-mail, by post, etc.). Also, include where it came from (e.g. from customers, colleagues or suppliers, etc.).

From the information you collected, were you able to make accurate records? If not, why not?

Next, select a couple of examples where you have made detailed records. Imagine you are going to pass on this information to someone else who needs it, *in writing,* in order to maintain reliable customer service. Now write down the information you need to pass on, following the guidelines 1–3 above (and 4 if you are using e-mail).

Compare what you have written to other written communications you have sent in the past. Consider the differences. Do your writing skills need any adjustment to ensure your written communications are effective?

The impact of legislation on recording and supplying customer service information

Working in customer service, you may often be in a position where you ask for, receive and have access to a great deal of information about your customers. You need to know about and understand (in relation to your customer service role) the legislation concerned with the privacy of the individual and access to, and disclosure of, information — as well as consumer legislation.

Data protection

Not all records are kept on paper. Increasingly, e-mail is used to pass information from one individual to another via a computer. People tend to communicate informally by e-mail – they record information

Working in customer service involves understanding your role and responsibilities in connection with consumer and data protection legislation

almost as if they were talking on the telephone to the other person. Because of this, some people can record in an e-mail information that is frivolous and unnecessary.

If you deal with the processing of customer service information by whatever means, you need to ask yourself the following questions:

• Why is this information being collected?
• How is it going to be used?
• Who will have access to it?

Principles of data protection

The Data Protection Act 1998 established eight enforceable principles of good practice which you need to know about when you are involved with the processing of personal customer service data (i.e. information about your customers) (see Figure 1.17).

As already mentioned, these principles are enforceable through the Data Protection Act 1998, which came into force on 1 March 2000 and which updates previous legislation (the Data Protection Act 1984). The Act makes provision for regulating the processing of information relating to individuals, including obtaining, holding, using or disclosing such information. Personal data covers both facts

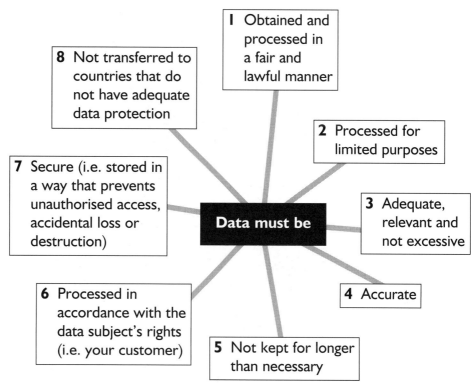

Figure 1.17 The eight principles of good practice when processing personal data

and opinions about your customers and applies to personal data in computerised, manual or any other format.

The Act gives the customer certain rights. To:

- be informed where the data is being processed
- a description of the details being held
- know the reason why the data is being processed
- know to whom the data may be disclosed.

Sensitive information

As a general rule, information concerning race or ethnic origin, political persuasion, religious or philosophical belief, trade union membership, health or medical condition and sexual orientation may not be collected and processed *unless* your customer has given his or her explicit consent. It is the responsibility of the 'data controller' – your organisation – to obtain this explicit consent.

Liability

As just noted, the person responsible for compliance with the Data Protection Act and who will be liable in the event of a breach is the data controller. In most cases, this will be the organisation itself or, in the case of a partnership, the partners or, in the case of a sole trader, the sole trader him or herself.

Active knowledge

Find out your own role and responsibilities in connection with the Data Protection Act. What does your organisation expect you to do to comply with the eight enforceable principles of good practice?

Case study

Whilst trying to find some dividend vouchers for a customer of his bank, Damian came across some old interview notes that had been typed up on to an interview card. He was interested to read that, in 1978, his customer had seen the bank manager and had been declined a loan of £2,000 to purchase a car. This wasn't the only information on the interview note, which is shown in Figure 1.18.

Damian was surprised to read how the interview note had been written and quickly realised that, had this note been written now, it would contravene the principles of the Data Protection Act.

What is wrong with the way in which the interview has been recorded?

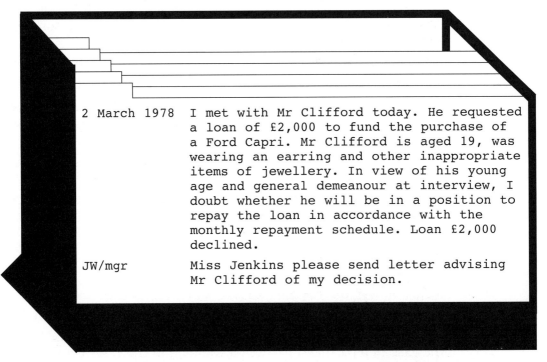

| 2 March 1978 | I met with Mr Clifford today. He requested a loan of £2,000 to fund the purchase of a Ford Capri. Mr Clifford is aged 19, was wearing an earring and other inappropriate items of jewellery. In view of his young age and general demeanour at interview, I doubt whether he will be in a position to repay the loan in accordance with the monthly repayment schedule. Loan £2,000 declined. |
| JW/mgr | Miss Jenkins please send letter advising Mr Clifford of my decision. |

Figure 1.18 What is wrong with the way this interview has been recorded?

Effect of legislation on forms

Some sections of industry will be particularly affected by legislation on human rights and data protection. If you are involved in any way with application forms (for instance, in recruitment), you will need to consider the impact of this legislation on what is put on the forms. After all, any application form is a way of extracting information from your customers.

The nature of the questions on a form will naturally depend on what information your organisation is trying to obtain. In the case of recruiting people, applicants will be needed to fill a specific role, and the questions will be tailored to suit that particular job. However, legislation may no longer make it possible to ask some questions that may previously have been asked.

Look at the specimen job application form for a general manager shown in Figure 1.19 overleaf. The details are marked on the figure with a ? or a X. The ? means that, in future, it may not be legal to ask these questions. The X means that to ask for these details is now illegal. Why do you think this is the case?

As you can see, there are currently many question marks, as the law is unclear. We suggest you approach your organisation if you are in any way concerned at the questions you are required to ask of your customers.

Copyright

If you work in a library and a customer asks you to photocopy an article from a magazine, are you able to do so? If you are surfing the net and come across a useful web page you wish to include in a training programme you are designing for your call centre supervisor, are you able to copy it?

The answer to both these questions is 'no' unless you have obtained the express permission of the person who 'owns' the work. This is because the law treats that work as the owner's property – it is the owner's *copyright*. Anyone else who wishes to make use of it must obtain the owner's permission to do so and sometimes a fee is payable. There are now a number of agencies that exist to collect fees – for example, the Copyright Licensing Agency (CLA) and the Performing Rights Society (PRS).

The copyright owner has the exclusive right to:

- copy the work
- issue copies of it to the public
- perform, show or play the work in public
- broadcast it or to include it in a cable programme service
- adapt it.

HAWTHORN RECYCLING (ACTEA COUNCIL) – JOB APPLICATION FORM

Vacancy – General Manager

CANDIDATE DETAILS

Name:

Sex: **?**

Age/date of birth: **?**

Marital status: **X**

Do you have a partner? **?** If so, are they male or female? **X**

Do you have any children? **?** If so, what is the age of the youngest? **X**

Do you have any dependants? **?**

Education

List your qualifications obtained at school/university ....

....

....

Date obtained: **?**

List your qualifications relevant to this role: ....

Date obtained: **?**

Where obtained: **?**

Health

Current and recent health problems: **?**

Absence record in last job: **?**

Hobbies and interests

Membership of clubs and societies: **?**

(Include union and political party membership): **X**

Figure 1.19 A specimen job application form: **X** = invalid; **?** = law not yet clear

Literary, dramatic, musical and artistic works are protected during the author's lifetime and for 70 years after death. Literary works include e-mails and web pages. Sound recordings and broadcasts are protected for 50 years from the date of first publication/first broadcast.

Can you think of any instances where the supply of customer service information to others will involve *you* in a breach of copyright?

Consumer legislation

In addition to legislation dealing with the recording of information, there is also legislation that may affect your customer service role if you deal with transactions involving goods and services and where you supply information.

The main legislation you need to be aware of is:

- the Sale of Goods Act 1979
- the Supply of Goods and Services Act 1982
- the Trade Descriptions Act 1968
- the Consumer Protection Act 1987
- the Consumer Credit Act 1974
- the Financial Services Act 1986.

These Acts apply to England and Wales – the situation in Northern Ireland and Scotland is similar, but some Acts have different names and dates.

The Sale of Goods Act 1979

Goods bought or hired from a trader (i.e. from a shop, a street market, by mail order or door to door) are covered by the Sale of Goods Act. This includes goods bought in sales. This Act aims to prevent customers being deceived into buying goods which are not fit to be sold. The goods for sale, therefore, must be as follows.

As described Where there is a contract for the sale of goods your customer will expect and be entitled to receive goods according to the description you have given or the customer has read about in your organisation's literature. For instance, a customer who has been told the blouse she is buying is 100% silk would not expect to get home and find the blouse is made of cotton. A new item must look new and unspoiled as well as work properly, but if the goods are second-hand or seconds, a customer cannot expect perfect quality.

Of merchantable quality The goods being purchased must meet the standard a reasonable person would regard as acceptable, bearing in mind the way in which they were described, what they cost and any other relevant circumstances. This covers the appearance and finish of the goods, their safety and their durability. Goods must be free from defects – even minor ones except when such a defect has been brought to the attention of the customer by the seller. For example, the words 'shop-soiled' or 'rejects' or 'seconds' are often seen on items for sale.

Fit for the purpose for which they are intended You must not tell your customer the item he or she is interested in buying will do things it was not designed to do. So you would not try to sell a phone to a customer who has told you he or she wants an answer phone facility when the phone you are trying to sell him or her does not in fact have this function.

Remember

It is the seller who is responsible under this Act, not the manufacturer.

If goods are not of a satisfactory quality, your customer is entitled (if he or she acts within a reasonable time) to reject the goods and ask for his or her money back. A customer has been deemed to have accepted goods by keeping them (without complaint) after he or she has had a reasonable time to examine them. What is reasonable is not fixed; it depends on all the circumstances. However, if there has been a delay in the customer telling you about the fault, the customer may lose his or her right to reject the goods.

Giving refunds – your customers' rights

If the goods bought do not conform to any one of the three criteria (i.e. be as described, of merchantable quality and fit for purpose), a customer may approach you for a refund (see Figure 1.20).

You may work in an organisation that has goodwill policies that go beyond a customer's statutory rights. For example, some shops will allow customers to exchange goods that are not faulty, such as clothes that are the wrong size.

The Supply of Goods and Services Act 1982

If you are a hairdresser, exhaust fitter or, perhaps, a computer repairer, you are providing a service. This Act deals with the terms with which these and other jobs that provide a service will be carried out. It aims to protect customers against shoddy workmanship, delays and exorbitant charges. The Act states the service will be carried out as follows.

With reasonable care and skill A job should be done to a proper standard of workmanship. The exhaust fitter would not fit an exhaust that falls off as the customer drives home.

Within a reasonable time Even where your customer has not actually agreed a definite completion time with you, the service you provide should be within a reasonable time frame.

For a reasonable charge, if no price has been fixed in advance If a price was fixed at the outset, a customer cannot complain later it was unreasonable.

- If the customer prefers, he or she can accept a replacement or repair but you are not obliged to offer anything except cash compensation.

- Your customer does not have to accept a credit note.

- Your customer has the same rights when buying sale goods as any other goods, so notices saying 'no refunds on sale items' are illegal. However, if an item is in a sale because it is a 'second' and is described as such, a customer cannot bring it back and ask for a refund because of that particular fault.

- There is no legal obligation on the customer to produce a receipt. Again, you must not display a sign that says 'no refunds without a receipt'. You may ask for proof of purchase – perhaps a cheque book stub or credit card copy sales voucher.

- If the item being rejected is bulky, your customer is not legally obliged to return it at his or her own expense; the customer is entitled to ask you to collect it. This does not apply where the customer complains about faults after having accepted the goods.

- Your customer is not entitled to anything if he or she has had a change of mind, has decided that something doesn't fit, has damaged the goods him or herself or knew about the fault or should have seen it.

- Only the buyer has statutory rights, so if your customer received the faulty goods as a present or gift, it is the person who gave the gift who is covered by the Act. However, you should think about the possible loss of goodwill if you insist you want the latter to make the request for a refund and not the person who has received the present.

Figure 1.20 The customer's rights to a refund

The Act extends the protection of customers provided by the Sale of Goods Act to include goods supplied as part of a service. So, the perming lotion, car exhaust or computer part must all be 'as described, of merchantable quality and fit for purpose'.

The Trade Descriptions Act 1968

This Act aims to prevent people giving false or misleading information about goods or services. This includes:

- selling goods that are wrongly described by the manufacturer (e.g. shoes described as 'made of real leather' when they are not)

- implied descriptions (e.g. a picture or illustration giving a false impression)

Which piece of legislation aims to prevent people giving false or misleading information about goods or services?

• false descriptions of other aspects of the goods including quantity, size, composition, method of manufacture, etc.

The Consumer Protection Act 1987

This Act provides for liability for damage caused by defective products (i.e. it is an offence to supply consumer goods that are not reasonably safe). It is also an offence to offer or agree to supply unsafe goods or to possess them in order to supply them.

The Act also deals with the pricing of goods and services. It is an offence for a person to give a customer a misleading indication of the price at which any goods, services, accommodation or facilities are available. So it is wrong to make a false comparison with a 'manufacturer's recommended price' (e.g. saying '£10 less than the recommended price' if no such price exists). Similarly, you should not make a false comparison with a previous price (e.g. 'goods were £19.99 and are now £9.99' if they were never sold at £19.99).

The Consumer Credit Act 1974

This Act regulates consumer credit and consumer hire agreements for amounts up to £25,000 (see Figure 1.21). It does not apply to agreements made between traders and corporate bodies, such as limited companies.

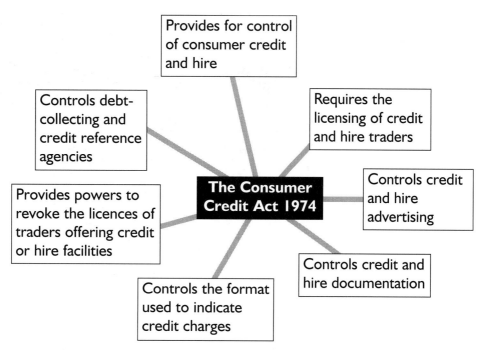

Figure 1.21 The provisions of the Consumer Credit Act 1974

The object of the Act is to protect the customer (i.e. the borrower) by providing the fullest possible information about his or her legal rights and obligations. The three major provisions are as follows.

1 A credit agreement must be issued to the buyer in a form that complies with regulations made under the Act. It must contain details such as:

  • names and addresses of the parties concerned
  • the APR
  • the cash price, deposit and total amount of credit
  • the total amount payable
  • the repayment dates and amount of each payment
  • sums payable on default
  • other rights and protections under the Act.

2 Customers who buy goods on credit may have the right to cancel the agreement if they change their minds, provided they have:

  • signed the agreement at home or anywhere else except on the trader's business premises
  • bought the goods face to face with the dealer.

3 If your customer signs a credit agreement at home, he or she must be given a copy immediately. Every copy of a cancellable agreement must contain a box labelled 'Your right to cancel,' which tells the customer what to do. About a week later, a further copy or separate notice of cancellation rights must be sent to the customer

by post. Starting from the day after this second copy is received, the customer has five days in which to give you written notice of cancellation.

The Financial Services Act 1986

This Act will apply to you and your organisation if you work in the investment business dealing in stocks and shares, or life assurance or pension plans. The Act does not cover ordinary banking or building society deposits or other types of insurance.

The legislation is complex but key points include:

- investment advisers must state whether they are giving independent advice or working as the agent or representative for one particular organisation
- an adviser must find out enough information from their customers – the investors – to give the best personal advice to them. The adviser should not look to make the best deal for his or her organisation
- advertisements must not mislead (e.g. they must not make exaggerated claims for expected financial returns or miss out key information)
- independent advisers must reveal to their customers the amount of commission they will receive.

The Consumer Protection (Distance Selling) Regulations 2000

These regulations give new protection to customers who shop by phone, mail order, via the Internet or through digital TV. Customers have the right to:

- receive clear information about goods and services before deciding to buy
- receive confirmation of this information in writing
- a cooling-off period of seven working days in which the customer can withdraw from the contract
- protection from credit card fraud.

And finally . . .

E-commerce

The ability to shop electronically (e.g. through the Internet, digital TV or other electronic means) is rapidly changing the way in which customers buy products and services. One of the factors determining the success of e-commerce is whether customers are confident it is safe to shop electronically, and that they will be able to seek redress if things do go wrong.

Remember

Existing laws that govern the sale of products and services apply equally to online trading.

Consolidation

Read the following statements and decide whether a criminal offence has been committed and why.

1 Graham works in an off-licence and has *never* sold 'Really Regal Red Wine' at £4.99 a bottle. But the labels on his RRRW bottles say 'Was £4.99 now £3.99'.

2 Brian the builder built a conservatory for Graham for £10,999 but didn't tell him that the price of £10,999 was conditional on Graham buying a suite of conservatory furniture from him.

3 Marsha works in Dazzling Dry Cleaners, which has a poster in the window saying '24 hour/overnight service'. Brian took his trousers in to get a red wine stain out and was told they would be back the next day. When Brian went back the next day, his trousers were not ready.

4 Marsha is married to Graham, who went out to buy her a suite of conservatory furniture. It was ordered on 15 October and a delivery date of 15 November was given. The furniture did not arrive until Christmas Eve, at which time Marsha did not accept the goods, which were sent back on the delivery van.

Answers

1 Graham has committed a criminal offence because he has made a misleading price claim. *It is a criminal offence for traders to make misleading price claims about goods or services.*

2 Brian has also committed a criminal offence because he did not tell Graham that the price of £10,999 was conditional on another purchase. *It is a criminal offence for traders to make misleading price claims about goods or services.*

3 Dazzling Dry Cleaners have committed a criminal offence by making an *untrue claim* about the length of time it takes them to turn their cleaning around.

4 Marsha was within her rights not to accept the furniture, which *did not arrive when stated nor within a reasonable time afterwards.*

End-of-unit test

1 Write down nine statements which describe *reliable* customer service.

2 What resources are available to you when dealing with customers?

3 Give five examples of what you might do to demonstrate to a customer you are well organised.

4 When would you need to use a formal plan to help you deliver reliable customer service?

5 What are your responsibilities under the Health and Safety at Work Act 1974 and the Disability Discrimination Act 1995?

6 List five good practices you could adopt when your customers have to wait for you to deal with them.

7 What is the four 'D' system?

8 The Data Protection Act 1998 is concerned with the processing of information relating to individuals. What obligations does the Act place on you and your customer service role? What rights does it give to individuals?

9 What can you do to help a hearing-impaired person understand you?

10 What arrangements could you put in place to ensure you keep yourself up to date with your organisation's products and services?

11 What steps are involved in dealing with spontaneous negative customer feedback?

12 When seeking feedback from customers, name five subject areas you might ask questions about.

13 How might you go about seeking feedback from customers? What could you do with the feedback received?

14 True or false?

- The Sales of Goods Act 1979 includes goods bought in sales.
- The customer is not legally obliged to produce a receipt when returning goods.
- In terms of copyright issues, e-mails and web pages are covered as well as books and magazine articles.
- Signs saying 'no refunds will be given for goods purchased in the sale' are illegal.

15 How should you go about telling others about the feedback you have received?

Unit CL 2

Improve the customer relationship

It is fundamental fact of business life that, if you don't offer what your customers want, they will do their business with your competitors.

> Research undertaken by the Royal Mail has consistently found it costs seven to ten times more to attract new customers than it does to keep ones you already have.

At the same time, customer expectations have changed. Whilst in the past organisations concentrated on setting *overall* customer service standards ('We will answer the telephone within three rings' or 'We have a charter for customers that sets out our service standards'), this level of service is now taken for granted. Customers demand that organisations are able to respond to their *individual* needs. Good customer service, therefore, stems from approaches that:

- recognise customers as individuals or individual organisations
- acknowledge customers as having their own specific needs
- deliver a service that matches customers' expectations.

One of the most important aspects of delivering a successful customer service, therefore, is to make the best use of all your organisation's resources to provide your customers with the service they require. This unit looks at the ways you can improve that service.

The elements for this unit are:

2.1 Improve communications with your customers.
2.2 Balance the needs of your customer and your organisation.
2.3 Exceed customer expectations to develop the relationship.

- How to select and use the best method of communication to suit your customers' needs.
- The skills of communicating face to face, on the phone, in writing, by e-mail and through the Internet.
- How to take the initiative to keep your customers informed.
- How to adopt your behaviour to suit individual customers' feelings.

How to select and use the best method of communication to suit your customers' needs

It's been said most of us spend nearly all our working lives communicating with other people. If this is true it means that, for most of us, we spend the bulk of our working lives *listening* or *speaking* to others. When we are listening or speaking, the impact of what we are trying to communicate comes from:

- the words we use
- the tone of our voice
- our body language.

The reported statistics for the order of importance of these aspects of communicating with other people are:

- words (7%)
- tone of voice (38%)
- body language (55%).

If these statistics are true, they should have an enormous impact on the way we deal with our customers.

> The Disney organisation discovered that the staff who dealt with the most customer enquiries were the cleaning crew. As customers made their way around, the cleaners were the most readily accessible people for customers to speak to. So Disney had to make sure it had the right recruitment and training procedures to ensure its cleaning crew were friendly, polite and courteous – as well as able to cope with the cleaning routines.

Active knowledge

Who meets whom in your organisation? Who are the people who first meet your external customers? Do they meet them face-to-face, on the telephone or via the Internet? Who are the people who handle your customers' queries or problems: are they the same people mentioned above, or are they screened from the customer by an initial point of contact? What communication methods do they use in order to do their job effectively? Set out a table showing who meets whom and what communication methods the job requires.

The skills of communicating face to face, on the phone, in writing, by e-mail and through the Internet

Face-to-face communication

Communicating face to face has many advantages over other forms of communication. For example:

- you can observe your customers and thus obtain an idea of their needs (you are getting the most immediate form of customer *feedback*)

- you have more time to find out exactly what your customers want

- perhaps most importantly, you have an opportunity to remember your customers as *individuals* so that, the next time you meet or speak to them, you have a far better chance of recalling them personally.

Remember

Getting to know your customers personally is what distinguishes your customer service from that of your competitors.

So how do you go about building good face-to-face relationships with your customers? If the statistics above are accurate, when dealing with people face to face, perhaps the most important thing for us to get right is our *body language*: the way we stand, the way we look at the other person, the expression on our faces, and so on.

Remember

First impressions count. We make our minds up about other people in an incredibly short period of time – often seconds.

- *Shoulder tension* (combined with a wary gaze) indicates anxiety. Combined with an *averted* gaze, it means someone wants to be left alone.

- *Crossed arms* are often seen as a rejection of what is happening but can have less sinister meanings – it could simply be that someone is feeling cold!

- *Forehead raised* with slight lines across it means someone is thinking visually. If the forehead raising is very noticeable and lasts for a second or two, this is usually a sign of strong emotion – like bad news.

- *Sitting forward* indicates interest and even enthusiasm.

Figure 2.2 Posture

Posture Posture gives you clues not only to such things as a person's age and background but also to that person's thoughts and feelings (see Figure 2.2).

Active knowledge

Are you skilled at interpreting gestures and posture? At your next meeting with your colleagues at work, when you are not directly involved in the discussion, check the gestures and posture of the other participants:

- Did they reinforce the words the person was saying?

- Did the gestures and posture people adopted have any influence on the results of the meeting?

- Was there any difference between the gestures and posture adopted by the 'home team' and the 'away' team?

Behaviour in your customer's premises

Because you are on their 'territory', customers will not expect you to behave in any way that indicates ownership or superiority whilst you are on their premises.

Image and appearance

Whether we realise it or not, every day of your lives we make assumptions about people from the way they look. Not only that, but people are making the same assumptions about us.

Keys to good practice

Working on the customer's own premises

✓ Wait until you are invited to sit down.

✓ When you do sit down, sit upright: do not lounge and certainly do not put your feet on any item of furniture.

✓ If you have equipment with you that needs electrical power, make sure you check and ask permission before it is used.

✓ If your work involves the movement of any furniture, etc., explain what you want to do, ask permission and check constantly before items are moved to new locations.

✓ After you have finished your work, ask permission to replace objects that were moved and do your best to make sure things are returned to their previous state. This is doubly important if you are working in someone's home.

Case study

You take an electrical item into a shop to have it repaired. What would be your initial reactions about the following people, assuming they were all equally polite and efficient in dealing with your request?

1 A young but very overweight man, just out of college, wearing a T-shirt and jeans, hair shaved very close to his head and chewing gum. When you enter the shop, he barely manages to greet you.

2 A frail elderly man close to retirement, wearing a rather dirty cardigan, with very unkempt hair and smoking a hand-rolled cigarette. This man also barely manages to greet you.

3 A middle aged woman, immaculately dressed with carefully styled hair and a very purposeful approach. She asks you very brightly how she can help you.

Would your opinion change if the nature of your problem changed, as in the following circumstances?

1 You have brought in an electronic games player that does not want to load the latest software you have just bought.

2 You have a hair dryer that stopped working this morning.

3 Your portable computer has just crashed and you think you have lost a lot of your documents. You hope someone with the right technical knowledge might be able to recover them.

How you dress, how you style your hair, how you approach people, therefore, may all be a matter of personal choice – but you need to be aware of the image you are portraying to the world at large.

Active knowledge

What is the most sensitive situation you currently deal with by means of a standard letter? Is this letter doing its job? Could you improve its effectiveness by adding a more personal touch?

Draft a new letter and pilot it for a short period of time. Compare the responses to your new letter with the old one. Has the new letter made any difference?

Ensuring standards

Quality Include all the necessary information. You want to write one letter only, so marshal your facts before you begin.

Accuracy Get the personal details of the addressee correct. Misspelling names is particularly irritating.

Confidentiality Who is going to receive your documents and who is going to receive a copy? If you are writing a report that expresses opinions on a customer or that is going to be used in legal proceedings, you should always check meticulously who else will receive a copy of it. You should also check where and how the documentation (both printed and electronic) is going to be stored.

Urgency Sometimes speed is more important than presentation. On other occasions, however, accuracy will be more important and may justify a slower response. In either case, you must agree the priority with your customer or colleagues. When speed is more important

Advantages	Disadvantages
Can be quicker than airmail and is much cheaper	A fax's appearance depends not only on the quality of your own fax machine but also the receiving one
A fax can confirm the details of a telephone conservation	Not a good way of transmitting quality pictures
Faxed confirmations of telephone orders make it easy for the customer just to sign an order and then fax it back	If the fax is not legible you may have to ask your customer to send it again
If you are in a hurry, you can write a fax by hand. This is perfectly acceptable and businesslike	Handwriting can be difficult to read

Figure 2.6 The advantages and disadvantages of using faxes

than appearance, faxes can be the best method of communication to use (see Figure 2.6).

Keys to good practice

Style and grammar

✓ *Style* Keep letters as short as possible. Each part of the letter should be short, with short sentences in short paragraphs. Use lists and avoid flowery language ('I am writing with regard to your letter', 'in reference to', etc.).

✓ *Grammar* Write in plain English. Make sure letters are grammatically correct.

✓ Spell out *acronyms* (i.e. CSA becomes Customer Service Adviser), and *avoid jargon*.

✓ *Spelling* Spellcheck every letter and *read* all letters before printing them out. Spellcheckers do not pick up everything, particularly people's names.

✓ *Layout* Suggest everyone in your department uses the same format for letters to ensure a consistency of appearance. Make sure all letters are presented neatly.

✓ *Signing* Sign all letters personally.

✓ *Enclosures* If you've promised to enclose something with a letter, make sure you do.

E-mail and the Internet
E-mail

Because it enables you to send information to a large number of people in a very short period of time, e-mail has become a very popular way to link up with customers. Not only can organisations respond quickly to an individual customer they but can also send messages to each of their customers at the same time. E-mail messages also tend to be less formal because they can be sent and received very quickly. In some respects, they are like telephoning.

Dealing with incoming e-mails Because people use e-mail as an instant way of communicating, they expect your reply to be equally quick. If you work for a large organisation, your e-mail service may be available at all times. Hence you will be able to see immediately when you have received a message. For others who don't have this facility, it is important to check your in-box regularly.

You can set your e-mail facility to send out responses automatically to senders if their messages conform to certain specifications. If your business takes orders via e-mail, you can set your mailbox to inspect the titles and to send an automatic response (e.g. 'Thank you for your order, which is receiving our prompt attention').

Because an e-mail is electronic, you can key in a reply at the bottom of an incoming message and send it back. This shows you have dealt with the enquiry personally. Paradoxically, you should not reply straight away to a message that could be open to misinterpretation. In such cases, it is far better to use the phone to clarify the situation.

Many people leave their messages in their in-boxes until they decide to delete them. However, some kind of filing system would help you to keep your messages in order. Most e-mail programs have a facility for you to sort your messages into appropriately named folders.

Outgoing e-mails Sending e-mails rather than using the phone can have enormous advantages: the telephone is intrusive, you might not be sure you are phoning the right person and more and more businesses are using voice mail throughout the working day. And unlike the phone, your e-mail recipient does not have to be there to receive your message.

There are, however, occasions when it is better to use the phone (see also Unit 1, page 51). The telephone:

- can help when negotiating – you lose the give-and-take in an e-mail that is often necessary in a communication
- is more immediate when an instant answer is needed
- can be *more* intimate when discussing emotionally charged subjects
- can be *less* intimidating than words put down in cold writing
- is more secure than an e-mail, which you really don't know who will see.

While the same rules apply to outgoing e-mails as they do to incoming ones, there are a few points you might like to bear in mind when composing outgoing messages.

Most word-processors enable you to construct an e-mail message as a normal document and then choose to send your message as an e-mail. E-mail software also allows you to prepare drafts, so you have the opportunity to consult your colleagues before sending the message. Many people compose their messages once they have logged on to the Internet and only log off once they have sent them. However, you can compose e-mails off-line so you only have to log on to send all your messages in one go.

Sometimes your software makes it possible for you to retrieve a message, provided the recipient hasn't opened it. Also, in the same way as you can send back an incoming e-mail with your own comments on it, so can the recipient of your message. It is possible, therefore, for both you and your customer to hold the full text of a considerable number of messages on one message file. This can be quite useful if, for example, you need to review the progress of a complaint.

It is also possible to place a 'voting' button in your e-mail messages so you can request and count responses to questions you have posed in your outgoing message. This is an ideal way of canvassing your customers' opinions and getting immediate feedback.

You must establish guidelines for those people who use e-mail in their day-to-day communications. If you use e-mail to communicate with your customers, suppliers or distributors, you need to make sure they are treated in exactly the same way as letters or faxes. British law states that all business correspondence must contain certain information:

• the company's registration number
• the company's registered name
• its registered address.

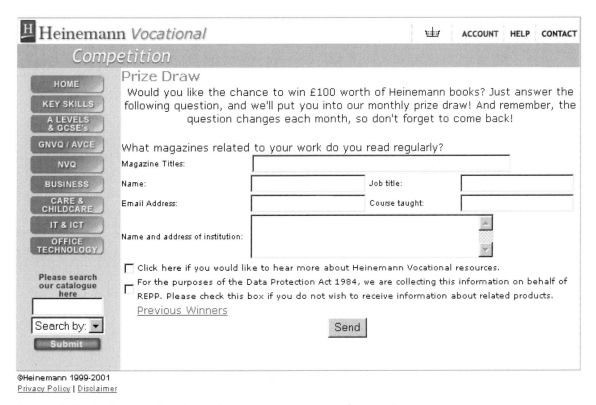

Figure 2.7 An interactive form for customers to mail in on-line

If you send commercially sensitive or confidential information, the law obliges you to inform the recipient the contents are confidential. Similarly, copies of important incoming and outgoing e-mails should be kept safely in case they ever need to be presented as evidence.

Websites

One of the benefits of the Internet is that it can cost the same whether one or one million people access your website. The major costs lie in setting up and maintaining a website and servicing any enquiries.

Using your website to give great customer service If your customers are able to access your organisation's website, it is worth spending a considerable amount of time making sure it is well designed and carefully thought out. If the information is detailed and constantly updated, customers will have a much better opportunity to do business with you.

The test of a good Internet service, however, is when something goes wrong, and a lot of complaints about Internet shopping are based on a lack of after-sales service. A well designed and easy-to-use website, therefore, should reduce the numbers of enquiries or complaints you have to deal with over the phone (see Figure 2.8).

Providing information for your customers We have already mentioned the importance of keeping the information on your site absolutely accurate and up to date. Many sites also have a section called 'Frequently asked questions' (FAQs). At the click of a button, information can be sent almost instantly to your customers that you would normally have to repeat countless times a day.

Your site could similarly include interactive forms for customers to mail in on-line (see Figure 2.7). The site could also contain e-mail links to relevant staff or to the customer service department. You can also place 'voting' buttons on your site to make it easy to obtain feedback from your customers (see above). Another common feature of most websites is a link to other sites relevant to your customers. Your organisation can also arrange reciprocal links with other websites to encourage more people to visit your own site.

Obtaining information from your customers As we have noted above, the more interactive your website is, the more you are to be able to generate good levels of customer response.

Cost Even though maintaining a website is relatively inexpensive, it can be costly to set one up as you may need to employ the services of a specialist web design company.

Figure 2.8 A well-designed website

Active knowledge

When considering communicating via the Internet, it is important to ask yourself the following questions. (If you can, for each of these questions, make a note of the reasons for your answers.)

- What proportion of our *current* customers and *prospective* customers are we likely to make contact with via the Internet?

- How will we ensure we give the best level of service we can to support our website?

- What part of our service could be more easily dealt with by a website or via e-mail, and what part needs personal contact with a member of staff?

How to take the initiative to keep your customers informed

If things are not going to plan, initiating a call or letter to your customers gives you an advantage in that you have time to prepare what you are going to say. Initiating this first contact means you are also less likely to be caught off-guard by irritated customers. It also shows the customers your organisation is willing to make the effort to put things right if something has gone wrong.

No matter how well you handle any kind of communication, there will always be some difficult customers to deal with or complicated problems to solve. The main point to remember is that, when problems arise, they should always be dealt with at the earliest opportunity (dealing with negative customer feedback is covered in detail in Unit 1, pages 35–38).

Holding people on the phone

Putting people on hold during a telephone call is acceptable; *how* you do it is critical. Always tell the customer what you are going to do: 'I am going to put you on hold while I check . . . This may take a few moments, but I will be back.' If you keep the customer on hold longer than a minute, come back with: 'I am still checking the details (or asking for information, etc.). I will be with you shortly.' If the customer is on hold too long, he or she will assume you've forgotten him or her and may well be annoyed when you return – if he or she hasn't hung up already!

Customers who are on hold do not have an accurate perception of how long they have waited (see Figure 2.9). The bottom line is that, when you have customers on hold for more than two minutes, their perception of the response time changes drastically.

Regardless of how conscientious and quick you are, however, remember to inform customers at all times about exactly what is happening:

• I am downloading your account now.
• I am updating your new record.

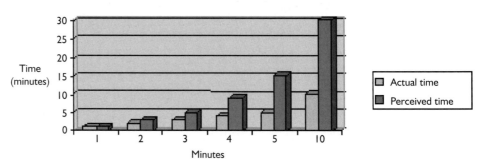

Figure 2.9 Customers' perceptions of how long they have been on hold

- I am reviewing all our records.
- I am checking the availability of this service.

If you have to put the customer on hold while checking various screens, the problem can be handled with a simple: 'I need to look at several screens. Please bear with me whilst I read the current information we have. Our records indicate . . .'

Transferring calls

If you have to put a customer on hold while you connect him or her to your manager or supervisor, tell your customer it may take a few minutes to connect him or her to the relevant person. Use those few minutes to give clear, concise information to the third person so he or she has all the information needed to speak confidently to the customer. Good service means the customer *not* having to repeat the same information again.

Putting it in writing

There may be times when you have to plan a long-term and significant change to your products or services. In these cases it may be more appropriate to write to all your customers, advising them of the changes and what they must do to take advantage of them. If you are conducting your business or service via the Internet, you have the ability to make immediate contact with all those customers for whom you hold an e-mail address.

Active knowledge

If your organisation faced a severe breakdown in the supply of its products or services, what steps could you take to keep your customers informed – not just immediately but also over an extended period of time?

How to adapt your behaviour to suit individual customers' feelings

Listening skills

Whilst we speak at a rate of 125–150 words per minute, most of us can listen to and assimilate information at the rate of 450 words per minute. This means we are able to assemble our thoughts into an immediate response – but it also means we may only be concentrating on what is being said for approximately one-third of the time. For the rest of the time we are either distracted by the noises that surround us or are already preparing our answers to what is being said.

There are two basic things to consider about the art of listening.

1 *The acknowledgement*. This is usually the initial phase of a conversation. You need to set the right ambience (or mood) to gain your customer's confidence.

2 *Obtaining information and responding to feelings*. You must concentrate on collecting the relevant information while responding positively at all times to your customer, even though your customer may be angry or even threatening.

Acknowledgement

It's essential to acknowledge customers when they are speaking to you. This acknowledgement could be established by simple sounds or through such words and phrases as 'Oh, I see', 'Yes', 'Thank you' or 'OK'. Particularly when using the telephone, people may think you're not listening when you are, simply because they have not been given a response. So it is doubly important to acknowledge your customer with words if you are on the telephone.

Active knowledge

Arrange over a period of, say, one or two days to observe one of your colleagues in your workplace and to be observed in return. Evaluate your colleague's acknowledgement skills. (You may have to repeat the process a few times to get over the effects of any self-consciousness that may have influenced the first session.) Give constructive feedback to your colleague and ask for similar feedback when you are observed.

Collecting information and responding to feelings

The basis of all good listening skills is assessing the importance and relevance of the information you are being told and providing a competent reply. However, as noted above, good listening also means taking care of the person speaking to you.

Make use of the silences, hesitations and pauses in your conversations. *You* know you are looking something up, waiting for the computer to catch up or making notes, but the customer may not. So the same rules for holding someone on the phone given earlier apply equally to face-to-face conversations.

Active knowledge

Have you ever been told 'there are problems with your credit card'? What thoughts went through your mind? If you can, make a list of the possible problems that can occur with credit cards and work out phrases you could use in each of those instances to allay the fears of a customer having 'problems' with his or her card.

If you can, write down key information and possibly some notes on how to respond to your customer's points (note-taking is covered in detail in Unit 1, Element 1.3). If the information is complex, *confirm* your understanding by repeating it: 'Just let me make sure I have understood all your points. You said that you ... ?' Ask *questions* if you are unclear about anything: 'Did you want the PC with ... or the laptop with ... ?' *Repeat* critical (to the customer) information (e.g. the spelling of the customer's name or the numbers in an address or phone number).

Barriers to effective listening

Noise It may be possible to gather routine information when you are surrounded by the noise of colleagues and customers, but it is very unlikely you will be able to deal with more intense problems in such an environment. If your job involves you dealing with customers' feelings, you should make sure you have a private, quiet room you can use.

Interruptions If you can provide an uninterrupted time for individual customers you are saying to them they are important and that you are concerned to listen to them. If you are meeting a customer personally, you should make it clear to your colleagues beforehand you do not want to be interrupted.

If you are making a vital phone call, make a postcard-sized notice saying: 'This phone call is really important. I'll contact you as soon as I have finished it.' Then you can wave this at any potential interrupters. Ideally, you should find yourself a quiet spot, but in many open-plan offices this is just not possible.

Attitudes Our attitudes colour what we hear and how we respond.

Stereotypes We all like 'people like us' and we all make assumptions about people from what they look like, how they behave and what they have to say. By making assumptions, we make it difficult to prepare an appropriate response to what people are really saying. We then add insult to injury by arranging our responses to fit our preconceived prejudices.

Daydreaming When you find your thoughts drifting away to what you saw on television last night or to the argument you had with your family this morning, you cut right across your efforts to promote effective listening. Bring yourself back to earth by doing any of the simple exercises shown in Figure 2.10.

Active knowledge

What are the barriers to effective listening in your workplace? Write down briefly how these barriers could be overcome.

Advantages	Disadvantages
Closed questions	
You get the facts	You have no way of confirming your *understanding*
Can be used to bring the conversation to a close	They do not allow you to clarify the situation
They allow you to control the conversation	The customer doesn't know if you *really are* listening
Open questions	
You get a more accurate picture of what the customer wants	They take longer to ask
They help to improve your understanding	The customer's conversation may drift from the issue at hand
They open up the possibility of thinking about alternatives	You can lose control of the conversation

Figure 2.11 The advantages and disadvantages of open and closed questions

Consolidation

Organisations meet their customers in many different circumstances and internally the staff meet and cooperate with each other in a variety of ways. Consider the people who work within your organisation or, if it is large, the people who work within your department or team.

Who meets whom on a face-to-face basis? What skills do they need? What can your organisation do to ensure they communicate as effectively as possible? What good practice can you suggest to improve matters?

Now repeat the process for:

• staff who meet internal or external customers over the telephone
• staff who communicate in writing or via e-mail
• staff who provide Internet support.

WHAT YOU NEED TO LEARN

- How to explain to your customers if their needs and expectations cannot be met.
- How to identify and negotiate alternative solutions for your customers either within or outside the organisation.
- How to assess the costs and benefits of alternative solutions to your organisation and to your customers.

Whilst it is important you recognise and acknowledge other people's feelings, you need to separate *your own* feelings from the actions that are taking place. This acknowledgement but ultimate separation is a skill, often called 'empathy'. This skill takes time and experience to perfect.

To do a competent job, you need to develop empathy for your customer's situation and, at the same time, positively convey that empathy to your customer. People with natural empathy are those considered most suitable for service jobs, but everyone can use a number of techniques that are effective ways of conveying empathy.

Unit 1, Element 1.2 discusses dealing with spontaneous negative customer feedback and the need to empathise with your customers in such situations. In this element, we consider the action you can take if your organisation cannot meet your customers' needs, and what you could do to balance your customers' needs with those of your organisation. What is said in Unit 1 about dealing with negative customer feedback could apply equally to the things discussed in this element.

How to explain to your customers if their needs and expectations cannot be met

Adapt a positive approach

If for whatever reason you cannot fulfil a customer's request, make sure you keep your approach *positive*: tell the customer what you *can* do, not what you *cannot* do (see Figure 2.12). Note in that last example in the figure the friendlier and more neutral *and* rather than the more negative *but*. If you can change your approach to using 'and' rather than 'but', you will take a significant step to ensuring a positive approach to customer service.

Don't say	Do say
I'm sorry, I can't help you	Let's see what other options there may be
I don't know	Let me check and find out
Your last name is what?	Can you help me with the spelling of your last name?
Wait for a minute and I'll come back to you	It may take me a few minutes to get that. Are you able to wait while I check?
I would like to help *but* I am very busy	I would like to help *and* I am very busy, so what I can do is . . .

Figure 2.12 Keep your approach *positive*

Active knowledge

Write down ten phrases you use regularly when talking to customers or other members of staff, replacing 'but' with 'and'. How do these phrases improve the impression of the service you are giving?

Is the customer always right?

We have all heard the exhortations that 'The customer is always right' or 'The customer is king'. Studies have found that customers cause about a *third* of the problems they complain about. There are very few of us who carefully read the instructions on a new product we have just bought, but we still put it together, switch it on and wonder why it does not work. Then we get in touch with the company and tell them it is not working properly or even not at all!

This means you should *not* automatically believe (or behave as if you believe) the customer is always right, as this can be harmful both to you and to your customers. There are a number of reasons why customers may not be right:

- they don't know enough about your products and services
- they may have formed a mistaken opinion about your service based on incomplete information
- they haven't paid enough attention to the terms and conditions of your sale or service
- they don't appreciate that third parties may be involved (e.g. delivery services) who are not covered by your service standards.

There are times when you will need to take steps to educate your customers about the details of your products and services. What you have to do is to get the balance right between correcting false impressions and ensuring you give the best possible service – regardless.

It is important you don't fall into the trap of following the 'Customer is always right' rule in an unthinking way.

• Sometimes customers believe things that are patently untrue or inaccurate. If you insist the customer is always right, you won't be able to solve their problems. You can't correct a problem or a customer's misunderstanding if you cannot admit it exists.

• You need to distinguish between providing a service and becoming a servant. Providing a professional service does not relegate the provider to a lower position. If you believe the customer is always right, you run the risk of becoming a servant.

• When something goes wrong, as it often can, it must be *you* who is wrong. The principle simply cannot apply that you must be wrong in *every* situation!

Active knowledge

Write down three examples of when customers who were complaining to you were not right. How did you handle these situations? What approach did you take to these customers? Could you improve your approach to such customers if similar situations arise in the future?

How to identify and negotiate alternative solutions for your customers either within or outside the organisation

If you are unable to supply the product or service your customer needs, it is particularly important you try to find an alternative from other sources. This is the key to providing the sort of service that keeps customers returning to your organisation. Customers will understand if you ultimately have to admit defeat but what they do not appreciate is to be turned down completely.

It is vital to remain positive and to advise the customer, not what *cannot* be done, but what your organisation *can* do for him or her. If a piece of equipment is beyond repair but initially you thought it could be fixed, say: 'The problem is more serious than I expected. It's such an expensive job to repair, you may want to consider getting a new one.'

Negotiating alternative solutions for your customers

When two organisations are competing closely and there is little apparent difference between their offers, the approach they take when their normal service promise cannot be met will be the deciding factor in whether customers will stay with them or go to a new supplier. Service *recovery* is just as important as service *delivery*, and supplying alternatives is a major part of service recovery.

Should you ever recommend a competitor's product if you are unable to supply your own? The answer is yes – if you have made every effort to supply your own but to no avail. Your customer will value your personal attention and will invariably return to you in the future.

Many organisations are reluctant to allow staff to use their individual judgement on what needs to be done if the customer's needs cannot be met. They forget that people buy from people, not from impersonal organisations. Decisions on meeting customers' needs should be kept as close to the initial point of contact as possible. If you are unable to resolve matters for your customers immediately, make sure you retain the customer – preferably physically – until an alternative arrangement can be found. If this is not possible, make sure you obtain sufficient contact information for you to be able to

People buy from people, not from impersonal organisations

make an alternative available to your customer as soon as your manager has agreed it.

Active knowledge

Give two examples of situations where you had to work hard to find alternative solutions for your customers. One should be a time when you were successful in providing the alternative; the other a time when you were unsuccessful. What made the difference between the two situations?

How to assess the costs and benefits of alternative solutions to your organisation and to your customers

There should be many opportunities for you to offer alternatives to your customers that should cost your organisation very little when compared with the cost of the goods or services originally requested.

- became reluctant to customise products or services or to make one-off arrangements with existing customers
- stopped asking the customers questions, either because they had lost interest in them or because they assumed they knew the answers
- switched their resources into creating special deals for new customers instead of for existing ones.

Relationships with customers are longer term than the initial contact or sale. When you commit yourself to a customer, you need to remember the customer needs to be serviced over a substantial period of time.

Active knowledge

Does your organisation know if it has lost customers to competitors? Can you measure the numbers lost? Can you find the reasons why they may have left? What could you have done to prevent them from leaving?

Consolidation

Organisations that can balance what they have on offer with what their customers expect, and manage still to exceed their customers' expectations, have truly found the answer to excellent customer service. What steps can your organisation take to ensure that your customers are fully informed about the offers you have and the terms of business that relate to those offers? Are there areas that can sometimes lead to dispute and, if so, what steps could your organisation take to improve the communication involved? What happens if, after taking all the usual precautions, you find yourself with a dissatisfied customer? Has your organisation trained its staff to be able to recover these situations? In disputed cases, what does your organisation usually do?

Suggest some ways in which your organisation could ensure that its staff know what to do to recover service failure.

WHAT YOU NEED TO LEARN

- The importance of customer loyalty to your organisation.
- How to recognise opportunities to exceed your customers' expectations.
- How to exceed your customers' expectations within the limits of your own authority.

The importance of customer loyalty to your organisation

In the past, many organisations relied on traditional market research to discover what new products or services customers wanted. Today, organisations have access to a much more powerful tool – a database that reveals their customers' buying habits. This database is built up from information stored on customers' 'loyalty cards'. The data is collected when the cards are swiped at the till or at a customer service information point.

What interests organisations when they analyse this information is discovering, for example, the impact of the organisation's promotional offers on people's buying patterns. Who, for example, is taking advantage of 'two for the price of one' offers?

Analysts have come up with four categories of buyer:

1 the *deal seeker* who buys promotional lines only
2 the *stockpiler* who buys in bulk
3 the *loyalist* who buys more of a favourite line when it's on special offer
4 the *new market* customer who tries a special offer and keeps on buying it when it returns to its normal price.

This sort of analysis helps organisations to find out if they are attracting new long-term business or just generating a short-term boost.

Loyalty cards are not the only way of generating information about your customers, and you can often devise ways of obtaining customer information much more cheaply. For example, companies often offer prizes to visitors who leave their business cards at their stands at exhibitions. This is a simple yet relatively inexpensive way of collecting information about prospective customers. While this approach will not give you the detailed analysis of customer spending loyalty cards can produce, it will form the basis of a mailing list with which you can begin to develop a service strategy.

Whatever technique you use, it should be devised in such a way it will collect as much detailed information as possible. You are trading the cost of the prize against the value of the information you are collecting. And if you can add to your potential customer's pleasure by making the whole thing fun and profitable, you have begun to establish the sort of relationship that will retain a customer's loyalty over an extended period of time. Some customers, however, will remain loyal while others will flit from supplier to supplier, seeking the best deal – which usually means the lowest price.

Remember

It costs much more to generate a new customer than to retain one you have already. You will readily appreciate, therefore, the importance of delivering a service that exceeds your customers' expectations (see below).

Some of the booksellers now operating on the Internet have made it their priority to know who is buying which books. Using a database of customer preferences and buying patterns, they treat people as individuals. Returning customers are greeted by name and are offered a list of recommended titles based on the books they have already bought. While you may not have a web-based facility, you can still record information about those customers who have responded to a 'special offer' – provided, of course, you have asked for information as part of your 'deal'!

Active knowledge

What methods could you devise to obtain information about your customers that will enable you to promote loyalty schemes? Give two examples of how these approaches could be used in your own job.

How to recognise opportunities to exceed your customers' expectations

We have noted again and again that repeat business takes less than 5% of the effort needed to generate new business. Yet people normally do not expect to get 100% of what they want from one company. They often settle for far less because they do not appreciate what is available from the full service. By giving your customers the full 100%, you will absolutely guarantee your transactions with your customers will go smoothly.

There is a very famous story of parachute packers in the Second World War, who achieved a quality rate of 99.9% and felt very satisfied with that result. Needless to say, the thousandth parachutist did not share their satisfaction. One day it was decreed that, once a week, the packers would make a jump with parachutes chosen at random. The error rate promptly sank to zero. We don't know whether this is a true story, but it illustrates the point that, if 100% is available, we should always achieve it – just being 'good' isn't enough.

Keys to good practice

Exceeding your customer's expectations

✓ When dealing with a problem for a customer, take a little extra time at each step to explain what you are doing and what you expect the result to be.

✓ If you can't help in the first place, instead of referring your customer to another source, make arrangements with that third party to call your customer.

✓ Send a regular note to all your current customers thanking them for their continuing custom and expressing your pleasure at doing business with them.

These extra efforts do not involve you in massive amounts of extra work; they just add that gloss which ensures a good response from your customers and a better sense of job satisfaction for you.

Active knowledge

Do you use any of these approaches in your job? If so, give an example of each one you use. If not, can you identify any opportunities where you could adopt these approaches?

How to exceed your customers' expectations within the limits of your own authority

Some marketing experts tell us we do not buy goods and services. What we buy instead are *good feelings* and *solutions to problems*. For example, we don't just buy clothes, we buy a sharp appearance, style and attractiveness – good feelings. We don't just buy a computer, we buy the benefits of new technology and all these can achieve – solutions to problems.

So what happens when your organisation provides the same price, delivery arrangements, benefits and reliability that similar organisations provide? The answer lies in providing your customers with good feelings and solutions to problems.

- Writing to or telephoning customers who have complained to thank them for so doing. They have given you the opportunity to fix something in your systems, and they have also given you the chance to regain their loyalty through your service recovery.

- Writing a note or sending an acknowledgement (or even a discount) to someone who has increased his or her level of spending or commitment to your organisation.

- Adding something extra to your service for customers, who then have the opportunity to promote your service to others – such as adding a free car wash to each car your garage services.

Many people feel they are powerless to give service over and above the normal because they feel they do not have the opportunity or authority to add value to what is on offer. The examples given above, however, should not reduce your organisation's income or profit: you do not need to spend vast amounts of money and resources to create the good feelings your customers want.

There will be times, however, when you will not be able help a customer, no matter what! The best solution in such cases is to turn the customer over to someone else. Perhaps a colleague would be better suited to dealing with this customer because of his or her personality, because of the specific questions the customer is asking, because of his or her experience, etc.

This is why it is so important you and your colleagues co-operate to maintain the service offered by your organisation. If you get it wrong when dealing with a customer, you run the risk of damaging all the good service the customer has received from your organisation.

Remember

A customer sees *all* the staff with whom he or she has dealt personally as an embodiment of your organisation. Constantly improving the relationships you and your organisation have with your customers will, therefore, always reflect well on you personally.

Active knowledge

Give two examples of times when you were able to exceed your customers' expectations: the first when you were able to take action within the limits of your own authority; the second when you had to obtain clearance from a senior member of staff. Give one example of a time when you were unable to help a customer but, by calling in a colleague, you were able eventually to meet your customer's needs.

Consolidation

Exceeding your customers' expectations is a critical factor in delivering excellent customer service. However, it is more easily said than done. Many organisations simply give up if they are asked to do more than provide a basic service. On the other hand, some organisations take great care to cultivate customer loyalty because they recognise the benefits that it can bring. What actions does your organisation take to reward customer loyalty? Do they involve measures which can lead to customers' expectations being exceeded? If so, how is it done? Would a change in the limits of authority make it easier for staff to exceed expectations? If your answer was *yes*, how could you demonstrate this? If your answer was *no*, what other steps could be taken instead?

End-of-unit test

1 Which of your communication skills have the greatest impact when talking to a customer **a** face to face and **b** on the telephone?

to improve customer service. This may be the option put forward from one group or it could be a combination of ideas.

A variation on a buzz group is:

Round robin

Here everyone works on his or her own on the customer service issue for 5–10 minutes. Just jot down some ideas you have to improve customer service. After the allocated time, individuals meet back together and contribute *one* idea to the whole group. Ideas are recorded on a flip chart or similar so all can see the options. What you then have are several ideas from different people that can be taken forward to produce a plan to improve customer service.

Reversal

Now here's an interesting thought! What do you think would happen if you thought about ways of making customer service worse? This may sound daft but reversing the issue you wish to take forward can often be an excellent way of coming up with new ideas.

For instance, 'how to ensure the answer phone facility is only switched on out of hours' could become 'how to ensure the answer phone facility is switched on 24 hours a day'. Answering the reversed question would doubtless throw up some wild answers but may also allow you to consider carefully the responses to see if slight adjustments may actually allow you to make plans for what you really want to achieve (i.e. have someone available to answer the phone).

5 Ws and the H

The questions *Who? What? Why? Where? When?* and *How?* together make a good all-round prompt or checklist to generating ideas. Go through each prompt/question in turn to see what the impact is on your issue/task in hand.

By sharing ideas with others you can generate a greater range of options for customer service improvement than would be produced by people working on their own.

How to contribute your ideas

You may work in an environment where it is acceptable simply to discuss your ideas with others or you may need to produce a formal report to submit to those who have the authority to put plans into action. Either way, the following are the areas you may like to think about when contributing your ideas.

Keys to good practice

Presenting your ideas to improve customer service

✓ A brief description of the process/issue/plan you are contributing ideas to and why you consider it important to put the improvement into place (i.e. *your idea*).

✓ A brief outline of how you came up with your idea.

✓ A description of the current situation/how the current process works.

✓ Details of any particular steps in the processes/issues that are causing problems.

✓ Details of any customer feedback you have.

✓ What the expected benefits will be (e.g. speedier service, wider product knowledge, cost reductions, etc.).

✓ A summary of the impact of your idea on other processes/services/departments, etc. (i.e. any potential downsides).

✓ A summary of the support you or others may require to put the idea into action, plus a summary of the resources required to make your idea work.

✓ The role you play in the plan to improve the customer service you are contributing to.

✓ What the risks of doing nothing are.

Active knowledge

Identify an area of customer service that concerns you and define it in terms of a short statement (e.g. identify which newspapers you should advertise in, ways of improving telephone handling, how to speed up dealing with customer complaints, etc.).

Next, seek the support of others to help you generate ideas. Use one of the techniques above and select the best way forward. Produce a short report using the keys to good practice.

The limits of your own authority and when you need to seek agreement from others

If everyone you worked with came up with great ideas for improving customer service and attempted to put them into action without first checking if they had the authority to do so, there might be some unfortunate implications!

For instance:

- If your photocopier breaks down, would you immediately go to the local shop to do your copying or call them out to repair it?
- Would you order a bouquet of flowers for someone who has complained?
- Would you place an order for more comfortable seating for your customers?
- Would you offer a discount to customers because they are complaining?
- Would you write to customers to tell them about a new product?
- Would you change your working hours?

The answer to these might be 'yes', but it should only be yes if you are sure you have the authority to act. The implications of 'doing your own thing' without authority could be quite high.

1 Cost implications for your organisation:

- Just how many bouquets of flowers have you bought?
- The contract on servicing the photocopier states only authorised repairs should be carried out; your intervention has invalidated the contract.
- Everyone now wants a discount!

2 Legal implications:

- The chairs you bought do not comply with fire regulations.
- The bunch of flowers you sent in response to a threat to instigate legal action implies your organisation was responsible.

3 Implications for you:

- You have constantly to explain your actions and it might not be possible to undo what you have done.
- Your performance is called into question.

Increasingly, it is becoming more common for individual members of staff to have a budget to use to compensate customers who complain, so much will depend on the culture of the organisation in which you work. This budget might be used to make monetary refunds, or to arrange for flowers or perhaps a bottle of wine or chocolates to be sent. Acting with authority to do so without referring to another person might enable a quick resolution to an escalating problem. You should always make sure you know how the budget is supposed to be used.

Knowing the scope and limits of your own authority is not just about what you can do with money. It is also about such things as whom you are able to negotiate with, what you are able to make decisions about and which equipment you are entitled to use.

If you do not have the authority to act, it's best to check first. If you find you didn't need to ask permission, a precedent has been set and you will know what to do the next time.

Active knowledge

Find out in what circumstances you need to seek agreement with, or permission from, others when providing customer service.

Your organisation's customer service goals or targets and how they are set

You may be responsible for setting personal objectives that relate to your own performance and that of others. In addition to personal objectives, your organisation may have its own customer service goals or targets. You need to understand the role you play in helping your organisation reach these targets.

First, we will look at why setting organisational goals and targets is important. Without goals and targets, your organisation would lack direction, have nothing to aim for and become static and unresponsive to changes in the environment in which it exists. It would lose sight of the fact that customer expectations change and would not be able, at the very least, to keep up with what its competitors are doing. Indeed, it may not be enough just to look in terms of 'keeping up'. Much more may need to be done to move your organisation forward, to make it profitable and to ensure its long-term survival. Having something to aim for (i.e. setting goals and targets) will help to achieve this.

There are many ways this can be done. If you are not responsible for setting (or contributing ideas for setting) targets, you should find out who can help you find this information.

The following are some ideas about how organisations go about setting goals and targets.

PEST analysis

The organisation may look at such external factors as the **P**olitical climate, the **E**conomic climate, **S**ocial-cultural influences and **T**echnological changes. This is known as a PEST analysis. A PEST analysis is normally used to develop a marketing plan. However, it is also useful when setting goals and targets because it stimulates people to consider these external influences. The following are some examples of what might be considered by those setting your organisation's targets.

Political factors

• Will government policy influence laws that regulate or tax your organisation's business?

aims. Under each quadrant would come the specific goals/targets/objectives that need to be met or exceeded to achieve the aims of the overall BBS.

So under 'customer perspective' an organisation may include such goals as:

- undertake two customer satisfaction surveys by the end of the year
- develop a strategy during quarter 1 for evaluating our ability to deliver what we promise
- pilot this strategy during quarter 2.

Putting it all together

These are just some of the tools or methods for going about setting targets or goals. It is also important to remember that everyone involved in helping reach these goals must understand:

- what is expected of him or her (i.e. the role he or she plays)
- what each goal or target means – it must be crystal clear.

Clearly, each goal or target must be communicated to everyone in an organisation who can help improve customer service through meeting the goals or targets. It is often helpful to spell out what the consequences might be to all concerned if targets are not met. This

'Motivation is the art of getting people to do what you want them to do because they want to do it' (Dwight D. Eisenhower)

helps to put things into context and, also, some people find it very motivational.

Goals/targets are not motivational if they are unrealistic. So, whilst it might be great for organisations to set a goal of having world-class customer service by the end of the year, is it realistic and what does 'world class' mean?

Because the goal of being world class is so huge, it would be much better to break the goal down into smaller chunks for people to work on. These smaller chunks are often called *objectives*. When looking at the objectives together, they should all add up so that achieving them would mean the organisation has reached its goal or target.

SMART formula

The SMART formula is used by some organisations to assist everyone both to set and to achieve objectives. Using SMART enables people to know what they are aiming for – and it also makes measuring results easier. This is what SMART stands for.

Keys to good practice

Writing SMART goals/targets/objectives

✓ **S**pecific – be clear about the what, where, when and how something must be done. Avoid being woolly – don't use words like 'better', 'improve', 'good'. Say exactly what has got to happen in terms of quantity – if applicable, put numbers on it.

✓ **M**easurable – your organisation will not know whether it has achieved its goal or target unless it is written in a way that means someone can check off activities that contribute to success.

✓ **A**chievable – targets should be a challenge but they become pointless if the resources available to help meet them are not taken into account.

✓ **R**ealistic – be sensible about what can be achieved – is the level of change too great?

✓ **T**imebound – put a date on it so that what's going to be done by when is known.

So, an organisation's goal of being 'world class' in customer service could be broken down into many SMART objectives. A PEST analysis and/or a SWOT could also be done. The organisation could then have as its main goal being 'world class', and could use the outcomes from the PEST and SWOT to inform how it writes a BBS or sets targets to communicate this main goal to the employees.

Figure 3.3 suggests some ideas for how SMART objectives might be written. Are there any in the figure you think *you* could improve? For instance, the last objective about establishing competitor activity is a bit vague. What is missing from it? You can read more about SMART in Unit 8 of this book

Active knowledge

Find out about the way in which your organisation sets its customer service goals or targets. Are they written in the SMART format? If you are not clear what they mean, *ask* someone to explain them. What part do you play in helping your organisation reach these aims? What will it mean to your organisation if the goals or targets are not met?

The impact other people have on the products and services you provide and your role when working with others to improve customer service

You may be brilliant at customer service, but life would be difficult if those around you did not do their bit too! This does, of course, work both ways – sometimes when people try very hard to do the right thing they end up upsetting the colleagues they work with! Does this sound familiar to you?

To obtain an impression of how you work with others (and how others work with you) to improve customer service, you first need to identify exactly who these people are, where they work, their role and the nature of your relationship with them –

in other words, just who depends on whom?

Think about all the people you deal with whom you help and also those who help you to deliver customer service. We don't mean their names necessarily, just the types of people who are involved!

> All customer-contact staff to attend a three-day workshop in customer care by the end of June.
>
> The operations manager to lead the team during September in conducting a telephone survey of the top 20 clients to establish their level of customer satisfaction.
>
> Reduce the number of complaints by 5% year on year.
>
> Establish details of competitor activity within a 30-mile radius.

Figure 3.3 Examples of SMART objectives

Active knowledge

Make a list of the people you deal with in your customer service role. Include people working in your organisation and those external to it. Next, mark with an asterisk those whom you would consider as colleagues. Now consider the ways in which you work with your contacts:

- Is there any difference between how colleagues treat you and vice versa?
- What about dealing with people whom you never meet face to face?
- What relationships have you developed that you consider are the most successful in helping you to improve customer service?
- Why are they successful?
- Where do you consider the working relationship could be improved?
- What is it that makes the difference between the relationships that work well and those that are not so good?
- How can you improve the relationships for the benefit of customers and yourself?

When reviewing your responses to these questions, what you are actually doing is assessing how other people work with you and you with them. You will probably have established that some relationships tick along just fine, whilst others don't seem to get anywhere. Perhaps you have to ask more than once to get something done on behalf of a customer. Perhaps there are some people whom you just don't trust to get something right the first time and so you end up doing it yourself. Perhaps there are other occasions where colleagues know you so well you don't even have to ask for help.

Why do some of your relationships work well and others not so well?

Impact on the customer

Irrespective of whether we are talking about people working in the same organisation or about people working elsewhere, your customers receive service from *you*. They will not want to know that something has gone wrong because someone working 100 miles away for another organisation did not respond to your phone calls. It is, therefore, vital that your teamworking skills are well developed. Without this you will find that people who depend on you may not be able to do so 100%, and vice versa. In the context of improving customer service this does not bode well.

You will learn more about teamworking in Unit 8. Even though this is

Good customer service involves communication and building relationships

an optional unit, if you do not choose to take it we would encourage you to read it to learn more about teamwork and its effect on customer service. This should help you with this unit. In the mean time, however, you will not know how good you are at teamworking unless you actively seek feedback.

The following are some pointers to help you understand what teamworking means when working with others to improve customer service. Try giving yourself a score on this out of 10! You may also like to consider asking the people you have identified in the previous exercise to complete it as well. If you do this, however, be ready to be surprised by what people say about you – they may not share the same opinion as you! There is also no point in asking for feedback if you are not prepared to learn from it and develop your knowledge and skills.

You may like to think about what is meant by the last point in the list – being *professional*. Whilst this will probably mean different things to different people, Figure 3.4 suggests a few things you might like to consider in relation to unprofessional behaviour. What do *you* consider as unprofessional behaviour when you yourself are a customer?

Keys to good practice

Using teamwork to improve customer service

When working with others to improve customer service:

✓ I make sure everyone knows the importance of co-operating with each other to achieve my organisation's customer service goals and targets.

✓ I keep the promises I make.

✓ I am alert to things that may affect plans to improve customer service and ask for contributions from others to improve our service.

✓ When people disagree about what to do, I help the team to explore any differences in a positive way.

✓ I accept help and give help to others working in other parts of my organisation as well as to those who work outside my organisation.

✓ I share information, ideas and suggestions to improve customer service with people inside and external to my organisation.

✓ I am professional in the way in which I deal with others.

Consolidation

Imagine you are going to explain to your boss how two or three of your ideas to improve customer service have helped your organisation to achieve its goals or targets. What would you say? Remember to include what you had to do, how the ideas helped plans, how you co-operated with others and the impact your ideas had on customer service.

* Smoking in the presence of colleagues when there is a no-smoking policy or where you know others object to people smoking.

* Not being punctual when attending team meetings.

* Negative attitudes.

* Complaining about your organisation or those whom you work with in the presence of customers.

* Complaining about your organisation's policies or your income in the presence of customers.

* Using offensive language.

Figure 3.4 Unprofessional behaviour

Element CL3.2 Monitor your own performance against plans to improve customer service

WHAT YOU NEED TO LEARN

- The roles and responsibilities of other people in your organisation.
- The relationship your role has to the customer service performance of others.
- How to develop a positive working relationship with others to improve your customer service performance.
- Ways of monitoring the way in which you work with others.

Everything you do (or don't do) when working in customer service impacts upon your customers, your organisation, your colleagues and others. What you do and the way in which you do it also have a direct influence on the assessment of your own performance.

In Unit 1 we looked at ways of monitoring your own performance and methods of obtaining feedback – you should refer to these sections to help you with this element.

The roles and responsibilities of other people in your organisation

Do you really know what other people are responsible for in your organisation? Have you ever asked them? Clearly, that would be a quick and simple way of finding out! In addition to asking questions, your organisation may have written descriptions of the various jobs people do. These can come in many different formats and can sometimes go into a great deal of detail. They are known as *job descriptions* and are simply statements about the purpose, scope, responsibilities and duties that make up a particular job.

Reading one of these would tell you much about a job. In practice, however, you may not work in an organisation that completes job descriptions in such fine detail. Looking at the headings in a job description will, on the other hand, help you understand the sort of information you might like to ask about. Figure 3.5 gives examples of some of the categories that could be included in a job description.

Well, that's the theory! In practice, you may not be able to track down job descriptions or you may simply not have access to them. So let's think about why knowing about the roles and responsibilities

Job title	This should be kept short and should reflect the nature of the job
Department/unit/division	Information to help identify where the job fits in with the rest of the organisation
Location of the job	Where the job-holder normally works
Main purpose of the job	A brief statement that explains the general aim of the job in order to show how it helps to fulfil the departmental/unit/organisational objectives
Duties/responsibilities/tasks	A list of specific tasks underneath main headings that explain the job-holder's duties/responsibilities
Responsible to	The position of the person whom the job-holder is immediately responsible to
Relationships	Contacts inside and outside the organisation
Judgement	Details of any judgements/degree of discretion the job-holder has
Physical working conditions	The working environment (e.g. the physical, psychological, workload, posture, etc., demands of the job)
Social working conditions	The size and nature of any group work involved in the job
Economic working conditions	Hours, pay, holidays, etc.

Figure 3.5 A job description

of others in your organisation could help you to improve customer service, and what some of the key areas are that will help you to do this (see Figure 3.6).

Answering the questions in Figure 3.6 may help you to learn more about other people and the jobs they do in your organisation. Most importantly, it will give you an insight into why things happen in the way they do and will help you to understand who is the best person to go to to help customers.

alter suggestions and ideas to make them fit into agreed plans and systems.

Team worker

Team workers give personal support and help to others. They build on other people's ideas and suggestions and take steps to draw in team members who are not contributing to a discussion, etc. They are likely to be the people who step in to avert or overcome any disruptions to the team.

Resource investigator

These people introduce ideas and developments of external origin into the team. They take the initiative to contact others outside their immediate work area, and are also likely to be the people who engage in any necessary negotiations.

Completer/finisher

These people want to see a project finished. They take steps to push things forward to ensure this happens, sometimes giving the proceedings a sense of urgency. They will be the people who have an eye on targets and schedules, and who look for errors or oversights. This may involve them in galvanising others into action.

As you can see, people play many different roles in terms of their contribution to a team. In making plans to improve customer service, it is likely you will play one of these roles.

Active knowledge

Which category do you fit in to? How does this affect your impact on other people? If you can, write down three examples of how your role in team meetings has affected the outcome of those meetings.

What would happen if there were no completer/finishers in a team?

Team development

Having established the roles people play within a team, we will now look at the stages teams go through in their development. Researchers have identified four key stages. Katzenbach described the stages as forming, storming, norming and performing. Blanchard called them orientation, dissatisfaction, integration and performing. Schutz didn't identify a fourth stage but said teams go through stages of belonging, role search and collaboration.

We don't need to worry too much about the names; however, we *do* need to take a look at what happens at each stage of a team's development. A team can be defined as any group of two or more people who come together for a common purpose or outcome. The team then goes through a series of stages of development.

Stage one

When a team first comes together, there is often a tendency to have a 'honeymoon period'. Individual differences between team members are overlooked whilst matters are discussed and people get to know each other. Morale can be quite high during stage one and productivity low. What people want to establish is who is in and who is out of the team (put coldly, whom do they want to work with and who is going to make things happen). In terms of leadership, the most effective leader during stage one will be someone who leads by telling others what to do. This style of leadership is known as *directing*.

Stage two

After a team has come together and established who is in or out, people's roles and responsibilities become the priority. Control of the team becomes a priority. A hierarchy starts to be established and power struggles may occur. Smaller mini-teams might form, favouring one leader over another. Morale tends to be low although productivity may have increased from that seen at stage one. The most effective leadership style during stage two is *coaching*.

Stage three

This stage is reached only when the chaos and internal politics seen during stage two have been settled. Relationships and hierarchies stabilise or 'norm'. When this happens, morale and productivity increase, and people have a desire to be open and honest with each other. An effective leader in stage three is someone whose style is to *support others*.

Stage four

Internal politics have now stabilised and the attention of the team is focused on the task in hand. Morale is high, as is productivity. It is important at stage four that any disagreements and misunderstandings are resolved quickly, or the team may revert to stage-two type behaviour. The most effective leadership style in stage four is *delegating*.

In terms of a timescale, these phases can all occur on one day or each can last over a considerable period of time.

Active knowledge

You may be a member of several teams. Identify one group of people whom you work with when establishing plans to improve customer service.

Which stage of development is this team currently at? Can you identify when and how the team made the transition from the earlier stages to where you are now? What needs to happen for your team to move on to the next stage or, if you are at stage four, to stay there?

What has been the impact of your own behaviour on the team? In general terms, do you have a positive working relationship with others?

Teamwork is discussed in more detail in Unit 8.

How to develop a positive working relationship with others to improve your customer service performance

The most effective relationships tend to be those that are built not only from what you *do* with other people but also from what you *feel* and *think* about other people. The way you think about other people is critical to your success, since your thoughts (whether conscious or subconscious) influence your behaviour towards others. Likewise, your behaviour might well be mirrored by the people you are dealing with. So it makes sense to be professional at all times – you are then more likely to receive the appropriate behaviour back.

Remember

Behaviour breeds behaviour: 'Smile and the world smiles with you, weep and you weep alone.'

Active knowledge

Think back to the customers or colleagues you have dealt with in the past few days:

• Were you smiling as you spoke to them – on the phone or face to face?

• Were they smiling at you?

• Was there any difference in the way in which the transaction went?

Opinions and beliefs

It is only human nature to have our own perceptions about what other people are like, whether our customers or the people we deal with at work. Often our beliefs are formed before we get to know

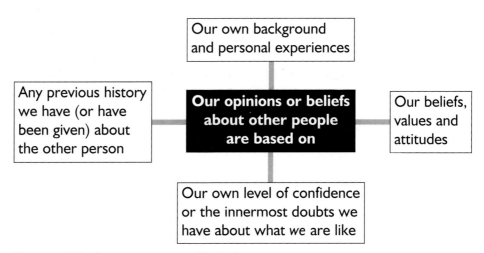

Figure 3.7 Our opinions and beliefs

someone (see Figure 3.7). All it takes is a few seconds when someone walks into a room for us to form an opinion.

Once all these thoughts are firmly planted in our minds, it is often difficult to change our beliefs or even to question whether the first impression was accurate or not. Clearly, this can, and often does,

Keys to good practice
Forming positive working relationships

✓ Make people feel welcome around you – give them appropriate time and attention.

✓ Look at people when they talk to you – but be genuine when showing an interest – and actively listen to what someone is saying to you – make appropriate nodding gestures with your head and say the right verbal acknowledgements too!

✓ Sound interested when you talk to them and think before you speak!

✓ Ask questions – enquire if you're not sure you've understood what's been said.

✓ Involve yourself with others – become part of a team. This might mean not just work but social life too.

✓ Show a keenness to help others but know when to stand back.

✓ Be sensitive to the needs of others – but be honest and open in what you do and say.

✓ Keep your promises.

✓ Be fun to work with.

present problems. For instance, if you have been told by a colleague that the supervisor working on the help desk doesn't seem to get on with people who are significantly younger than her, this will probably affect your own working relationship with this supervisor. Or if you have a personal dislike for people who wear shoes that are scuffed and who generally don't dress according to your own standards, it is likely you will treat these people as being less than professional, irrespective of how they behave towards you.

There are all sorts of things you could do to try to ensure your working relationships are positive (see the Keys to good practice list on page 133), with the result that your customer service improves.

Ways of monitoring the way in which you work with others

So, we have looked at what makes people tick! Now you should turn your attention to understanding how well you are doing at reviewing your own performance with others. For the purposes of this unit, this means concentrating on looking at the ways in which you assess your own work with others in relation to improving customer service.

This pulls together everything you do to improve customer service in your organisation and the implications this has for the activities you undertake with other people. You might like to ask yourself now how often you meet with other people to review progress against set

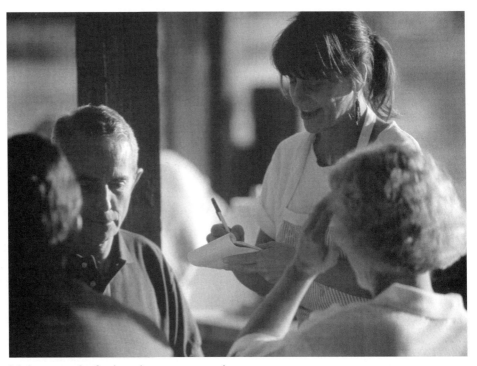

Make people feel welcome around you

targets. Do you initiate such discussions, or do you wait for someone else to chase you?

Remember

This is not just about reaching a particular goal or target but also about the manner in which that target is achieved or exceeded.

For instance, if you run a small business and have a goal of attracting more people to use your 'services' in the next 12 months, it will not be worth achieving this goal at the expense of losing colleagues who leave your business because they cannot stand the pressure. This might leave you continuously having to recruit and train more staff.

Think about how this small business owner might have placed his or her staff under too much pressure. The goal, whilst commendable, became 'too expensive' to meet. So, at a review meeting, the small business owner would have been wise to have an eye on staff morale and its impact on staff turnover. This will only happen if a monitoring process ensures the 'whys' are looked at as well as the hard facts.

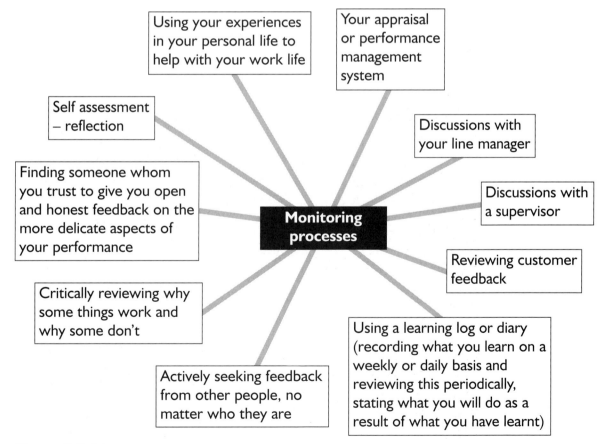

Figure 3.8 Monitoring processes

First, however, you need to have acquired the discipline of monitoring your progress. Sometimes this will come naturally from the existing procedures organisations have in terms of appraisals or performance management. If you work in such an organisation, make sure you make maximum use of these processes.

You should establish what sort of monitoring process best suits the way in which you work with others. Figure 3.8 gives a few suggestions.

Remember

This process can be as formal or as informal as you like. What is important is that you have the discipline to stick to it!

How often should you monitor what you do, and how you do it? There is no right answer to this question, especially as the best form of monitoring probably consists of a combination of all these methods. As a guideline, you might like to think about having a monthly discussion with a line manager or supervisor, with a formal meeting taking place quarterly and backing this up with a weekly check using some of the other methods listed.

Consolidation

Think about a customer service project or plan you have been involved with recently. Write a story (case study) about this that shows how you have worked with other people to achieve the aims of the project.

Include:

- how you set about understanding what goals or targets were necessary and how these linked in with your organisation's aims
- how you understood your own role in the project
- what you did to find out about other people's roles and responsibilities in relation to this project
- what you did to monitor your own performance
- how you monitored progress against the goals or targets
- what you did with the feedback you received about your own performance
- how your positive working relationship with other people helped you to improve customer service.

Monitor joint performance against plans to improve customer service

WHAT YOU NEED TO LEARN

- How to review the progress of joint plans to improve customer service.

- How to take action with others to improve joint customer service performance.

- The contribution you make when working with others to improve customer service for your organisation and for your customers.

In Element 3.2 the focus of your attention was on *your own* performance. Element 3.3 is all about *joint* performance (i.e. how the team or group of people involved with improving customer service work together to improve customer service).

Remember

These people may be inside or external to your organisation.

How to review the progress of joint plans to improve customer service

The way in which you monitor joint progress will be influenced by the nature of your relationship with the other people. For instance, it may be comparatively easy to hold a meeting with colleagues who work under the same roof, but less easy to bring people together who work at different sites. Luckily, technology has helped here. The phone, e-mail, your organisation's intranet and video-conferencing will all assist to help people talk with each other even if not in a traditional face-to-face review meeting.

When looking at joint performance, it's a good idea to be a bit more formal with the process you use than when looking at your own performance. By this we mean that, when you work on your own to conduct your own personal review, you are largely your own boss. Whilst others might input their thoughts, the actions that need to be taken as a result of the feedback you receive are largely down to you.

However, with joint performance, everyone has a stake in the monitoring process. Have you noticed how people moan very quickly (and quite rightly) about how much time is wasted in meetings that seem to be about nothing or have nothing to do with them?

You may be responsible for arranging review/monitoring meetings or you may be someone who participates but doesn't get involved with the background work. Either way, there are some points to consider.

Planning a team review
- Has the purpose of the team review been determined?
- Does everyone know? How have they been told?
- Is a formal agenda necessary?
- How will you meet to discuss these things (e.g. in a formal meeting, a discussion over lunch, e-mail, the company's intranet, video-conferencing, etc.)?

The information needed for the review must also be identified. This information could include such details as shown in Figure 3.9. Does everyone know what information he or she needs to bring with him or her? Finally, how will you know if the review meeting has been successful?

Assuming the right people to attend the review have been identified and are available to join in, the following are some pointers about what should be included.

Team reviews must have a clear purpose

Figure 3.9 The possible information needed for a team review

During the review

- Has the purpose of the meeting been restated?
- Is everyone clear about why he or she is there?
- Do *all* individuals need to make contributions to the discussion? If so, how is this going to be handled within the time allocated for the meeting?
- Has all the information prepared by individuals been discussed?
- Is there sufficient and reliable information to take further action to improve customer service?

Everyone at a team review needs to be clear about why he or she is there

- Should the meeting take no action if the information is judged to be insufficient or inaccurate?
- What action needs to be taken in the light of a positive review?
- What action needs to be taken in the light of a negative review?
- Whose responsibility is it to take action points forward?
- How does this impact on the original goals and targets?
- If goals and targets are not being met, is there agreement within the meeting as to why?
- How does the customer benefit from holding this review meeting?

It is essential that, after a review meeting has been held, everyone is clear as to what needs to be done, by whom and by when. If you do not do this you might as well have *not* held a meeting as nothing will change.

It is also a good idea to have set a date or at least an estimate of when the next review meeting will happen. Nothing focuses people's minds more on doing something they are committed to doing than seeing a deadline date looming up in the diary!

Remember

You could use your own contributions to review meetings to assess the way you behave with other people.

How to take action with others to improve joint customer service performance

If you have taken part in a *successful* review meeting, you should have no difficulty in sorting out what needs to be done. You will have had a golden opportunity to co-operate with other people in the achievement of your aims, as well as those of others.

Failure to seek agreement during the meeting can often lead to difficulties directly afterwards. All good intentions to put thoughts into actions go by the wayside if inappropriate people have been tasked with taking action points further.

This comes back to:

- understanding the roles and responsibilities of others
- working with others in a positive way
- understanding what you as an individual can do within your job
- knowing when you need to seek agreement with, or permission from, others.

Everyone depends on everyone else to make customer service a success. So if your joint efforts are not producing the desired results, your review meeting will probably shed some light on this.

When deciding on how you will work co-operatively with others, you would be well advised to remember the keys to good practice on using teamwork to improve customer service (pages 124–125) and on developing positive working relationships (pages 133–134). If you try to follow the tips contained in these two checklists, you will be well on the way to being successful in your relationships with others. This does, of course, work both ways. You should also consider what you are going to do if you do *not* receive the appropriate behaviour back.

Part of the monitoring process should include reviewing the process itself. If your meetings are not producing the desired results, this could be something to do with the way the meetings are conducted. Something as simple as motivating people to want to take part can make a big difference to the outcome.

Similarly, you should make sure the action points you agree on are SMART:

Specific
Measurable
Achievable
Realistic
Timebound.

This will make a significant difference to the customer service you provide.

Active knowledge

The next time you are a customer yourself and receive service you think could be bettered, imagine you work there:

- What would you do to set about getting people to work together to improve customer service?
- What plans would you need to make?
- How would you ensure these plans are followed?
- Why should people want to help you to improve customer service?

The contribution you make when working with others to improve customer service for your organisation and for your customers

When was the last time you were thanked for doing something well? Chances are, if you have been praised or if someone bothered to write a thank-you letter, you will not have forgotten about it. People like to be recognised for what they do well. What people are not so good at is telling their colleagues other people have sent congratulations on a job well done or have simply said those two important words 'thank you'.

To identify what you are doing to improve customer service you are going to need to think about all the sources of information that are available to you that give you feedback on what you do.

Active knowledge

Make a list of the ways in which you can obtain feedback on your own contribution to improving customer service. Identify which sources you actually use and which you do not.

Your list may have included some of the following sources of information:

- customers
- colleagues
- line managers/supervisors/team leaders
- suppliers
- manufacturers
- reports and statistics available to you that show how customer service has been improved.

Having established where you might get this information from, it will not be sufficient to say: 'I got a thank-you letter from Mr X!' You will need to explain a bit more. You should think about adding *why* you got

When you receive positive feedback from customers, think about what it is that they are thanking you for

Yet the average business receives complaints from only about 4% of its disgruntled customers. An amazing 96% of unhappy customers suffer in silence. So why does this happen? Most dissatisfied customers don't complain because:

• it takes effort to make a complaint
• to complain is a hassle.

It is easier to stay quiet and go elsewhere.

There are three basic reasons why customers choose to 'vote with their feet':

1 they think we do not care
2 they do not think anything good will happen, even if we do care
3 they do not have the courage.

The flow chart in Figure 4.1 illustrates some of the stages when dealing with customer complaints. (*Note*: *comments* are 'early warning' signs which might indicate something could become a complaint.)

Remember

Complaints should be seen positively as they provide early warning signals.

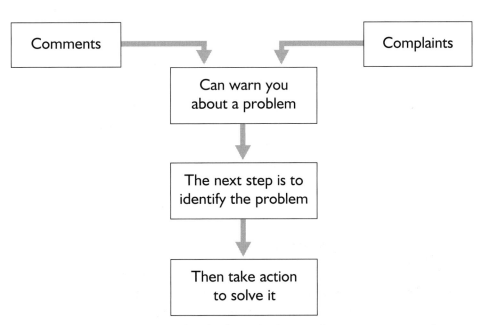

Figure 4.1 The stages involved when dealing with customer complaints

The introduction to this unit explained why it is important to solve customer service problems. This element asks you to consider what you can do for customers who have problems.

When dealing with customer service problems you need to remember the following:

- you are not working alone but are part of a team
- your organisation has guidelines which are there to help both you and the customer.

WHAT YOU NEED TO LEARN

- Respond positively to customers' problems in line with organisational guidelines.
- Solve customer service problems by working with others or on your own.
- Check at all stages that the customer is satisfied with the actions you are taking.
- Anticipating and solving problems in the service system.

Respond positively to customers' problems in line with organisational guidelines

> It is a well-known fact that complaining customers who are properly handled can become even more loyal than customers who have never had a problem (Theodore Levitt, Marketing Professor at Harvard University).

You need to make the most of customer complaints.

Just because you do not think it is a 'big deal' does not mean your customers do not think it is a big deal. When your customer says 'it *is* a big deal', it *is* a big deal. And when your customer says 'it is not a big deal' it is *still* a big deal. Otherwise, why would they bring it up?

Keys to good practice

Making the most of customer complaints

✓ When you have an opportunity to address a complaint face to face, *listen*.

✓ Treat complaints as an opportunity.

✓ Be assertive in seeking customer feedback.

✓ Encourage your colleagues to ask for feedback.

✓ Negative feedback should be used to improve performance, not punish people.

Active knowledge

What are the most common causes of complaint you have to deal with? How do you deal with these complaints? What happens to the complaints after you have completed your action?

When a customer complains he or she is frequently angry. And that customer may have been passed from one person to another, or you could be first person he or she meets! One way to protect yourself from customer anger is to focus on the facts. Customers may become

When dealing with an angry customer, try to focus on the facts

> 1 *Listen* and try to understand what your customer is saying – get the facts.
> 2 *Repeat* the facts back to your customer to show you heard and understood him or her.
> 3 *Act* on what your customer is complaining about.

Figure 4.2 How to calm an angry customer

angrier because they are confused and disappointed. The more you and your disappointed customer focus on the hard facts, the less you will get caught up in the customer's anger. You will have a happier customer in a shorter time and you will not become stressed! The three steps to calming an angry customer are shown in Figure 4.2.

How do you react to complaints?

> - give in
> - be apologetic
> - show fear
> - fail to get your way.
> If you do this you are being *submissive*.

> - attack
> - demand
> - show anger
> - get your way at the expense of other people.
> If you do this you are being *aggressive*.

> - remain calm
> - show concern for others
> - ask for what you want
> - get what you want without offending others
> - stand up for your rights without violating others' rights.
> If you do this you are being *assertive*.

Conflict brings out natural instincts – to stand and fight (*aggression*) or to take flight (*submission*). Aggression can give you a sense of power and can make you feel good but for only a short time. The long-term effects on customer relations can be harmful. Submission avoids causing unhappiness to others and so customers get what they want. It can mean you accepting blame for things that are not your organisation's fault. Being over-submissive does not create good long-term customer relationships.

> ✓ *Can produce a 'win-win' situation* Your own and your customer's opinions are respected so you both can feel you have 'won'.
>
> ✓ *Confidence* Assertive behaviour tends to produce success without heated arguments. This success makes you more self-confident. Customers 'feel' this and, as a result, have more confidence in the organisation.
>
> ✓ *Greater self-responsibility* You do not blame others (aggressive) or constantly say you are 'sorry' (submissive). You take responsibility for achieving what you want to achieve and you take responsibility for making the customer satisfied.
>
> ✓ *Greater self-control* Your mind is concentrated on achieving mutually acceptable solutions. You are not giving in to control by others. In addition, you have not lost your temper in an emotional and aggressive outburst.

Figure 4.3 The advantages of adopting assertive behaviour

Assertive behaviour, on the other hand, can be better than both aggression and submission and is the best way to deal with customers who come to you with a complaint or problem. Figure 4.3 summarises the advantages of assertive behaviour.

The technique of bypassing emotional issues (such as anger, frustration and disappointment) is known as *conflict resolution*. What you should try to do when resolving a conflict is achieve a 'win-win' situation. Perhaps this is really a 'I win and you win' situation: you have kept your respect and your customer has got a solution in a positive way. The relationship with the customer is undamaged and may even be enhanced.

The alternatives to a win-win situation are:

- 'I win – you lose': you did what you thought was correct but the customer will not come back again

- 'I lose – you win': you may have allowed the customer to win at a cost to the organisation

- 'I lose – you lose': you may have lost your cool with the customer and he or she leaves and does not return.

So you need to ensure the outcome is win-win! By being assertive, you can deal with customers in a calm and efficient manner and, at the same time, gather information that will help you to identify the problem. The three steps to being assertive, therefore, are:

Always try to achieve a 'win-win' solution to a problem

Step 1 Listen and say you understand the customer's view. Listening skills are a vital part of assertiveness.

Step 2 Say clearly what you think or feel.

Step 3 Say clearly what you want to happen.

'However' is a good word to link to step 1 with step 2. For example: 'I can appreciate you want it straight away. *However*, we are not able to supply the goods until the end of next week.'

'So' is a good word to link step 2 with step 3: ' … *so* I can recommend that …'

So conflict resolution is nothing more than realising you have a responsibility to understand and deal with a customer's problems. You need to keep the tasks in perspective and the emotions at bay, and you need to see your customer's problems resolved to everyone's satisfaction. The basic rules are:

1 *Listen* Understand so that the customer's problem becomes your problem while **not** taking the customer's anger or frustration personally.

2 *Repeat* Clearly communicate expectations.

3 *Act* Solve the problem.

Remember

By being assertive you will stay in control of the situation.

Have you ever asked yourself why your customers leave your organisation and go to your competitors? In Unit 2, Element 2.2 we saw that most customers leave an organisation as a result of being treated indifferently or as a result of being ignored by that organisation. To overcome this problem, John Hartley (a trainer with a large hotel group in Florida) came up with the idea of HEAT.

Keep your customers by taking the HEAT

HEAT stands for:

Hear
Empathise
Apologise
Take ownership

Everyone who comes into contact with customers will, at some point, have the opportunity to apply the HEAT technique. What you say or do will determine whether customers are likely to remain yours or to go somewhere else.

Active knowledge

Think about a time when you made a complaint. Do you remember what the person hearing the complaint did? Did he or she:

- listen, interrupt, argue?
- seem indifferent?
- pass you over to someone else?
- worse yet, not even seem to care?

Now think about what *you* did when a customer complained to *you*. Either write down what happened when a customer last complained or start to keep a record of how you handle complaints. Are you applying the HEAT technique?

By learning and applying the HEAT technique, you can turn a negative situation into a positive one. HEAT works well either in person or over the phone and it allows you, first, to meet the customer's *personal* needs and then to focus on meeting his or her *practical* needs.

Applying HEAT
Hear

A dissatisfied customer wants to know someone is willing to listen. It is important to be quiet, to pay attention and to listen carefully to what the customer is saying, without being distracted or sounding impatient. *Do not interrupt.* To do so may cause the customer to argue, to withdraw, to hang up or to go away.

Empathise

After being given the opportunity to express dissatisfaction, the customer wants to know someone understands and cares. Listen and respond with empathy to acknowledge the customer's feelings (upset, frustrated, disappointed, etc.) and the facts of the situation that are causing those feelings. To empathise effectively, you should:

- acknowledge the customer's feelings
- acknowledge the facts of the situation
- let the customer know you heard him or her
- let the customer know you understand how he or she feels and why he or she is upset.

Apologise

The customer wants to hear you are sorry about the problem or inconvenience. Expressing empathy before apologising shows the customer you understand the feelings behind the complaint, which legitimises your apology. Unless the problem is your fault, you can apologise without accepting blame. You can say, for example, 'I'm sorry you feel you weren't treated fairly'. However, be careful not to apologise too much. Doing so might make your organisation appear incompetent. You should admit fault only if it is clear the organisation is to blame.

Take ownership

Customers complain because they feel something needs to be done. If the problem can be fixed on the spot, do so! If the problem cannot be fixed on the spot, *some* action needs to be taken. This may include calling in a supervisor or transferring the customer to the appropriate department. Commit to *follow up* if appropriate – and it would be hard to imagine an instance where some form of follow-up is not needed.

The benefits of HEAT

Figure 4.4 summarises the benefits of using the HEAT technique.

Hear	Allow the person to speak without interruption. Acknowledge what he or she says.
Empathise	'I'm sure _____ (fill in the blank) was upsetting. I'd be upset if _____ (fill in the blank) happened to me.'
Apologise	'I apologise for the situation. I'm sorry you were inconvenienced.'
Take ownership	'I'd like to take care of this right away. Let me call my supervisor and get some help.'

Figure 4.4 The benefits of using the HEAT technique

Using this technique will take the HEAT out of the situation and you will have a cool customer! And finally, HEAT pays in:

- customer loyalty
- business success
- customer satisfaction and retention
- employee satisfaction.

Active knowledge

Working in pairs, role play these situations. See if you can take the HEAT out of them! Take turns to be the customer and the employee:

1 A customer has bought an expensive camcorder using a debit card. The company has accidentally taken out the money twice. As a result, the customer has been charged by his or her bank for an unauthorised overdraft.
2 A regular customer at a hairdressers has been double-booked. He or she is offered and accepts a junior stylist but is very upset by the result.

Acknowledging the situation

When dealing with a customer's problem your customer needs to know you are going to *do* something about the problem. This is known as *acknowledging the situation* and it requires more than an apology. Instead of apologising by saying 'I'm sorry we sold you a faulty washing machine' you should say: 'I know how inconvenient it is when a washing machine breaks down and the distress it must be causing you. Now let me see what we can do to get it working for you again.' By saying this you are acknowledging the situation and you are focused on taking action and moving towards a solution.

Taking action to resolve customer service problems

The customer needs to know:

- how you are going to solve the problem (and you need to communicate this clearly to the customer)
- that you are doing everything within your power to help him or her
- that the proposed plan will satisfy him or her and that it is within company guidelines
- that you will follow up the proposed action to ensure it has been implemented.

It is not always possible to satisfy the customer 100% but, by providing a quick, fair solution and showing empathy for the customer, he or she will feel as though he or she has been treated fairly.

Solve customer service problems by working with others or on your own

The four steps to problem-solving are:

1 *understand* the problem
2 *identify* the cause
3 *discuss* possible solutions
4 *solve* the problem.

Understanding the problem

To understand the problem you need to:

- get all the facts
- listen non-defensively
- repeat the problem back to the customer as you understand it.

It does not matter whether the problem is big or small. To be effective you must first find out what the problem is and then set out to solve it. If you attempt to solve the problem before you have all the facts this could to lead to customer dissatisfaction.

Think of a time when:

- a *customer* identified a problem
- *you* identified a problem which might have affected a customer
- a *colleague* identified a possible customer problem.

It is important to recognise these three ways of spotting problems. All three form part of the customer service chain and, if one part of the chain is missing, it will not work effectively.

Case study

Mrs Hilton's car's air conditioner stopped working last summer. Hoping all it needed was a new fuse, she took her car in, only to find out it wasn't that simple. After asking Mrs Hilton a lot of questions and checking out several things, Mike (the mechanic at the garage) discovered a whole series of problems had occurred. A fan bearing had failed, causing the car to overheat. This caused something else to blow, which produced more problems.

The net result was the air conditioner, radiator, radiator fan and whole fuse assembly all had to be replaced. But that was not the real problem – at least from Mrs Hilton's viewpoint. The real problem was that the car was just out of warranty by about two months.

After taking the time to understand Mrs Hilton's problem thoroughly, Mike told her all this did not just happen at one time, it probably had begun a few months ago, and that he would go back to the manufacturer to see if they would help on the parts. He could have been talking a foreign language for all Mrs Hilton knew, but she felt he honestly cared about helping her.

The next day he called Mrs Hilton and explained that the manufacturer had agreed to supply all the parts if she would pay for the labour. Mrs Hilton was thrilled and genuinely grateful for his help.

1 How did Mike go through the four steps to problem-solving?
2 Why was Mrs Hilton so pleased?
3 Had Mrs Hilton's problems actually been solved?
4 Why was this a win-win situation?

Removing negative emotions when problem-solving

It is easy in the midst of problem resolution for egos to surface and to spoil everything. When this happens, good judgement flies out the window. Many customers are lost this way. At the first sign of problems you can react in these ways:

- deny or duck the problem – acting as if it doesn't exist
- attempt to push the blame on to others
- react to the customer's anger or negative actions by automatically demonstrating the same behaviour
- patiently and calmly getting people talking, expressing what they think and feel and by you listening.

Your first objective is to *understand* the problem to get all the facts. Listen non-defensively and repeat back the problem, as you

Remaining calm and listening non-defensively is the best way to diffuse a customer's anger

understand it. Asking questions and listening is the best strategy to diffuse people's anger or hostility. When you meet their negative tones with calm, sincere understanding, they will often change, because it takes two to do battle.

The following are some questions you can ask to help you understand people's problems and to defuse their hostile feelings:

• So I can understand, would you please explain to me what happened?
• When did you first notice this problem?
• Would you please explain to me everything that has happened?
• Now, to make sure I understand, would you please explain all this once more?

If you can get people to explain their view of the problem twice, they'll talk out their negative feelings or anger. Then, if you will listen non-defensively without interrupting or arguing, the customer's negative emotions may disappear.

> The Ritz-Carlton Hotels have a policy that, when any employee spots a problem, he or she is to 'take ownership' of it. It becomes the employee's problem to handle as best as he or she can.

If you practise all the above you will have more confidence in the face of problems and you will discover a way to deepen your relationships with your customers.

Keys to good practice
Understanding problems
✓ Get all the facts.
✓ Listen non-defensively.
✓ Repeat back the problem as understood.
✓ 'Take ownership' or responsibility for the problems. When this is done with a sincere desire to understand and solve problems, it can turn negative customer attitudes into positive ones.

Identify the cause
To solve a problem you have to identify the cause – the *real* cause – then remove or remedy it. There are many causes of problems. They can be *functional* – the goods are broken – or *personal* – the salesperson's attitude or the manner in which the customer was treated. Some problems are preventable and some are not.

To identify the real cause, you can ask these questions:

• What has happened?

- What should have happened?
- What went wrong?

It is only by asking these questions that you will be able, eventually, to solve the problem.

Keys to good practice

Identifying the problem

✓ *Specify the problem* Find out exactly what has happened and what the problem is.

✓ *Identify the background to the problem* What were the circumstances? Who was involved?

✓ *Find out the present situation* Has someone else been involved? Has anything already been done to try to solve the problem?

✓ *Check the scale of the problem* Is this a 'one-off' problem or have other customers had the same problem? Could the problem put a customer in an unsafe situation?

✓ *Identify what the customer really wants* Does he or she want a refund, a replacement, a credit note or some other action?

✓ *Check your role in the problem* Are you in a position to help the customer or do you have to pass the problem to someone else?

✓ *Check all the facts* If you do not have all the facts you will not be able to find a satisfactory solution to the customer's problem.

Case study

An organisation was keeping inaccurate customer records over a period of time. A number of complaints were received from customers:

- One customer said: 'I have been a customer of this organisation for five years, but they have no record of me!'

- Another customer commented: 'Their records on me were over two years out of date!'

- An invoice showing the wrong amount was sent to another customer.

- A letter demanding payment was sent to a customer, even though the customer had not ordered a product or service.

- A customer who ordered a product some time ago had received nothing; there was no record of this customer's order.

Although the complaints were different, the problem was the same – inefficient and inaccurate customer record-keeping.

1 What actions does this company need to take concerning the complaints?
2 What does it need to do to ensure such problems are solved in the future?
3 What could be the consequences to the company of not acknowledging the complaints?

Egos, emotions and attitudes

Problems or complaints are not usually logical; nor can they be solved by mere reason. When people's emotions enter the picture, reason often goes out the window. This makes problem-solving difficult and is why, occasionally, people fail to solve problems or complaints.

In complaining, people often place themselves in a position where their egos won't allow them to retreat or accept solutions. This is why you should do everything possible to neutralise negative emotions. One effective way to neutralise these harmful emotions is to admit it is your fault. To say with your words and actions, 'Hey, it's my responsibility – the cause of the problem can rest on my shoulders. I'll take full blame. My main objective is to correct the problem and make you happy'. When this is your attitude, you will undoubtedly neutralise the hostile and enraged emotions your customers can have.

Rather than putting the responsibility of the problem or its cause and cure on your customer's shoulders, place it on your own, but do not allow yourself to become trapped into discussing where the blame should rest. You cannot win that game.

How much does an unresolved complaint cost your organisation?

Few organisations have any idea how much an unresolved complaint costs them!

Case study

An auto-parts company owner said: 'Whenever customers have a problem or are unhappy, I ask them what they feel needs to be done to correct it and whatever they say, I do.'

'Really? Anything?' someone asked.

'Yeah', he responded. 'Look at it like this. If I have to give a part away, I still come out ahead – even if I'm right and they're dead wrong.' He went on: 'If I have to pay for a part, it is still a lot less than losing the several thousand pounds their future business would have brought in.'

'The real issue,' he explains, 'isn't what their complaint is. The real issue is what I'll lose in future business if they decide to take their business elsewhere.'

Does this man really know what an unresolved complaint could cost him? Give the reasons for your answer.

It is important to understand how much an unresolved complaint costs you. The following are some of the factors to consider when you assess your real costs:

• what the issue at hand will cost to satisfy the customer

• what the future purchases of this customer will be

• what future business will be influenced by this customer – if he or she is happy or unhappy.

Active knowledge

Think of an example from your workplace where a customer has complained about a product or service. How much does that product or service cost? How much would it cost your organisation to replace that product or repeat or redo the service? How much money would be lost if you lost the customer's future business?

Identifying the cause of a problem helps to avoid conflict
Listening non-defensively

As you attempt to understand the cause of a problem, it helps to listen non-defensively. That is listening without preconceived notions or prejudice. This is not easy to do, but you can make it a habit by practising it. Someone used to using this technique has said the following.

> I've learned to let them talk (no matter how long), and I'm more aware of listening non-defensively. I realised the customers were ready for me to be defensive and when I didn't act that way, solving their problem became painless for both of us.
>
> Before, when a dissatisfied customer came to me, my attitude was, 'Here we go again'. Now problems are easier because I know they will be solved positively. I now have the awareness and control to change situations into the right perspective.

Without the ability to listen patiently and with an open mind the problems will only increase and cause dissatisfied customers.

What's the cause of most of your problems?

Take a moment to think of the most common problems you experience with customers. Most problems can fall into these four main categories.

1 *Functional* The product or service did not work correctly.
2 *Misapplication* The customers did not put it together or use it correctly.
3 *Human element* Imperfect people do not make things that are perfect nor do imperfect people perfectly use or maintain them.
4 *Ego* This problem causes people to look good or bad in the eyes of themselves and others.

Look at these four categories again. Does number 4 account for about 80% of your problems? The cause of most misunderstandings can be traced back to ego.

Having *identified* the cause of the problem, *analyse* it. The five main steps when analysing a problem are:

1 prioritise the problem
2 identify the cause
3 collect the information
4 define the problem
5 recognise the problem.

Check at all stages that the customer is satisfied with the actions you are taking

Customers will help us solve most of our problems with them – if we will only let them! One way you can move towards problem resolution, as well as show your concern to people, is to discuss possible solutions with them. Not only does this create an air of professionalism but it also helps you move beyond arguments, conflicts or discussions about who should shoulder the blame. You will resolve conflicts much faster and keep your customers happy when you seek out options and then help them select the best ones.

This works for the simplest situations to the most complicated ones.

Active knowledge

Think of an occasion when you had to ask someone else to help you find solutions to a problem. What was the situation? Whom did you turn to for advice? Make notes about this.

When you have identified a solution to a problem, do you have to seek authority from others to carry out the solution? If your answer to this is 'yes', who are these people? Why is it necessary to seek their authority?

Remember

You are part of a *team*: you may not have the authority to act on your own to provide the solution the customer wants.

Case study

An elderly couple went to their doctor's surgery and told the receptionist they had an appointment and gave her their name. She looked at her appointments book and informed them their appointment was at 11.00 am, not 10.00 am. Confused, they looked at each other and the man said to the woman: 'But you told me it was at 10.00 o'clock.'

She replied: 'I did not, I told you I didn't remember. You said it was at 10.00.' He wasn't too thrilled at that and grumbled his displeasure, which precipitated a couple of minutes of rather active dialogue between them.

All the time the receptionist just sat there and didn't say a word. Sizing up her problem, the woman asked the receptionist: 'Well, what are we going to do? It's too far to go back home and we don't have time to go to Tesco and do the rest of our shopping!' The receptionist just looked at the couple and didn't say a word.

Again, one asked the other: 'What will we do for the next hour?' Neither knew. Both seemed very confused. Again the receptionist didn't help. She didn't offer any options or say anything. After a painful moment of indecision, the man asked her if they could just sit in the reception room and look at magazines for the next hour. The receptionist replied dryly 'Yes', and they sat down.

1 Why wasn't the receptionist more sensitive?
2 Did this doctor's receptionist realise she could have helped them solve a problem?
3 How do you think the elderly couple felt about this incident?
4 What might be the consequences for the doctor?

A problem may be large or small but it's still a problem and, for almost any problem, you can discuss possible solutions by practising these action steps:

1 suggest options
2 ask for the customer's ideas
3 agree on the best course of action.

When you apply these steps methodically, you will usually get very positive results.

Suggest options

When you have a problem with a customer, what different solutions or alternatives can you offer to make the customer happy? The doctor's receptionist mentioned above could have offered the following solutions when the elderly couple's problem was identified. She could have:

- invited them to sit down and read magazines while she got them a cup of tea

- spoken of her concern for their situation and told them about a nice tea shop down the road

- suggested they might like to look round the park, which was only five minutes' walk from the surgery.

But she did not. She gave up a great opportunity to cement her relationship with the couple.

Active knowledge

Think about a complaint you have had to deal with recently. Make a note of the problem. What solutions did you offer? What was the customer's choice? What might another customer have chosen?

Ask for the customer's ideas

You need to consider all alternatives before offering the customer a solution. Ask the customer what he or she is expecting you to do:

- give him or her a refund
- credit his or her account
- replace the item.

Agree on the best course of action

Psychologically speaking, when you ask for a customer's ideas about the best course of action, you usually cause the customer to become more lenient and forgiving. Customers soften from the often firm positions they feel forced to defend. It makes it 'all right' for them to compromise.

The question 'What do you feel is the best solution?' often makes disgruntled people much more pliable and easy to work with.

Ask if the customer is satisfied with the solution

A follow-up call to the customer to see if the customer is happy with the solution will reinforce customer satisfaction. When you follow up like this, you lay yourself open to potential happiness or unhappiness – and it is here you make the greatest impression on people. Your genuine, sincere desire to know how the customer is doing will impact positively on people with optimum results. The reason is simple. Few people actually take the time to say 'Thank you' or 'How are you doing, feeling or liking what you have bought?' or 'What is your level of satisfaction?'

You will cement strong customer relationships. And this is actually only common courtesy.

Anticipating and solving problems in the service system

Take corrective action

You have your own special problems to solve. Your professionalism shows when you have a good grasp of the common problems your customers have and when you know what corrective action to take once the cause of a problem has been identified. It is here your sincere desire to help customers can be shown further. Your attitude is demonstrated in your actions.

When people see you want to help them, your trust and rapport will be increased. This gives you a terrific opportunity to cement relationships with customers so they will want to continue to do business with you. It is the manner and attitude with which you take corrective action that influences much of your customers' satisfaction. Where corrective action is taken in a grudging, suspicious, surly way, the customer will not be happy. It all depends on your attitude.

Remember

- *One* complaint on an issue is an inconvenience.

- *Several* complaints on the same issue are the tell-tale signs of a major problem.

- Do not make the mistake of dealing with individual inconveniences when you should really be tackling the *major problem*.

- You do *not* get a second chance to be your customer's first choice.

Customer complaints

So what are the most common causes of complaint? Figure 4.5 lists the most common. The following is an extract from the *Royal Mail Code of Practice*.

- Delivery not made when promised.
- The product or service not living up to expectations.
- Delays in responding to enquiries.
- Mistakes.
- Unprofessional behaviour from the staff (e.g. rudeness) – this may or may not have been intentional.
- Not being able to get through to the person or organisation because of poor communication.
- Limited choice of product.
- Limited choice of *when* and *how* services are delivered.

Figure 4.5 The commonest causes of customer complaints

What do you do if you do have a problem?

Complaints

We want to know when customers are not satisfied with our services so that we can try to put matters right. If you have any problems or complaints, please ring your local Customer Care unit.

We aim to:

- Tell customers that we have received their written complaints and claims for compensation within 24 hours of receiving them.
- Deal with them quickly.
- Resolve those for the inland post within 6 weeks.

As you can see, there is a clear commitment here that a customer's problem will be acknowledged and that it will be treated as being important.

Consolidation

If you were asked to brief a colleague new to your section on the following, what would you say?

1 The three most common complaints are …

2 This is how they are dealt with …

3 The way I handle a difficult customer is by …

Identify repeated customer service problems and options for solving them

In the previous element you learnt how to identify and analyse a customer service problem. This element is about how you can identify repeated customer service problems and the options available to you for solving them.

WHAT YOU NEED TO LEARN

• How to identify repeated customer service problems either on your own or with colleagues.

• The options for dealing with repeated problems and the advantages and disadvantages of each option.

• Work with others to determine an agreed way forward for solving repeated problems.

How to identify repeated customer service problems either on your own or with colleagues

If customer complaints are not collected and analysed, the organisation will not know what are 'repeated' problems and will not be able to take the appropriate action to prevent them happening again. Hence repeated problems are important and you are part of a team that contributes to the process of identifying and preventing repeated problems from happening again. Not only do repeated problems cause customers problems but they also cost the organisation money.

Remember

'Unhappy customers do not fight – they switch' (John J. Franco, former President of Learning International, Stamford, Connecticut).

You should record problems because:

• if the customer comes back again and you are not there, someone else knows what the situation is
• they can indicate patterns and trends in the service your organisation is providing
• they will show repeated customer service problems.

Case study

An elderly lady rang a company to complain about a bill that she had paid the previous month. She had a receipt to prove it. Her account details were taken, but the payment did not show up in the company's records. She was asked to bring in the receipt. She explained she was not able to, and she was not happy to post it as it was the only proof she had paid the bill.

Although it was not part of any complaint procedure, a company employee was given permission to visit the customer, collect the receipt and leave a signed note to say the company had the receipt. Once the details on the receipt were checked, it was obvious the company had made an error: the payment had not been entered into the computer system. The customer was telephoned and a letter of apology was sent to her.

1 In your opinion, was the elderly lady's complaint dealt with well?
2 What system was at fault?
3 What code of practice could this company establish as a result of monitoring this complaint?

The options for dealing with repeated problems and the advantages and disadvantages of each option

If a customer has a problem or makes a complaint, it could be there are a number of possible solutions. It may also be you can solve the complaint:

- using your own authority (a solution you know about and could implement yourself)
- through negotiating with others in your own team
- through negotiating with others in other teams or departments.

It may not be possible to solve all problems with 'standard' procedures and so you may need to work with others to find other solutions. You also need to remember that you have to work within your organisation's guidelines: you have to balance the needs of your customer with those of your organisation.

Active knowledge

Think of a complaint you have dealt with recently for which there were a number of solutions. Which solution would have given the most advantages to the customer? Which solution would have given the most advantages to your organisation? Give the reasons for your answers.

Types of recurring complaints

There are a number of recurring complaints which will generally fall into one of these categories:

- the quality of products or services
- the availability of products or services
- the organisation's systems and procedures
- individual members of staff.

The quality of products or services

Complaints about quality include such things as:

- a product is faulty or damaged
- a service engineer fails to turn up
- a customer has difficulty getting through on the phone.

Recurring product and service quality problems can be sorted out if they are recorded and passed on to the appropriate people.

The availability of products or services

Complaints about availability include such things as:

- the product is not in stock
- the service or product is not provided by your organisation
- an engineer is not immediately available and you cannot say when one will be.

Recurring problems about product or service availability can be solved by noting regular requests. When solving these problems, you need to look closely at regular requests if something is frequently going out of stock or is only available at certain times. It could be you need to ensure that higher levels of this particular product are always available.

If a certain service no longer matches the customers' needs, services may need to be adapted or updated to meet these changing needs.

Dealing with information

Simply collecting information is worthless unless the information is examined and acted on.

Keys to good practice

Solving recurring problems

✓ Accept there is a problem.

✓ Look closely at the complaints you and your colleagues have received.

✓ Study each one to see if you can find the cause.

✓ Take each recurring problem seriously and think of ways in which each can be dealt with to prevent further complaints.

Active knowledge

Think of any of the people you have told about recurring problems (e.g. managers, colleagues, etc.). How did you pass on this information? What procedures are in place in your organisation for passing on complaints? Does this system work well in your opinion?

Work with others to determine an agreed way forward for solving repeated problems

What do you do if there are no alternative solutions? Saying 'no' is hard, especially as you do not want to lose your customer.

Keys to good practice

When there are no alternatives to a problem

✓ Tell the truth but do not make your customer feel rejected.

✓ Give reasons, explaining *why* you cannot help, and do not make up excuses.

✓ Keep calm. Some customers will not take 'no' for an answer, so just repeat your message until the customer hears it. Be polite and matter of fact.

✓ Offer alternatives (e.g. 'We do not stock that product, but we do sell a similar one which has the same features and is cheaper.' The customer might not have thought about other options).

✓ End politely. If a customer is still angry and dissatisfied, thank him or her for bringing the problem to your notice. Say this is obviously an area that needs attention and at least he or she has told you about it.

Consolidation

Think about the most frequently repeated customer complaint in your organisation and consider the following points:

• What you have done to resolve the problem.

• What your colleagues have done to resolve the problem.

• What you would say to a customer when there are no alternative solutions to the problem.

At the beginning of this unit you learnt *how* to keep your customers informed of the steps you are taking to solve their problems. This element is about how you negotiate and take action to avoid customer service problems being repeated.

WHAT YOU NEED TO LEARN

• The purpose of complaints procedures.

• How to use complaints procedures to action changes to customer service systems and procedures.

The purpose of complaints procedures

All organisations should have a procedure for dealing with complaints. This may be just one procedure or a series of procedures. You need to get to know all the complaint procedures in use in your organisation so you can deal with problems efficiently and effectively. The procedures are there to help you find the best solution.

Why does an organisation need complaint procedures?

The main reason for instigating complaint procedures is because customers have a legal right to expect products or services to be of a reasonable quality. Complaint procedures have been developed to help organisations meet customers' rights and needs.

There are three main Acts of Parliament which outline customers' rights to goods and services of a reasonable quality:

1 The Sale of Goods Act 1979
2 The Supply of Goods and Services Act 1982
3 The Consumer Protection Act 1987.

Full details of these Acts of Parliament are given in Unit 1, pages 59–62.

Helping to find solutions

Complaint procedures should give information about how the customer can complain and what the organisation is responsible for. They should give some indication about what the customer can expect when making a claim. This information should help you and your colleagues to come up with the best solution and to treat each customer fairly.

Remember

Good organisations use their complaint procedures to put problems right and to help improve their service. Rather than looking at complaints in a negative way, they use the information to prevent further complaints of the same nature (recurring problems).

Customer information

Many organisations supply information to customers about:

- the products or services they provide
- how they promise to satisfy their customers (their *guarantee*)
- what the customer can do if they fail to keep their promises (this might include how to claim for compensation).

Customers may receive this information in a charter, leaflet or booklet that is distributed by, or freely available from, the organisation. For example, British Telecom has a customer charter that outlines the services it provides and what it promises to do. The charter covers:

- what the service is and what it includes
- when the service will be provided
- how faults will be repaired.

Charters usually contain a section on how to complain if the service as stated is not provided.

Active knowledge

Look at the details of your own organisation's customer service information. Consider one service or product guarantee by answering the following questions:

- What is the service or product?

- What is included in the guarantee?

- When will the service or product be provided?

- Is there anything else your organisation promises to do?

Sometimes the customer may have to agree to do certain things if he or she wants to receive the service or product. For example, if you want a telephone you have to agree to:

- pay any charges – including rental and call charges
- use the correct sockets and wiring
- use the equipment correctly and safely
- allow entry to your premises for installation and repairs
- not damage or misuse the equipment.

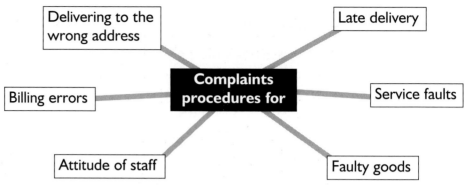

Figure 4.6 Complaints procedures

Your organisation is likely to have procedures for the situations noted in Figure 4.6. An organisation's complaint procedures should also state the following.

• The guarantee (or promises) and what is *not* covered by the guarantee.

• What the organisation will do if it breaks its promise.

• What the organisation is able to do if events occur that are beyond its reasonable control.

• What happens if the customer breaks his or her side of the agreement.

• What will happen if any matter cannot be resolved by the organisation or the customer.

• The types of compensation a customer can claim.

• Details of how to complain or make a claim. This should include:
  – the period of time allowed in which to make a claim (from when the problem arose)
  – where to complain or make a claim – an address, telephone number, fax number or e-mail address for the customer to use.

Active knowledge

Read your organisation's complaint procedure. If there are several, choose the one you use most frequently. Consider the relevant parts of the complaint procedure using the headings shown in Figure 4.7.

You may need to choose more than one procedure to solve a customer's problem: procedures are not meant to be a set of rules but *guidelines* to assist you to solve problems. The solution will depend, amongst other things, on:

Complaint procedure	Relevant points
Any guarantees (or promises)?	
What is *not* covered by the guarantee?	
What will the company do if it breaks its promise?	
What types of compensation can customers claim?	
When matters cannot be resolved, who will help?	

Figure 4.7 The relevant points about your organisation's complaints procedures

- the exact nature of the complaint
- the customer's willingness or unwillingness to help find an acceptable solution
- how the problem arose
- whether the problem is covered by a guarantee.

Active knowledge

Review some recent customer service complaints and decide which category they fall into – product or service quality or availability, staff errors or some other reason. Could they have been avoided? Does the procedure need changing? Is another department involved?

To provide solutions to a customer service problem you need to have the necessary *resources*. Resources fall into three categories:

1 *human* – the people in your team or in other parts of the organisation and their different experience and expertise

2 *financial* – the money available to solve customer service problems

3 *other* – equipment available to help you do your job, etc.

If all the complaints you received were identical, your job would be much easier. You could apply the same solution or complaint procedure to solving every problem. In fact, you could probably solve the problem once and for all. But problems do not stay the same. Customers' requirements and expectations change. What is acceptable today may not be acceptable tomorrow. You must aim to provide a continually improving service to your customers.

Many organisations try to reduce complaints by sending questionnaires to their customers to see how satisfied they are (see

Customer feedback can improve almost any type of service

Unit 5). As was noted before, for every complaint they receive, there may be several customers who have not bothered to complain and may simply have taken their business elsewhere. As a result of customer feedback, the organisation will often improve or change its product or service to meet customer needs and, consequently, to reduce customer complaints.

Active knowledge

Can you think of any changes that have been made to your organisation's products or services as a result of changing customer requirements? If so, note these down, giving the reasons why the changes were made.

How to use complaints procedures to action changes to customer service systems and procedures

Finding creative solutions to customer problems requires you to be flexible in the way you carry out your job. It may be necessary to change a procedure because it is not meeting the needs of the customer or the organisation. Perhaps the procedure needs modifying or a new procedure needs to be implemented. It is unlikely you will have the authority to do either of these, but you can make recommendations to those responsible for drawing up the procedures. This may be your team leader or quality manager.

You will need to present them with the *reasons* why the procedure needs to be amended or introduced. As customers' needs and expectations change, it may become obvious that current procedures do not cover their complaints. At these times, a new procedure might be needed.

Figure 4.8 is an example of a complaints procedure form.

Customer Complaint Form

Name and address of customer:

....

....

....

....

Name of person who received complaint:

....

Date received:

....

Description of complaint:

....

....

....

....

....

Action taken (by whom and when):

Customer feedback

Complaint resolved (by whom and when)

Figure 4.8 A complaints procedure form

Active knowledge

Think of a customer complaint that was not covered by existing procedures. Could an existing procedure be changed to meet the problem, or should a new procedure be introduced? Who would you discuss these changes with?

Consolidation

Consider the value to your customer, your organisation and to you of having written complaints procedures.

What could happen if there were no written complaints procedures?

End-of-unit test

1 Are the following statements true or false?
   - With careful planning, all problems can be anticipated.
   - There is only one solution to most problems.
   - Management should not go looking for problems.
   - Talking with colleagues can often help to solve problems.
   - The customer will always expect you to have the solution.

2 Is everything perfect if customers do not complain?

3 Is it important if the customer only has a minor problem?

4 Does it really matter if your organisation loses a customer?

5 What does the term HEAT mean?

6 Why is it important for an organisation to keep accurate customer records?

7 What is meant by conflict resolution?

8 Why is it important to identify repeated customer service problems?

9 What types of complaints are likely to recur?

10 Why does an organisation need a complaints procedure?

Unit CL 5

Promote continuous improvement

This unit is about one of the key competencies of the customer service professional: looking at ways of improving the service you provide to your customers. This should not be a one-off activity but something that is built in to everything you and your organisation do for your customers.

This unit discusses how to collect customer feedback, how to analyse this feedback and how to suggest improvements to customer service. In addition, you will learn how to implement your suggested customer service improvement and, most importantly, how to evaluate the effectiveness of these improvements.

The elements for this unit are:

5.1 Plan improvements in customer service based on customer feedback.

5.2 Implement changes in customer service.

5.3 Review changes that promote continuous improvement.

Why is continuous improvement important?

Customers are free to choose whichever organisation they want to do business with. If organisations are to stay in business, they need to ensure they retain their customers. If they improve the service they provide, they should increase their numbers of customers and therefore their profitability.

A common method organisations use to calculate a customer's value is to identify a specific customer's annual spend and to multiply this by the potential number of years that customer will do business with the organisation. However, this calculation is only valid if you *retain* your business with the customer.

Experts in customer retention have worked out that if you keep 5% of the customers who would otherwise have taken their business elsewhere, you can *double your profits*. This is the main reason why shops like Sainsbury's and Tesco have loyalty cards. (There is more about loyalty cards in Unit 2, page 105.)

WHAT YOU NEED TO LEARN

- How to gather customer feedback.
- How to identify areas for improvement.
- What the effects of any improvements will be to the customers and the organisation.

How to gather customer feedback

Listening to customers must become everyone's business. With competitors moving even faster, the race will go to those who listen (and respond) most intently (Tom Peters, *Thriving on Chaos*).

There are three areas you need to consider:

1 *What* information do you want to gather?
2 *How* are you going to collect this information?
3 *When* are you going to ask the customers?

It is likely you want to ask the customers how satisfied they are with the service your organisation provides. This is called 'customer satisfaction'. Over the years, business has done a pretty fair job of convincing customers to suffer in silence. Now, when we want, need and are beginning to respect the value of this kind of informed feedback, we have to *coax* customers to provide it. There are many reasons for this state of affairs.

- In some cases we have lulled ourselves into thinking 'no news is good news' or that it is better to 'let sleeping dogs lie'.

- Sometimes we fear that, if we seek and receive customer complaints and no corrective action ensues, we might be perceived in a worse light than if we had left well alone. Research, however, contradicts that assumption: *it is better to have asked and not acted than not to have asked at all.*

- In some cases, we simply have not worked out how to ask for complaints effectively without sounding masochistic: *please tell us how bad we are.*

- Some of us have asked incorrectly, making the process of registering a complaint so difficult or obviously pointless we fail to get helpful information.

To satisfy your customers, you need to find out what they want

• And some of us have simply given up asking – often because it isn't seen as important by the organisation.

Improving customer service

Many organisations do not undertake customer surveys because:

• they know so much about their customers from other activities (like marketing focus groups) they feel they do not need to do specific customer surveys/questionnaires
• they are frightened about what might be said
• the management think they know exactly what it is their customers want so they do not need to ask them
• they have very little idea how to go about a survey and have almost no data about their customers and do not know how to contact them to ask for opinions.

You need, first, to consider what service the customer expects from your organisation (e.g. fast delivery, responsive, pleasant staff, after-sales service, product availability, etc.). You then need to consider the following:

• every customer will have different expectations
• customers change and develop and so your service or product needs to change and develop too
• you can never know the likes and dislikes of all your customers.

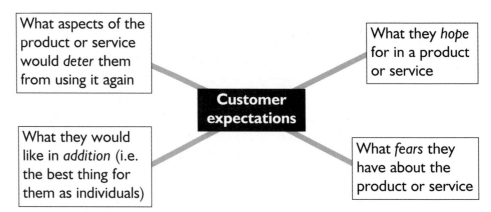

Figure 5.1 Customer expectations

Customers' expectations are based on a variety of feelings (see Figure 5.1). Whether or not your organisation can satisfy these customer expectations will often mean the difference between keeping or losing your customers. The two key questions are, therefore:

1 What do customers want?
2 Is my organisation providing it?

To get the answers to these questions you need to ask your customers for feedback. We looked briefly at obtaining customer feedback in Unit 1, Element 1.2. Here we look more closely at the methods you can use to obtain feedback from your customers.

How to gather customer feedback

There are two main methods of collecting customer feedback: *formal* and *informal*. We will consider the informal methods first (see Figure 5.2). By *observing* the behaviour of customers you become more aware of their feelings (e.g. customers may make loud remarks if they are standing in a long queue or may walk out without being served). *Talking* to the customers makes the customers feel as though the organisation cares about them and their opinions. A great deal can be learnt in this way (e.g. by using the customers' names and asking them if they are happy about the services the organisation is giving them).

This informal feedback should become part of your everyday customer service and should give you information to action yourself or pass on to others.

Figure 5.2 Informal methods of obtaining feedback

Case study

A restaurant manager noticed his regular customers were not booking as frequently as usual. He decided the only way of finding out what was wrong was to put himself in his customers' shoes. This was difficult as the staff obviously knew him and would be on their best behaviour, so he asked his cousin and her husband to spend an evening at the restaurant. They rang to book a table and the phone was answered – eventually. When asked if they could have a table in a non-smoking part of the restaurant, this appeared to be difficult. On their arrival at the restaurant they were asked to sit at the bar because their table was not ready. This was not true as, when they were shown to their table, it had been empty and laid when they had arrived. It was a wet evening and there was nowhere to hang their coats or put their umbrellas. The food was good but they felt rushed and pressured into leaving before they were really ready.

1 Why might the customers have felt dissatisfied about the way they were treated?
2 Name one action the manager could take.
3 Do you think the plan of sending the cousin was a good one? Can you think of any drawbacks?

The *formal* methods of obtaining customer feedback are shown in Figure 5.3. Figure 5.4 compares the advantages and disadvantages of each of these methods.

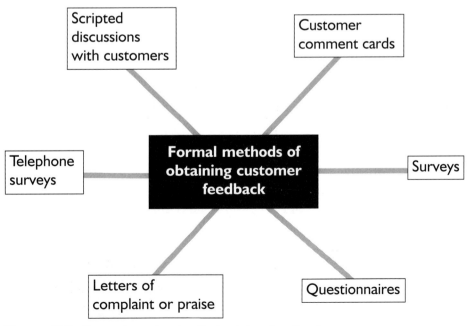

Figure 5.3 Formal methods of obtaining feedback

Method	Advantages	Disadvantages
Customer comment cards	• simple format • usually take a short time to complete • data easy to collect	• customers overlook them and do not complete • range of information may be limited
Surveys	• specific questions can be asked • a group of customers can be targeted • can be personalised • may be verbal or written	• can be expensive in time and resources • customers may not complete
Telephone surveys	as for Surveys (above) but the last point obviously does not apply	• people frequently feel their privacy is being invaded if rung at home
Questionnaires	• may be presented in a manner which encourages the customer to complete • specific questions can be asked of a particular customer group	• questions need to be very carefully written • can be expensive in resources – paper, post, etc. • customers may not complete
Scripted discussions with customers	• every customer is asked the same questions • responses received in a similar way • actual customers can be targeted	• may not capture all the customer's response • the people asking the questions need training to ensure consistency
Letters from customers (complaint or praise)	• unprompted feedback from customers	

Figure 5.4 The advantages and disadvantages of formal methods of obtaining feedback

Methods for obtaining formal feedback
Written questionnaires

This method involves a one to four-page document that asks a series of specific questions tailored to the needs of your organisation and

Have you created a savings plan in the last five years?	☐ Yes	☐ No
Do you have children still living at home?	☐ Yes	☐ No
Would you like to be contacted more frequently by your agent?	☐ Yes	☐ No

Figure 5.5 A customer survey from an insurance company

addressing the specific concerns of the customer or staff group you are surveying. The questions asked are usually phrased in one of three ways:

1 yes/no questions
2 poor/excellent questions
3 degree questions.

Yes/no questions These are closed questions, meaning they are phrased in such a way they prompt a simple 'yes' or 'no' answer (see also Unit 2, pages 95–96). These questions are most commonly used to gather general information about the customers. The customer simply circles or ticks the yes or no boxes. Figure 5.5 is an example from a customer survey conducted by an insurance company. Because closed questions are black and white and offer no shades of grey to choose from, they tend to give limited feedback. Therefore, they should only used to gather basic information and in combination with other styles of questions.

Poor/excellent questions These are usually open questions that begin with the words 'How' or 'What' and are answered either by circling or ticking a number or word that best reflects the respondent's opinion (see Figure 5.6).

The more numbers you have in the scale, the more work and tabulation you have to do when processing the responses. If you decide to make graphs from the answers you get and your questionnaire has a rating scale of 1 to 4, your graph only has to chart four categories. If you have a scale that goes from 1 to 8, the graph

How would you rate the overall service you receive from our reception staff?

☐ Poor ☐ Fair ☐ Good ☐ Excellent

What is your overall evaluation of our account department? (*Circle one*)

1	2	3	4	5	6
(Poor)					(Excellent)

Figure 5.6 Poor/excellent questions

> To what degree does our newsletter keep you informed on important trends?
> (*Circle one*)
>
> Not all   To a small degree   To a moderate degree   To a large degree

Figure 5.7 Degree questions

requires twice as many sets of numbers to chart eight categories. It is recommended you never have less than four rating categories (numbers or words) or more than eight.

Degree questions These are open questions that usually start with the words 'Did', 'Does', 'Do' or 'To what degree'. They usually refer to specific experiences or events and are rated by circling one of four specific words (see Figure 5.7). A variation on this theme are statements that offer a scale of possible answers that range from 'Strongly disagree' to 'Strongly agree'. The person answering the questionnaire is asked to circle the number or words that best reflects his or her opinion (see Figure 5.8).

If you are using numbers format and want to avoid middle-of-the-road answers, use an even series of numbers, such as 1 to 6 rather than an odd series of numbers such as 1 to 5. By circling a 3 in the odd series, the respondent has not indicated a preference of any sort and, in sitting on the fence, may not give you the kind of data you are looking for. By using an even series of numbers, you remove the middle number option and the respondent has to get off the fence and express a preference in one direction or another.

The quick response card

This is a shortened version of the full questionnaire. These are the short, one piece, often postage-paid questionnaires you find included with products you purchase at your hotel bedside or sitting between the pepper and salt pots on restaurant tables. This option is a good one if you cannot conduct a full survey or the nature of your business lends itself to this method. However, customers who will fill out

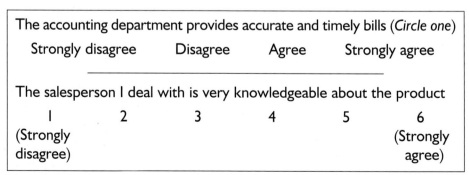

Figure 5.8 Strongly disagree/strongly agree questions

response cards are usually at either end of the spectrum – those who are very happy or very unhappy with your service.

Telephone surveys

Sometimes distance, time constraints or other factors make the telephone the ideal way to undertake a survey. Telephone surveys come in two basic styles:

1 ask and answer
2 discussion.

Ask and answer These surveys follow a pre-designed set of questions devised to be asked in one way only so as to obtain consistency. The interviewer, after explaining the type of rating scale he or she is using, reads each question to the respondent and makes a note of the answers. Because ask and answer telephone surveys are basically written questionnaires that speak, they do not necessarily require an interviewer who has any familiarity with the industry he or she is surveying. These surveys are frequently undertaken by companies who specialise in providing this service.

Discussion These telephone surveys ask more spontaneous and exploratory questions and can only be conducted effectively by an interviewer who has a good understanding of the nature of the business being surveyed. A good interviewer in this situation will pick up on part of an answer and then probe the respondent for more details. This discussion format allows for greater depth and often the discovery of issues that were not identified prior to speaking with the customer. For example:

Interviewer: What was your impression of the service mechanic who checked in your car?

Customer: He was okay.

Interviewer: Was there something he could have done better?

Customer: He seemed to be in a bad mood.

Interviewer: Was it something he said?

Customer: Not exactly, it was more the way he said 'Good morning'. He sounded kind of gruff, as if he had just had a fight with his boss.

Focus groups

Focus groups are groups of eight to ten of your customers who come together, at your invitation, to answer service-related questions that are prepared by you and then presented by your moderator. Because of the group dynamic, focus groups usually provide a lot of rich feedback in a relatively short period of time. The average focus group usually lasts between an hour and an hour and a half.

Customers are invited, by letter (usually followed with a confirmation phone call), to participate in a focus group. Breakfast or lunch is often served as a courtesy if meetings take place during the working day. Some companies invite their customers to participate in the evening and serve light refreshments.

The success of any focus group depends largely on the facilitator's or leader's skill. The facilitator can be an external consultant or someone from inside your company. Armed with a few pre-designed questions, the facilitator's main role is to:

• ensure everyone around the table has an opportunity to speak
• keep the group on track
• probe for the most in-depth information possible
• take detailed notes that will be written up.

The initial questions asked by the facilitator are usually conversation starters, such as:

• How is the overall level of service of this company?
• What would you like to see this company improve or change?
• How is the company's response when you have problems?

It is usual to invite 50% more customers than you want to attend. Doing so allows about a one-third no-show rate, which is fairly normal.

Face-to face-interviews

When you want to get the most anecdotal information from your customers in the most personal format, a face-to-face interview method is used. These are one-on-one meetings that are useful when dealing with issues such as:

• finding out why a customer has stopped doing business with you
• getting feedback from customers who deal with competing companies
• approaching senior executives for whom a group setting would be inappropriate.

It is recommended you do not use tape recorders or video cameras when you are in a face-to-face meeting. This equipment is far too obtrusive. The only acceptable method of recording your customer's feedback in this type of setting is by taking notes.

Although it takes a little more work and co-ordination, you get the best survey results by using a combination of different survey methods to poll your customers (and staff). Combining focus groups with written questionnaires, one-on-one interviews with telephone interviews or employing any other combination of methods provides the best mix of general and specific feedback, as well as qualitative and quantitative data.

Customer satisfaction questionnaires

There are two major types of customer satisfaction questionnaire formats:

1 checklist   **2** response.

Face-to-face interviews can provide valuable anecdotal information

The checklist format

For each item in the questionnaire the customer is asked to answer 'yes' or 'no'. The more items answered yes, the better the service (see Figure 5.9). A bank decided to ask customers what they thought of their service and devised the questionnaire as shown in Figure 5.10.

Please indicate whether or not each statement describes the service you received.

Check 'Yes' if the statement describes the service or 'No' if the statement does not describe the service.

	Yes	No
1. I could get an appointment with the salesman at a time I wanted.	……….	……….
2. The salesman was quick to respond when I arrived for my appointment.	……….	……….
3. The salesman immediately helped me when I entered the premises.	……….	……….
4. My appointment started promptly at the scheduled time.	……….	……….

Figure 5.9 Checklist format

Please tick the box which describes the service we provided.

	Yes	No
1 I waited a short period of time before I was helped.	☐	☐
2 The service started promptly when I arrived.	☐	☐
3 The teller handled transactions in a short period of time	☐	☐
4 The teller took a long time to complete my transaction.	☐	☐
5 The teller talked to me in a pleasant way.	☐	☐
6 The teller was very personable.	☐	☐
7 The teller carefully listened to me when I was requesting a transaction.	☐	☐
8 The teller knew how to handle the transactions.	☐	☐
9 The quality of the way the teller treated me was high.	☐	☐
10 The way the teller treated me met my expectations.	☐	☐
11 I am satisfied with the service you provided.	☐	☐

Figure 5.10 A checklist format as used by a bank

The response format

This format was designed by R. A. Likert and is still one of the main formats used today. It enables the customer to respond in varying degrees to each item that describes the service or product (see Figure 5.11, opposite).

Examples of customer satisfaction questionnaires

Figure 5.12 (page 192) is an example of a customer satisfaction questionnaire designed to get feedback from patients attending a dental practice. If you are starting from scratch and have never conducted a survey before, you may like to modify the questions shown in this figure as well as in the example shown in Figure 5.13 (page 193) and to use these examples as a basis for getting your own survey underway.

When you have decided what you are going to ask, you need to *introduce* the questionnaire to the customer. The introduction needs to explain the purpose of the questionnaire and how to complete it:

You recently received service from our organisation. Please indicate the extent to which you agree or disagree with the following statements about the service you received from (*your organisation's name*). Circle the appropriate number using the scale above.

or

In order to improve our customer service, we would like you to comment on the quality of the service …

Very poor	Poor	Neither poor nor good	Good	Very good
1	2	3	4	5

Strongly disagree	Disagree	Neither agree nor disagree	Agree	Strongly agree
1	2	3	4	5

Very dissatisfied	Dissatisfied	Neither satisfied nor dissatisfied	Satisfied	Very satisfied
1	2	3	4	5

1 I strongly disagree with this statement (SD).
2 I disagree with this statement (D).
3 I neither agree nor disagree with this statement (N).
4 I agree with this statement (A).
5 I strongly agree with this statement (SA).

	SD	D	N	A	SA
1 I could get an appointment with the salesman at a time I wanted	1	2	3	4	5
2 The salesman was quick to respond	1	2	3	4	5
3 The salesman immediately helped me when I entered the premises	1	2	3	4	5
4 My appointment started promptly at the scheduled time	1	2	3	4	5

Figure 5.11 Likert scales

Note this would normally be included on the questionnaire itself. You may, however, need to include a covering letter (see Figure 5.14, page 194).

A critical decision is also *who* is to receive the questionnaire:

• every 34th telephone caller to the Automobile Association gets a customer service questionnaire

• Kwik Fit gives customers reply-paid questionnaires with their receipts.

The final decision is *when* you are going to collect the feedback (e.g. one week or one month after the product or service you provided).

XYZ Office Supplies

Marsh Industrial Estate, Anytown AT3 6PS

Tele: 0610 355187 Fax: 0610 355189 Email XYZ@aserver.co.uk

16 July 2001

Dear Customer

We are committed to serving you, our customer, to the best of our ability. To this end, we have asked an independent consulting company to assess our customer service and commitment to the provision of a quality service.

Such a study requires we measure the perceptions of our customers. We would very much appreciate your taking a few moments to complete the enclosed questionnaire. It is designed for your candid feedback and evaluation of our company's customer service.

Please return the completed questionnaire in the postage-paid envelope to the following address by Friday, 27 July 2001.

BC Services
Old Road
Anytown
AT5 9BC

Thank you very much for your participation. We look forward to receiving your response.

Yours sincerely

A. Shamdasani
Customer Services Manager

Figure 5.14 A covering letter

Active knowledge

- What *formal* customer feedback is recorded and stored in your organisation? How is it recorded? How is it used? What is done with the results?

- What *informal* customer feedback is recorded and stored in your organisation? How is it recorded? How is it used?

If you can, suggest possible improvements to both these ways of obtaining and using the feedback you receive from your customers.

Communicate the results

The benefits of gathering feedback can be negated if the results are not followed through. Once an organisation has taken the initiative to invite feedback, it must take actions to correct at least some, if not all, of the problem areas highlighted. Going to the effort of gathering the information and then not doing anything about the problems identified is not only a waste of time and money, but can also increase the likelihood that future service improvement efforts will be viewed with scepticism.

For this reason, you must 'close the loop' in the surveys you have conducted by going back to the people who provided your organisation with the feedback. This not only confirms you have heard what they have said but also that you are making changes accordingly.

Case study

A large wholesale organisation undertook an extensive survey of their largest customers. They did this to find out what their customers really wanted and to see if the service they were providing was what their customers needed. After analysing the results they invited their customers to a breakfast meeting. The event was a 'thank you' to the customers who had given them the feedback. After breakfast the organisation presented the results – good and bad.

1 What were the benefits of this exercise to the wholesaler?
2 What were the benefits to the customers?
3 If in the future the company were to contact its customers again to undertake a similar survey, what would be the customers' response?

Analysing the results

Now you have collected the feedback you need to analyse it. This simply means you need to *count* the responses. For example, how many people:

- replied (e.g. out of 100 questionnaires sent, 45 were returned)
- responded in each category (e.g. how many answered 'yes' or 'no')
- answered 'agree' or 'disagree', etc.

A simple table can be very effective and provides a useful overall indicator of customer satisfaction. For example, part of a regular monthly report in a small restaurant could look like Figure 5.15. This format shows the results of the responses to each question. You may, however, want to select particular questions that identify whether your performance was good or bad.

Whatever way you decide to use the information, your analysis should highlight the main *trends* you can spot in the data you have collected. You should also compare the data you collected on previous occasions with the results you have just obtained. Once you have all this information, you will have a fair 'picture' of your feedback results.

Look at the customer comment slip responses for the Bay Tree Restaurant. What is your opinion of how well the restaurant is doing? What changes in the responses would the owner want to see in August and September? What follow-up research might the owners consider doing?

Presenting your results

If feedback is shown pictorially it has a far greater impact: information is always grasped more readily when it is presented this way. There is obviously more than a bit of truth in the old saying 'A picture is worth a thousand words'. Figure 5.16 suggests two ways you could present your findings – either as a pie chart or as a bar chart.

The Bay Tree Restaurant

Report on customer comment slip responses for: July

Number of responses received this month: 109

Q1   As a whole, how well do you feel we have met your needs on this occasion?

Very well	Fairly well	Not very well	Not at all
33	47	20	9

Q2   If a friend was visiting the area, would you recommend this restaurant?

Definitely	Probably	Probably not	Definitely not
13	50	25	11

Figure 5.15 Analysing the results of a survey

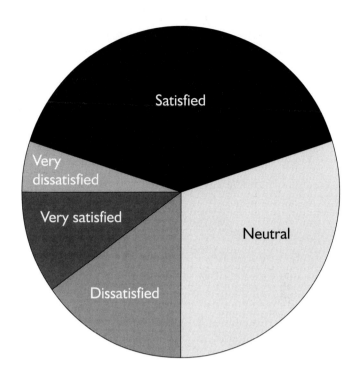

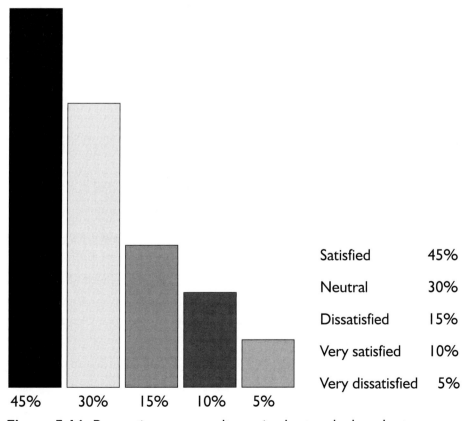

Satisfied	45%
Neutral	30%
Dissatisfied	15%
Very satisfied	10%
Very dissatisfied	5%

Figure 5.16 Presenting your results: a pie chart and a bar chart

Written reports are not the only way of presenting customer feedback – pictorial methods such as graphs can have a greater impact

How to identify areas for improvement

Customer complaints, customer satisfaction reports and problems identified by customers or staff are generally a good starting point for identifying areas in your customer service that need improvement. However, you should consider your *internal* as well as your *external* customers.

Possible areas *internal* to your organisation you could investigate include:

• your service (before and after delivery)
• your product (quality and suitability)
• your people (e.g. their attitudes)
• your systems (e.g. administration and documentation)
• other factors (e.g. suppliers, product faults, service-level agreements, contracts, legal requirements, etc.).

Customers will often say they want a *quality* product or service, but what do they mean? The true measure of quality is the ability of a product or service to meet the customer's needs. Quality is:

• fitness for purpose
• fitness for use to the extent the user expects.

For example, if you buy a toaster you expect it to toast bread. If you buy a toaster in a sale because it has a slight dent in its cover, it must still be able to toast! This is *fitness for purpose*. (Refer back to Unit 1, pages 59–60, for information concerning the legal aspects of fitness for purpose.) Suffice it to say that the costs of poor quality are conservatively estimated for most organisations to be in excess of 25% turnover!

We have looked at what a customer might mean by a quality service or product. We now need to consider service quality as a *system*. Figure 5.17 illustrates a system for providing the customer with a quality service. If you do not review each stage of the system constantly, you will not be providing the customers with the service they expect and will not be looking at improving the service.

If any part of this system is not working efficiently, you will not be delivering good customer service. You should therefore target that area for improvement. If your organisation has contractual or service-level agreements with its customers, these will provide clear guidelines as to what the customer can expect from your organisation. For example:

- delivery guaranteed within 28 days
- the item will be fully installed
- the old item removed at the time the new item is delivered.

What the effects of any improvements will be to the customers and the organisation

Any areas of improvement will impact on the customer and/or the organisation. However, if the cost of introducing an improvement is prohibitively expensive, such an improvement is unrealistic.

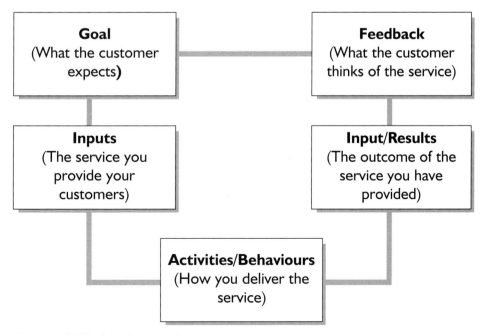

Figure 5.17 Service quality as a system

Service	Customers want to know whether the delivery will be am or pm Saturday deliveries
Product	Staff need greater product knowledge so they are in a better position to advise customers
People	Reminding staff of why it is important to smile at customers
Systems	The documentation required for customer service delivery should be available to all who need it at the time they need it. Not 'Sorry, the office is closed, I cannot help you'
Supplier and product faults	The organisation should review its suppliers. You are part of the team who reports back to the 'management' when things go wrong with suppliers
Service-level agreements and contracts	You are likely to be part of the team who are implementing or who are affected by these. Give feedback about any areas where there may be problems and which could be improved

Figure 5.18 Possible improvements to customer service

Remember that you need to balance the needs of the customer with those of the organisation. Some very small changes to systems or procedures, on the other hand, may dramatically improve the service to the customer at very little cost to the organisation. These are the areas your organisation needs to identify (see Figure 5.18 for examples of areas you might like to consider).

Active knowledge

Consider at least one area that would improve customer service in your organisation. How would this impact on the customer? Would it involve significant changes to the systems in the organisation?

Consolidation

If your line manager asked you to recommend one method of gathering customer feedback for your sector, what would you suggest and why?

You should consider both formal and informal methods.

WHAT YOU NEED TO LEARN

- How to recognise areas for change.
- How to plan and organise the changes.
- How to implement the changes within your organisational guidelines.

How to recognise areas for change

One of the greatest challenges organisations face is adapting to the pace of change. So what is *change*?

> Alvin Toffler (in *Future Shock*) states: 'Change is the process by which the future invades our lives.'

We are living in a world where change is inevitable – fashion changes each season, the decor in our homes goes in and out of style, kitchen appliances are 'improved' and updated. Change seems to be happening faster and faster. If change is happening in our private lives, it is certainly happening in business too. And organisations that do not change or 'move with the times' are unlikely to remain competitive.

Active knowledge

What changes have happened in your organisation in the past nine months? The following headings may help you to identify these:

- changes in personnel
- changes in service
- changes in a system or a product.

Change in *your* organisation is necessary because:

- competitors change and improve
- customer expectations change
- organisations around you change.

Therefore change is vital in any organisation. While people are often reluctant to change, if an organisation is to move forward, we all need to *plan* these changes. The causes for change are known as *driving forces* or *restraining forces* (see Figure 5.19).

> A driving force is often a need to change in order to solve a problem.
>
> A restraining force is one that is exerting pressure not to change.

Figure 5.19 Driving forces and restraining forces

The following are some examples of the driving forces that could affect your organisation:

- your *customers* – changing their buying patterns
- your *competitors* – their advertising and pricing policy
- *new technology* – e-commerce
- *new regulations for your industry* – new Acts of Parliament.

Any or all of the above will have an effect on your organisation and may mean a change is necessary.

Restraining forces (i.e. forces on your organisation *not* to change) are frequently to do with feelings or attitudes:

- we have always done it like this and there is no need to change
- a change will mean I have to change and I do not think I can.

If these forces are not recognised and addressed, the organisation is unlikely to change, which may stop the organisation growing and developing.

Types of change

A *reactive* change is often described as a change you cannot control but to which you need to react. A *proactive* change is one you can control. Reacting quickly to change is a key factor in the success of any business, and an organisation needs to be able to react innovatively and creatively.

Every member of staff needs to be able to accept and welcome change.

How to plan and organise the changes

As already noted, the key to implementing any change is careful planning. By careful planning you will increase your chances of success. To begin with you need to consider:

- what you are aiming to achieve
- how you are going to get there.

Planning in this way helps you to focus on several aspects of the proposed change:

- *who* is to be involved
- *what* needs to be done
- *why* the change is necessary
- *how* things are to be done
- *when* each step is to be undertaken and when it will be completed.

One way to get started is by drawing up an action plan (see Figure 5.20).

Proposed change:	To complete customer order within 3 working days.
Whom does this involve?	Our team, the packaging and despatch departments.
What needs to be done?	Our team to complete the order details on day 1, send to packaging for day 2 and to despatch for day 3.
When does this need to happen?	Each stage to be completed by 15.30 on each day.
Why does this need to be done?	To provide a better service to the customers who can get this service from our local competitor.
How can this be achieved?	Put a proposal together. Get agreement from my team leader and arrange a meeting between the various departments.

Figure 5.20 An example of an action plan

Remember

When planning change, consider Murphy's Law: 'If things can go wrong they will go wrong.'

In the example of an action plan given in Figure 5.21, an extra column has been added for 'Alternatives'. You need to plan for alternative courses of action should things not go exactly as planned. This is called *contingency planning* or 'What if ...?': if this goes wrong, then I would do this ...

Active knowledge

Draw up an action plan for a proposed change you might implement in your own organisation. Remember to use the *who*, *what*, *when*, *why* and *how* headings (see Figure 5.20) and to plan the contingencies.

Now you have your action plan and have identified who is to be involved, it is likely you will need to get agreement for your plan. This may be your supervisor or line manager. To implement changes, you will need permission from a more senior member of staff to ensure you are working within the organisation's guidelines. If your change involves members of staff from other areas or has a cost implication, it is vital you have management co-operation. You will certainly have to get the agreement of colleagues who are included in the plan.

Remember

Unless you involve everyone at this early stage, you will not get the co-operation you need to make your plan work.

The RED cycle

The RED cycle will help in the process of providing your customers with a better service (see Figure 5.22). RED stands for:

Research: you need to find out what your customers think about your organisation. This may be by surveys, questionnaires or one-to-one discussions.
Evaluate: do the research findings accord with the standards of service your organisation espouses (e.g. 'To provide the best cost-effective service')?
Determine: what changes need to be made to ensure your organisation meets the needs and expectations of your customers?

- Preparing a survey and analysing the results is the *research*.
- Comparing the level of service the organisation states it will provide with what it actually does provide is *evaluation*.
- Identifying the changes that need to be done is *determination*.

Everyone who is to be involved in your plan needs to know your reasons for the proposed change, and the benefits of your plan to the customers, to the organisation and to themselves.

How to implement the changes within your organisational guidelines

You now have all the information you would need to make a presentation to those people who need to approve your proposed changes. This could be in the form of a written paper or a verbal presentation (in either case supported by your research findings).

Action to be taken	Alternatives	By whom	By when

Figure 5.21 An action plan with an 'Alternatives' section

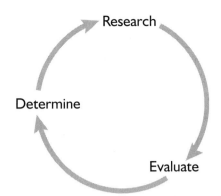

Figure 5.22 The RED cycle

As you begin to implement your proposed change you need to make notes of people's reactions and to consider if you need to make any adjustments to your plan. Your adjustments need to be based on the facts you have gathered using formal or informal feedback methods. You would then need to update your action plan to reflect the changes – this might mean involving different people and changing dates.

Case study

The Post Office decided to change the way it displayed its leaflets at the counters. As all the forms have identification numbers, the team decided to put them in numerical order with a list beside them on a display board explaining which number referred to which form.

After a week the counter staff discussed the changes and found they had been inundated by queries from customers who could not locate the leaflets they needed. So they decided to put 'like' leaflets together (e.g. all those to do with driving in one place). They reviewed the outcome at the end of two weeks and found they had had fewer enquiries from customers as to where to find the leaflets.

1 Why do you think the Post Office saw a need to change the way it displayed its leaflets?
2 Why did the initial change not work?
3 Who gave the feedback, and what type of feedback was it?

Consolidation

You have been asked to brief your team on a proposed change to customer service that you have suggested. What would you need to consider and prepare before your briefing meeting?

WHAT YOU NEED TO LEARN

• Collect and record the feedback on the effects of the change.

• Summarise the advantages and disadvantages of the changes.

• Use your evaluation of change to identify opportunities for further improvement.

• Share your findings with others.

Figure 5.23 is an example of a cycle of continuous improvement. You have completed this cycle as far as implementing the proposed change. You now need to consider the remainder of the cycle.

Collect and record the feedback on the effects of the change

When any changes have been made it is vital they are *monitored* and *evaluated*. Monitoring is reviewing what has happened as a result of the change. Evaluating is the identification of how effective the change has been. To begin the process of evaluation, you need to monitor the change by collecting feedback on your change. If you have decided on informal feedback, you will still need to record comments or statements in order to substantiate your findings.

Figure 5.23 A cycle of continuous improvement

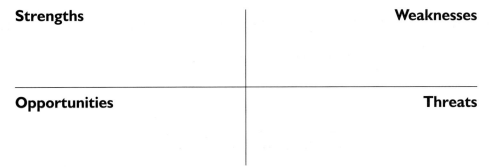

Strengths	Weaknesses

Opportunities	Threats

Figure 5.24 SWOT analysis grid

Summarise the advantages and disadvantages of the changes

One way of analysing your findings is by using a SWOT analysis. As you saw in Unit 3, SWOT stands for:

Strengths   usually internal to
Weaknesses   the organisation

Opportunities usually external to
Threats   the organisation

- Strengths identify the areas you can build on to ensure improved customer service.

- Weaknesses can be turned into strengths if identified at an early stage.

- Opportunities need to be identified and acted on as soon as possible.

- Threats need to be recognised and dealt with.

These are often set out as a grid (see Figure 5.24). SWOT is a well tried and tested form of analysis and can be used in many circumstances. For example, a team leader in a call centre decided to carry out a SWOT analysis on the team's performance (see Figure 5.25). By using a SWOT analysis in this way you can begin to identify the advantages and disadvantages of the changes you have implemented. It is important you consider customer expectations and the costs of providing the service. You may also have to consider how your industry's regulatory requirements affect the changes you have proposed and made.

Strengths	Weaknesses
A number of loyal customers supply us with repeat business	*Customers complain they cannot get through on the phone as it is always busy*

Opportunities	Threats
New product about to be launched	*New call centre has opened providing a quicker turnround on orders*

Figure 5.25 A completed SWOT analysis

Use your evaluation of change to identify opportunities for further improvement

It is at this point in the cycle you need to check your findings and to think about whether you need to make any further changes. You may have to go around this 'loop' several times until you feel confident you can take your findings to your supervisor or manager: it is not sufficient to go to your manager and say: 'I think the change is working but I'm not sure.' You need to have facts and figures and evidence of your findings. This is sometimes called a *business case*.

Your business case could include the following:

- customer and/or colleague feedback
- findings from the research you undertook *before* deciding what area of customer service you wanted to change
- records of meetings or discussions with colleagues
- a SWOT analysis
- a cost analysis.

A *cost analysis* may identify how much the change has cost in financial terms or in terms of staff time. You need to consider:

- how much staff time has been involved – and whether this has increased or decreased
- if sales have increased
- if customer complaints have been reduced
- if turnround time has increased or decreased.

The outcome of the cost analysis may identify that the change has:

- cost the organisation *x* number of £s but the number of customer complaints has reduced
- saved the staff from unnecessary administration
- streamlined a process or service, so becoming more efficient.

Your business case should identify the areas shown in Figure 5.26.

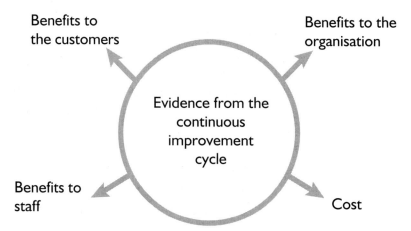

Figure 5.26 The areas identified by a business case

Share your findings with others

Now you have prepared a 'business case' you are in a position to share your findings with your supervisor and any of the other people involved. You need to *plan* how you are going to present your findings/business case. The *who*, *what*, *when*, *where* and *how* headings we have looked at previously are one way.

The *what* and *how* need careful consideration, however. Sufficient information needs to be given to justify the change you have implemented. If you give people too much information, it may become confusing! As stated previously, your presentation may be written in the form of a report, a verbal presentation with supporting written details in the form of handouts, or a visual presentation using acetates or PowerPoint.

Information should be clear and concise and based on the business case supported by evidence from the improvement cycle.

Remember

The well known saying: **P**erfect **P**lanning **P**revents **P**oor **P**erformance.

Three questions that will measure performance

Customer surveys, questionnaires and one-on-one discussions are all important tools – but a customer need only answer three questions to help you determine where questions should be asked during every single customer contact, particularly if the contact was the result of a complaint.

1 *Based on our performance, do you plan to continue doing business with us or purchase additional products or services from us?* If the answer is 'yes', you have met the minimum expectations of this customer and laid the groundwork for continuing contact and selling opportunities.
2 *Do you know of anyone else who could benefit from our services?* If your customer is willing to provide you with a referral, you know you have met the majority of this customer's expectations.
3 *Would you be willing to endorse our product/service to others?* If your customer is willing personally to endorse and support your organisation to others, pat yourself on the back – you have exceeded this customer's expectations.

As we said at the beginning, this should not be a one-off activity but built into the organisation's culture and involving all staff at all times.

Consolidation

If you were asked what continuous improvement means to you and your organisation, what would you say?

Why is it necessary to monitor and evaluate changes carefully? How might you do this?

End-of-unit test

1 What does customer feedback mean?

2 Name three ways of collecting feedback.

3 What is a focus group?

4 What are the advantages of a telephone survey?

5 What are the disadvantages of questionnaires?

6 When a checklist format is used in a questionnaire, the responses are always 'yes' or 'no'. Is this true or false?

7 Name two graphical ways of presenting the results of a survey.

8 Why should changes always be planned 'according to organisational guidelines'?

9 Why is it necessary to plan for contingencies?

10 What do the initials in a SWOT analysis stand for?

11 The key elements of a business case are benefits to the customer, the organisation and staff, and the costs – true or false?

12 What is the RED cycle?

13 What do you gain by planning changes?

14 Why is it important to evaluate changes?

15 What are the three basic questions that will measure performance?

Unit CL 6

Develop your own and others' customer service skills

If you are doing this unit you are probably someone who understands that we all learn from things in our everyday experiences. Even better if you are someone who does something with that learning to make positive changes. In the context of your role in customer service, making changes for the better (whether big or small) helps to improve your own customer service performance. By harnessing

What I **hear**, I *forget*.
What I hear and **see**, I *remember* a little.
What I hear, see and **ask questions** about, I start to *understand*.
What I hear, see, discuss and **do**, I *acquire* knowledge and skills.
When I **coach** others, I *master*.

Adapted from Confucius

your ability to make changes to your own performance, you can also help others to do the same.

The elements for this unit are:

6.1 Develop your own customer service skills.

6.2 Plan the coaching of others in customer service.

6.3 Coach others in customer service.

You can see from this that this unit is all about improving your own customer service skills and coaching others to do the same. When you coach or help people to develop, you do not necessarily have to be their manager, leader or supervisor. However, you will need to be skilled in helping people to help themselves learn and develop.

The unit starts by looking at your own performance.

Develop your own customer service skills

- What your organisation can do to help you and others develop.
- How to review your personal strengths and development needs.
- How to create and use a personal development and action plan.

What your organisation can do to help you and others develop

Before you start to look at your own performance, you need to understand what your organisation has in place by way of systems and procedures to develop its employees. This could be very wide ranging and you may be surprised at what you find is available.

We are not just talking about sending people off once a year on an 'everything you need to know about customer service in three fun-filled days' course. There are all sorts of systems and procedures an organisation can put in place to ensure they help their employees improve their customer service performance.

These can be processes that are done:

- *to* you
- *by* you
- *by* you *to* others.

One of the simplest ways of ensuring *you* have a say is for you to take responsibility for your own personal development and action planning. Figure 6.1 suggests some ways in which organisations support their employees with personal development.

Active knowledge

1 Which of the activities listed in Figure 6.1 are done:

- *to* you
- *by* you
- *by* you *to* others?

2 Think about the organisational systems and processes you have used to develop your customer service performance. What activities were the most successful? Why did they work?

Activity	What happens
What others can tell you about your own performance	
Performance appraisals	Discussions with a line manager (or someone who has direct responsibility for you) on your performance against agreed criteria/objectives/goals. These discussions are formal and are usually recorded in some way in order that your performance can be assessed over a set period of time. The outcomes of these discussions can be used to plan what you need to do in the future to be effective in your role. They can also be used to assess your contribution to the organisation for the purposes of reward and recognition (e.g. a pay rise).
Feedback	You ask for feedback or it is given to you without prompting. Feedback is often given spontaneously and is not always about your performance against agreed objectives – it can simply be about the way you handled a particular customer transaction. It does not have to be from someone who has direct responsibility for you. Some organisations operate a system called 360 degree appraisal. This is about obtaining feedback from colleagues, customers, suppliers, etc., as well as the more traditional feedback mentioned above. The coaching process will also involve giving and receiving feedback.
Changing roles	
Work shadowing	Having the opportunity to shadow (i.e. observe/ask questions of someone else about how he or she does his or her job).
Job swaps	Swapping your job with that of someone else in a different part of your organisation for a day or a week or two to get an insight into another role.
Secondments	Working in another organisation or a different part of your own organisation for a set period of time. This can be for many months and may involve someone else needing to do your job. Secondments in other organisations give you an insight into how other people deal with customer service issues.

Other processes	
Learning logs	A system of recording what happened, what you have learnt from the experience and how you will use the experience – a personal learning diary.
Personal development and action plans	A system of recording your learning and development objectives, what you have agreed to do to meet these objectives, details of any help you may require and notes made by you and/or others as to your progress.
Taking action on feedback	All the feedback you get or ask for will be wasted unless you do something with it. Some organisations actively look to ensure feedback is used.
Training and development activities	
Resource centres	Larger organisations especially have resources and facilities for their employees to use to develop their knowledge and skills. This might include a library where you would be able to obtain books, magazines, newspapers, periodicals and reports. Or perhaps using an interactive CD-ROM or using the Internet to learn about customer service. It could also involve watching a video or undertaking a computer-based activity.
Training courses and workshops	Some organisations will run their own; others will pay for you to go elsewhere to learn and practise customer service skills. It is important you know the objectives of the course you are attending to see whether it fits your aims. You should also discuss your attendance with your line manager (or whoever is responsible for you) before going. This is to ensure all parties get best value from the event – that you know why you are going, how it will help you and what is expected of you. When you come back you should also discuss what you have learnt and how you will use your new-found knowledge and skills.
Coaching	Having someone available to help you enhance your customer service performance.
Qualifications	Supporting you in terms of time and money to undertake a course of study. This might lead to a qualification in customer service (e.g. an NVQ).

Figure 6.1 The organisation's role in an individual's personal development

3 What changes have you made to the way in which you do things that are a direct result of what you have learnt from these activities?

4 How has the customer benefited?

5 How have your organisation and colleagues benefited?

6 What stands out as the key thing you have learnt which you think others might benefit from as well?

How to review your personal strengths and development needs

In this fast-moving world where so much changes so quickly, you need to approach life as an opportunity to learn. Clearly, you need to know what customer service skills you need in order to be effective in your role. In Unit 3 we talked about job descriptions. If you have a job description it may list the skills you need. If not, you should talk to whoever is responsible for you (or another appropriate person) to get a full understanding of the skills you require. A properly conducted appraisal discussion is another opportunity for you to do this (see Figure 6.2).

Name .... **Role Title** ....

Dept .... **Period Covered** ....

Reporting Officer/Supervisor/ Manager ....

Key Objectives
These are my key objectives I have agreed for this year
-
-
-
-

Success Measures
This is how I will demonstrate I have made progress towards and/or achieved these objectives
-
-
-
-

Achievements
This is what I have achieved in terms of my agreed objectives
-
-
-

This is what I have contributed outside of my agreed objectives
-
-
-

Development Actions
This is what I have done to develop the knowledge and skills I need to be a competent . . .
-
-
-

Figure 6.2 A sample appraisal discussion form

You can start to understand how skills affect your ability to be effective by first looking at your approach to personal development. The skills involved with your ability to learn and develop are shown in Figure 6.3. Of course, you have to *want* to learn! Like most things in life, your attitude to learning will determine whether you actually *do* learn anything and make positive changes as a result.

Your learning skills may involve you in:

- asking questions
- making suggestions
- looking for different ways of doing things
- taking some calculated risks (having a go)
- learning from mistakes
- reflecting and reviewing what happens
- sharing your learning with others
- taking responsibility for your own learning and development.

Whatever role you are in, there are probably some basic or key skills you will need no matter where you work:

- communication skills
- the skill of working with numbers (numeracy skills)
- IT skills

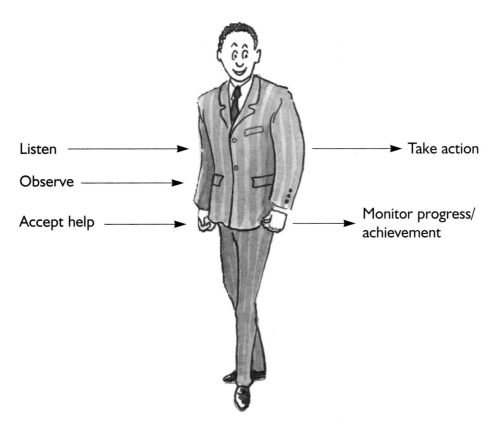

Listen ⟶

Observe ⟶

Accept help ⟶

⟶ Take action

Monitor progress/ achievement

Figure 6.3 The skills involved in learning and development

- the skill of working with others
- problem-solving skills
- the skill of learning and developing yourself.

A customer would probably say he or she would want you to be really good at communicating with him or her. Your supervisor or manager may say it is particularly important for you to be highly skilled in problem-solving. It doesn't really matter which is given priority since it is a *combination* of knowledge and skills working together that will make you effective in your role.

Only by knowing in some detail what customer service skills you require will you be able to learn how to develop them.

Active knowledge

Here are *some* suggestions for the specific customer service skills that make up your role:

- telephone skills
- influencing skills
- asking for help
- IT skills
- being flexible
- time management
- working alone
- using your own initiative.

Now in pairs or as a group, carry out a brainstorm. Continue the list by writing down all the skills that are needed to work in a customer service role. Then individually choose your 'top ten'. These are the ten skills that rate most highly. Finally, you could score yourself out of 10 on each of your top-ten skills. What does this tell you about your own performance?

Once you have established the customer service skills you require, the next step is to assess which skills you have, which you do not have and which need development.

When you are good at a particular skill you have a *strength* in that skill. When you need to do some work on a skill to be effective, you have a *development* need. You should remember, however, that just because you have a strength in something doesn't mean you should sit back and do nothing. There is usually something that can be done continuously to improve what you do. Nothing is ever perfect!

Your line manager, supervisor or whoever is responsible for you will help you to understand where your strengths and development needs lie. This is best done if you have first agreed with this person

Even when you are successful with customers, there is always room for improvement

which customer service skills are appropriate to your role. This is important as, without doing this, you will not know what you are being judged on.

It would also be a good idea to prepare yourself for any discussion by assessing your own strengths and development needs. Do this once you have understood fully the customer service skills you require. Figure 6.4 is a checklist of some quick questions you could ask

✓ What are the things I am doing well?

✓ How do I *know* I am doing these things well?

✓ What, if anything, do I need to do differently?

✓ How should I put these changes into place?

✓ Do I need any help?

✓ Has anything happened at work today I wish hadn't?

✓ How could I have dealt with the situation differently?

✓ What was I doing at the time?

✓ What have I done that has made me proud today?

✓ How have I made it easy for my customers?

Figure 6.4 Assessing your own strengths and development needs: a checklist

yourself to reflect and make a judgement on your own performance. A really good way of ensuring your answers to these questions (and any others that are appropriate to you) are used to help you learn and develop is to use a learning log.

Learning logs

There will be many times when you have been a customer yourself and have told yourself in your head you would never treat a customer in the way you have just been treated. The chances are, however, that you soon forget exactly what it was you promised yourself that you would never do. Similarly, what about all the times when you've said 'that was a great idea' or 'I really liked the way that person spoke to me'?

A learning log is simply a sort of learning diary that helps you to learn from experiences you have both at work and in your personal life. By having the discipline of recording what you have learnt you are more likely to *do* something with the learning.

Date	ACTIVITY What I did/ what happened	OUTCOMES What have I learnt	ACTIONS How will I will use this experience
23 Jan	Took call from distressed guest who had been ill in the night. This was followed up by another similar call.	I don't know how to handle situations where guests are ill. I didn't ask them if they needed anything nor did I make a note of their name or room number. I now realise there might also be legal implications for my hotel.	There is no process for dealing with this. I don't want to feel so helpless again so am going to speak to the General Manager about what staff are supposed to do. I am going to learn about the causes of food poisoning. I also need to know about the legal implications. But first, I will remember to ask guests what they need and to offer to get bottled water to their rooms.

Figure 6.5 Meena's learning log

Your learning log can also help you to discuss your strengths and development needs with the person who is responsible for you. This is because you will be recording how you have changed and developed as a result of what you have learnt. Look at the example of Meena.

Case study: Meena

Meena works on the reception desk in a hotel. Figure 6.5 is an example of part of a learning log Meena completes at the end of each day. Early one morning she took a call from a distressed guest who said she had been very ill during the night and, as she had only eaten in the hotel for the past couple of days, it had to be something to do with the hotel restaurant. Shortly after she had finished speaking to this guest, another call came through to her with the same problem.

1 How should Meena approach the General Manager with her thoughts?
2 From the entries in her learning log, do you think Meena has considered *all* the implications of how she dealt with the guests?
3 What difference will Meena make to customer service at the hotel by following through her course of action?

How to create and use a personal development and action plan

We have looked at how a learning log can help you to learn from the experiences you have. What is important is that you now convert this into *action*. Take another look at Meena's learning log. Notice the final column – Meena talks about what she *intends* to do, not how she will go about doing it. Translating intentions into actions can be done through the completion of a *personal development and action plan* – a PDP.

A typical PDP will include:

- your learning and development objectives (agreed between you and your line manager, if you have one)
- what you intend to do – the actions you will take
- details of any support you may require
- review notes – somewhere for you to record your progress
- a target date.

Figure 6.6 shows what Meena's PDP might look like. You can see that all Meena has had to do is to look at her learning log and then describe how she will bring her intentions to life.

Learning and development objectives	Action points	Support and resources required	Review notes	Target date
To understand the causes of food poisoning	Search the Local Council's Environmental Health website for information	None	Search completed – my new knowledge has given me further cause for concern about the lack of any system or process to deal with guests telling the hotel they have fallen ill	30 Jan
To know the legal implications/health and safety issues associated with guests complaining	Talk to training department	None	Hotel has no formal training/knowledge base	30 Jan
To implement a process for dealing with guest illnesses	Arrange meeting with General Manager to share info. Develop a solution	General Manager – time for meeting to discuss	Dependent on outcome of meeting	Meeting fixed for 5 Feb at 10.30 am
To become confident in the way I handle distressed customers	Ask colleagues for feedback	Seek agreement of colleagues to help me	On-going	On-going
To balance the needs of my customers with those of the hotel	Review outcome of meeting with General Manager	To be decided		6 Feb

Figure 6.6 Meena's PDP

Active knowledge

Find out if your organisation has a system for using learning logs and/or personal development and action plans. Then, using the forms your organisation provides for you or by drawing up your own:

- start to complete them in relation to developing your customer service skills
- ensure you review your progress and amend/update your PDP appropriately.

Sources of information to help you create a PDP

We have looked at how you can learn from experience. Figure 6.7 gives some more suggestions for where you might look in order to create a PDP and develop your customer service skills.

Agreeing actions

Some things we do to learn and develop can be very informal and do not require the agreement of someone else in your organisation. For instance, you may make an effort to read the financial pages of your newspaper to keep yourself up to date with competitor activities.

Learning opportunity	Thoughts for your PDP
Learning from experience	Translate learning log entries into actions
Attending training events/workshops/ courses/seminars/conferences, etc.	What do you need to do to put your new knowledge and skills into practice?
Reading magazines/press articles/ web articles	How does the information relate to you and customer service?
Asking for feedback from: • colleagues • customers • line managers	Am I happy the feedback I have obtained is accurate? What do I need to do?
Performance reviews	What have I agreed with my line manager to do?
Self-analysis	Critical review of my strengths and development needs
Learning from others when I am a customer	What do I like/not like?

Figure 6.7 Learning opportunities for completing a PDP

This may involve you changing the newspaper you buy or buying an additional newspaper once a week. Either way, it is probably something that can be done by you without seeking agreement from someone in your organisation. What you are doing is keeping pace with change.

However, you need to be sure that what you are learning is relevant to your role and to improving your customer service knowledge and skills. You can only really do this if you *agree the actions* you need to take. For this reason, you should never go on a course or any training event without knowing why you are going on it! What is it you are expected to learn, and how will this relate to your role? What will the benefits be for customer service? All this should be discussed with whoever is responsible for you before you attend.

Likewise, when you come back you should have a further discussion which sets out what you learnt and what you need to do to put your new-found knowledge and skills into practice. In other words, you are following the steps suggested when you complete a learning log and PDP.

You should also ensure the actions you agree follow the SMART method. Ask yourself if you can say 'yes' to the statements shown in Figure 6.8. (There is more about SMART in Unit 3.)

Having got this far with the creation of your personal development and action plan you will, of course, need to review and update it over time. How often you do this is up to you, but your reviews should be timed to enable you to put in place any necessary corrective action before the passing of time makes this impossible or difficult.

The personal development activities that have been agreed with the person responsible for me are:

Specific – written down in precise terms. No woolly words or ambiguous meanings

Measurable – we will both know when and how I carried out the activities

Achievable – what I have agreed to do is a challenge and all the resources/support I need are available to me

Realistic – I have agreed to a development action that will involve me changing what I do or know. This change is within my reach – it is not too huge for me to contemplate

Timebound – we have agreed a date when my development actions will be reviewed and/or completed.

Figure 6.8 SMART personal development activities

'Behaviour breeds behaviour' – if your body language is positive, it is likely to be mirrored back to you

Clearly, reviewing your PDP will involve you with obtaining feedback.

Before we move on to looking at how you might set about this we will first look at the *importance of behaviour*. This is because you will need to listen to feedback given to you and to be open and honest with what you are being told. This will involve you in either accepting or rejecting the personal feedback you have been given. The value you place on the feedback you receive will be directly related to your own views and opinions about the person giving it to you. The conclusions you reach about other people will be based on the way you see them behave. Likewise, the conclusions other people reach about you are based on your own behaviour.

Like an umbrella that stops you getting wet, we all wear an invisible 'behaviour blanket'. This blanket soaks up bad or ineffective behaviour which we then copy back. Or it gives out good behaviour that can be mirrored by the people we are with at the time (see Unit 2, pages 69–72, for more about body language in general). Raise your voice to someone and he or she is likely to shout back. Lowering your voice and speaking at a slower pace can help to calm an angry customer until he or she is also speaking in a more controlled and effective way. This is sometimes referred to as 'behaviour breeds behaviour'. Behaviour includes things like frowning, smiling, crying, shouting, whispering, doodling, fidgeting, pacing up and down, praising, criticising, being passive or assertive, being confident or shy. The list is endless (see Figure 6.9).

Figure 6.9 'Behaviour breeds behaviour'

Remember

Behaviour affects everything you do. Understanding this is crucial to your success as a customer service practitioner and as a coach for others. You are your behaviour. Behaviour is always observable, unlike the *reasons* for your behaviour: your attitudes, beliefs and emotional feelings.

Obtaining feedback

Obtaining *customer* feedback is covered in detail in Unit 1. Giving and receiving feedback in the context of *teamwork* is discussed in Unit 8. Here the focus is on obtaining and receiving feedback that is directly concerned with your own personal development.

If you are wondering if there is more to getting feedback than just asking a question and listening to the answer, you would be right. For a start, you need to find the right person – someone who knows enough about you and what you do so as to be able to give you some constructive feedback. It should not be someone who will take the easy route and say what you want to hear!

Keys to good practice

Obtaining feedback about your own personal development

✓ Choose the right person – someone you trust, who knows about the areas you wish to receive feedback on. For instance, you wouldn't ask your organisation's IT specialist to give you feedback on your complaint-handling skills but you might ask him or her to give you feedback on your IT skills.

✓ Try not to surprise someone with a request for feedback. Give him or her plenty of notice and tell him or her specifically what you need feedback on.

✓ Don't just say 'I want feedback on my customer service skills' – try to be more specific.

✓ Agree a date, time and location for the discussion. Try to make this somewhere private where you will both feel able to listen and talk.

✓ The day before, remind your person about the meeting – don't just turn up expecting him or her to be there.

✓ During the meeting, receive the feedback genuinely. Try not to become defensive or aggressive.

✓ Avoid justifying your actions if you disagree with what you are hearing. Clarify the situation by asking for specific examples.

tasks doesn't seem to help), finding a challenge can often be the answer. For instance, Meena's learning log indicates she is uncomfortable dealing with situations she is unfamiliar with:

• Do you think she is a confident person?

• What is the real issue here?

• Given the appropriate feedback and coaching, would a change to her daily routine expose her to a range of situations that might help her confidence?

Role playing

Meena didn't like having to deal with a distressed customer. Could she have found a colleague in the hotel to act out the part of a distressed customer in order for her to practise her skills? Ideally, an independent person, perhaps her coach, should be on hand to observe what happens and to give feedback.

Work-shadowing

Work-shadowing would involve Meena in spending time with another individual who has a similar role. Perhaps her hotel belongs to a chain of hotels. If so, it might be possible to spend some time seeing how other people handle customer calls to reception.

Secondments

Meena might be able to work at another hotel in her group for perhaps a week or longer.

Problem-solving groups

Meena's PDP clearly indicates she wishes to learn about food poisoning and then implement a process for dealing with guest illnesses. This shows a keenness to put things right on her part and also to share information with colleagues. Meena might work well in a problem-solving group set up specifically to find a solution to such issues.

Networking

Perhaps not so relevant to Meena's situation but don't shut the door completely on this opportunity to learn. Think about her situation – a hotel receptionist possibly working for a chain of hotels. Do the hotel employees meet either formally or informally – perhaps socially? Do hotel employees from a particular locality get together? There are plenty of opportunities to learn and develop by meeting with people from similar backgrounds, either from your own organisation or external to it.

Getting qualified

Meena will find there is nothing like achieving a professional qualification if she wants recognition for what she does. Plus, of course, the huge bonus of being able to develop her skills and knowledge at the same time. A coach would be able to explore this course of action with her.

Performance reviews

Meena should discuss the food-poisoning incident, how she handled it and what she has done since the event with whoever is responsible for her. The feedback she gets should help her to assess the effectiveness of her course of action.

In addition to these learning opportunities, Meena and her coach should ensure they know what support is available from the hotel – their organisation.

Relating this to your role as a coach, you will be in a position to explore options with your coachee. So as well as any naturally occurring opportunities, you should also know about the functions of your training and development department, if you have one:

- What support can they give?
- What training courses are available?
- Who can go on them?
- Are these classroom-based events or is there any relevant computer-based training?

Active knowledge

For those with an internal training and development department

Find out your organisation's policy on training and development for employees in customer service. Identify relevant customer service learning opportunities. For each event, make sure you know where you can get information on the aims, the target audience (i.e. who the event is designed for) and an outline of the course contents. Who pays for the training?

For those with no internal training and development department

Discuss with an appropriate person how you can best go about helping colleagues with their personal development. Think about the learning opportunities available to you apart from traditional training events. How should you approach helping colleagues to develop if your organisation has no provision for formal training?

As you can see, coaching can take place:

- *on-the-job* – i.e. in the normal work environment and whilst the coachee is carrying out his or her normal duties
- *off-the-job* – i.e. away from the normal place of work.

> ✓ Self-analysis/personal reflection.
> ✓ Observation by other people.
> ✓ Feedback from other people.
> ✓ Learning on the job from others who are more experienced.
> ✓ Discussion groups.
> ✓ Doing a qualification.
> ✓ Training courses and events.
> ✓ Work-shadowing and networking.

Figure 6.15 Developing colleagues' customer service skills and knowledge: a checklist

Figure 6.15 is a checklist of the key areas you could explore when looking for ways of helping colleagues to develop their customer service skills and knowledge.

How to plan and organise coaching sessions for colleagues

We have noted that formal coaching can have three main stages:

1 planning and preparation
2 the coaching itself
3 conclusion.

We looked at how to plan and prepare and how to organise the resources available to you in Unit 1, Element 1.1. Refer back to these sections because the planning skills you need when getting ready to coach are no different from those you put into practice for the delivery of reliable customer service.

Let's use Meena as an example. If you were her coach and were about to draw up a coaching plan for her, you would be thinking about three key questions in terms of her strengths and development needs:

1 Where is Meena now?
2 Where does she need to be?
3 How are we going to get her there?

This is a little like a journey – 'I'm at A, I need to get to B, and I'm going to get there by doing C'. Like any journey, there are many choices of what A, B and C might look like. It is your role as a coach to help Meena get to C in the most efficient way possible. In drawing up a coaching plan, you will therefore go through the following stages.

1 *Plan and prepare*. Set the context by:

- planning what needs to be done
- seeking agreement to coaching

- collecting any information you require
- identifying and agreeing strengths and development needs
- analysing and interpreting this information
- identifying and agreeing learning opportunities
- identifying priorities.

Agree the time, place and location by:

- considering the style and format of your coaching session (on-the-job coaching or one-to-one coaching requiring a private space)
- dealing with any administration needed to book a room, and by confirming details with your coachee.

2 *Run the coaching session* (see Element 6.3 'How to carry out coaching sessions with colleagues').

3 *Conclude*:

- deciding and agreeing how you will give feedback
- agreeing the next steps.

The choice is yours as to how you involve Meena with your planning and preparation. Sometimes it will be important to plan and prepare on your own. On other occasions it might be beneficial to do the planning and preparation together.

Work through the following case study, which gives one example of what might happen when a coach starts to help a colleague.

Case study

Meena has asked for feedback from her colleagues on the way she handles distressed customers. Several people have told her she is not assertive enough. This has been mentioned before by her line manager, who has told her she doesn't 'communicate in an assertive way'. Meena didn't understand what this meant and didn't ask for clarification at the time. Since then she has decided to ask someone to help her – she wants help in developing her self-confidence and she knows there is a training course available called 'Assertiveness and self-confidence development'.

Meena has a coach and she asks her for help on this matter. They both agree this would best be dealt with in the first instance by talking on a one-to-one basis.

Meena's coach draws up an outline coaching plan before the meeting, covering:

- *Aims* – what, in broad terms, does Meena want to achieve?
- *Objectives* – what should Meena be able to do as a result of the coaching?

- *Activities* – how can this be achieved?
- *Resources* – what resources are required?

1 Prior to asking her coach for help, Meena had already made up her mind she needed assertiveness training. What questions should the coach ask to check if this is the best option?
2 What can the coach do to find out Meena's preferred way of learning?
3 Apart from the training course, what other learning opportunities might be available to help Meena?

Consolidation

Imagine you are going to draw up a coaching plan to help a member of your family or a friend achieve one of his or her New Year's resolutions:

- What would you do to identify what he or she wants to achieve?
- How would you set about agreeing with him or her what he or she is good at and not so good at in connection with his or her New Year resolution (i.e. his or her strengths and development needs)?
- Draw up a coaching plan for him or her that includes:

1 the aims
2 the objectives (SMART ones!)
3 the activities
4 your responsibilities
5 the resources required
6 a space for you, the coach, to write any review notes.

It is up to you as to whether you actually carry out the plan with your friend. Why not work through the final part of this unit and then decide? You never know, you might just have some fun coaching him or her!

To recap, you have been working on the development of your own customer service skills and knowledge and you have looked at the steps you should take when planning to coach others. This element deals with running a coaching session.

WHAT YOU NEED TO LEARN

- How to carry out coaching sessions with colleagues.
- How to give useful and constructive personal feedback to others.
- How to help colleagues respond positively to personal feedback.

How to carry out coaching sessions with colleagues

So far, your role as a coach has taken you as far as:

- *setting the context* – helping to create a situation where your coachee has an awareness about, and takes responsibility for, his or her own personal development
- *planning and preparing* – supporting your coachee and challenging him or her when necessary to move him or her forward to where he or she needs to be.

Remember

Your coaching session is not about you telling someone what to do. Because of this, you may find coaching a little strange at first, since many people find it difficult to step back from providing advice because they want to help. Some people also give advice because it is the quickest thing to do. If you do this, you will not be *coaching*, you will be *instructing*.

You should be in no doubt that, to be a great coach, you will need to be highly skilled – in particular, with the types of questions you ask. But, first, what about the coaching session itself? How might it run? We will look initially at the sort of coaching that involves you helping someone to set goals and develop skills. This is all about identifying where the person is now, where he or she needs to be and how he or she is going to get there.

Step 1: set the scene

Start by asking questions that help you and your coachee to establish goals that are specific, measurable, attainable and relevant/realistic and that have a time frame – we are back to setting SMART objectives again. Draw on all the planning and preparation you have done (you may have already covered this bit before!).

Step 2: is this the whole picture?

Through the use of open and probing questions (see Element 6.2), you will ensure both you and your coachee are aware of the true situation. This may involve clearing out any assumptions that have been made. Always ask for *specific* examples: you are seeking to clarify the current circumstances and you may need to challenge what you have heard. Be supportive but avoid any attempts to problem solve at this stage.

Step 3: what are the choices?

Here you set about encouraging your coachee to think of as many options for reaching his or her objective as possible. Again, you may need to challenge your coachee for the less obvious options (such as doing nothing and the 'what if you could do anything?' option). You should offer suggestions carefully and you should ensure choices are made.

Step 4: do it now

Here you will obtain a commitment to action, identify any potential obstacles or barriers, make any action points (specific and time-phased) and agree on any support that may be required.

Let's see how Meena and her coach (Phyllida) deal with a coaching session. They meet as arranged to discuss Meena's wish to develop her self-confidence. They have 20 minutes available and settle down in the hotel's staff meeting room with a cup of tea and a notebook each.

Phyllida is keen to establish why the issue has arisen in the first place; all she knows so far is that Meena has asked for her help and has told her she wants to go on an assertiveness and self-confidence development course.

The following is a 'fly on the wall' account of how the coaching session went.

Step 1: set the scene

Phyllida (P): Meena, what exactly is it that you would you like to get out of the next 20 minutes?

Meena (M): Well, I'm not happy with the way in which I deal with distressed customers and I'd like to go on the assertiveness and self-confidence course.

P: Why is that, Meena?

M: I've been given some feedback that I'm not assertive enough and that I don't communicate assertively. I'm not too sure what that means.

Phyllida wants to establish that Meena's desire to go on the course is the best development option for her. She also needs to coach Meena to set herself clear development objectives. Phyllida starts to explore the whole picture *with Meena:*

Step 2: is this the whole picture?

P: You say you are not sure what the feedback you have been given means. What have you done to clarify this?

M: Nothing.

P: So, how do you know that going on this course is the right solution for you?

M: Well, thinking about it, I've been told that I use the wrong sort of words.

P: Please give me an example.

M: Recently, I had to deal with a distressed customer on the phone. Because I didn't know the process for dealing with guests who report they have fallen ill, I felt helpless and didn't help the customer in an appropriate way. She has now complained about the way I dealt with her and I just think the whole thing is terrible. If only I had known what to do this would not have happened.

Phyllida has now picked up on some words Meena has just used. For instance, had Meena felt more positive and assertive about her ability to influence her own performance, she might have used the words 'next time I will' instead of 'if only' and 'I've learnt from what happened' instead of 'it's terrible'.

Phyllida goes on to explore the reality of the situation. What else had happened to indicate to Meena she had a problem with her choice of words? Was Meena more confident in dealing with colleagues as opposed to customers? What plans has Meena made to move forward?

At this point, Meena shares what she has written in her learning log and PDP with her coach:

P: I see you have taken on board putting a process in place within the hotel for helping customers who have fallen ill. Is that the actions of someone who is lacking in confidence?

M: I see what you mean. I'm feeling better already! Perhaps it's just the way I talk to customers when I don't have the necessary background knowledge that's the issue.

By exploring the reality of the situation, Meena has come to understand she lacks confidence when her background knowledge is not up to scratch and that she doesn't follow up on feedback she gets but which she doesn't fully understand. She is, however, happy that she deals with colleagues in an appropriate way.

Phyllida moves on to the next step and explores with Meena the choices available to her:

Step 3: what are the choices?

P: OK, let's move on to discuss the options available to you. What are the benefits to you and to our customers of you going on the course?

M: I'm no longer sure it's relevant. I think I need to get some more feedback on the way in which I talk to customers after I have sorted out the process bit. I feel I should know what to do once my background knowledge is sound. So I think I'll just follow through what I've written down already in my PDP and, perhaps, I could ask you kindly to observe me at work on the reception desk?

Phyllida goes on to explore Meena's motivation to carry out her intentions by asking her when she will put her plans into practice, checking to see if she needs any support with developing her background knowledge and sorting out a new process for the hotel:

Step 4: do it now

P: I'd be happy to observe you, Meena. Let me know when you are ready.

M: Great! Thanks for your help.

Active knowledge

Revisit the approach you took to deal with the case study in Element 6.2. Compare and contrast the questions you might have asked Meena with the ones Phyllida asked:

- What might the likely impact be on Meena of your choice of questions?

- What was Meena planning to do as a result of the questions you asked her?

- Consider how the questions asked in this case study influenced the outcome of Meena's coaching session.

- How does the customer benefit when a coach gets to the heart of a development issue by using the right sort of coaching questions?

Step 1: set the scene

- What would you like to discuss?
- What do you want to achieve (short and long term)?
- How do you want to spend this session?
- What would need to happen during this session to enable you to move forward?
- What needs to change as a result of this session?
- When do you need to achieve it by?
- How will your goal benefit you/your customers/your colleagues/your organisation?
- How would you measure your success?

Step 2: is this the whole picture?

- What's going on now?
- Why do you think that?
- How do you know this is accurate?
- What have you done about it so far?
- How often does it happen?
- What's the impact on you?
- What's the impact on your customers/your colleagues/your organisation?
- Who else is involved?
- What have you tried so far?
- What (if any) are the key things stopping you moving forward?

Step 4: do it now

- What are you going to do?
- What do you see as the next steps?
- When are you going to do it?
- What might get in the way?
- How will you overcome any barriers?
- Who needs to know (if anyone) about what you are planning to do?
- What support do you need?
- How and when will you get that support?

Step 3: what are the choices?

- What could you do to change the situation?
- What are your options?
- What about other options?
- Who might be able to help?
- Would you like any suggestions from me?
- What are the pros and cons of your options?
- Which option do you like the most?
- Who benefits from your selected option?

Figure 6.16 Questions to use in a coaching session

Sample coaching questions to use

Whilst there is no one correct *set* of questions to follow, Figure 6.16 suggests questions that can be used and *built upon* throughout a coaching session.

Remember

Questions work in combination with one another. Concentrate on getting the *sequence* of your questioning right by following the four steps:

set the scene → find the whole picture → agree choices → do it now

You should now be aware of how the choice of questions a coach uses can influence the outcome for the coachee.

Active knowledge

Find out what systems and procedures are in place in your organisation to coach others:

- What has been the impact of this coaching on customer service and the personal development of your colleagues and yourself?
- If you do not work in an organisation that has a coaching culture, what do you need to do to ensure you are able to become involved with coaching?

If you are involved with the 'sitting next to Nellie' type of on-the-job training (which is used primarily to help someone develop a specific skill or to learn to perform a task), your coaching style also needs to consider how best to *explain* things to your coachee.

What you will be doing is *enabling* someone to observe you so he or she can learn from you and can, hence, perform a task or develop his or her skills, or you will be *explaining* what to do. Explaining means demonstrating what to do, letting him or her do it, explaining what to do again (i.e. giving feedback) and, finally, reflecting on what has happened.

Don't be put off by the amount of explaining in this sequence. You are right to think that coaching is not solely about telling – look at the sequence again:

explain → demonstrate → practise → feed back → reflect

During the stage where your coachee is actually practising the task, you may be in a position to give spontaneous feedback. If not, you will do so as soon as possible afterwards. Your coaching skills will come to the fore here and also when you help your coachee to reflect on what has happened.

Naturally, people can only absorb a certain amount of information at any one time – you wouldn't learn how to drive a car from just one driving lesson! So think about how best to break down what you need to explain into manageable chunks. You know if you have said too much in one go when your coachee starts to frown and look puzzled.

How good do you think people are at explaining things? Have a go at this 'be an artist' exercise, which is designed to see how good you are at giving explanations.

Focus on *behaviour* – this means talking about what you have seen being done or what you have heard being said. So you could say something like:

✓ 'Max, you answered the phone slowly' – *not*
✗ 'Max you're slow.'
✓ 'Max your desk is untidy' – *not*
✗ 'Max you are untidy.'

By giving feedback specifically about what a person does rather than focusing it directly on the person, you are more likely to encourage him or her to do something about it.

Think about it. People are more likely to react to being told their desk is untidy by tidying it up than they are to being told they *themselves* are untidy. Similarly, would you like to be told you are slow? Far better to be told you pick up the phone slowly – you are more likely to learn how to be quicker at this than to do something about a sweeping generalisation about being slow that has served only to make you angry.

You should speak for yourself. This means what you say should reflect *your* views, not what you think someone else might say or what you think the observed behaviour might mean to other people. So, say such things as:

✓ 'You dealt with that customer in a polite and fair manner' – *not*
✗ 'They think you are polite with customers.'
✓ 'I feel you have not done enough to learn about product X' – *not*
✗ 'The general feeling is that you haven't learnt enough.'

Take responsibility for the feedback you give. Use 'I': 'I know that …', 'I think …' and 'I feel that …'

There will probably be a mixture of positive and negative things you have to say. Helpful negative feedback enables people to see themselves through someone else's eyes. Mistakes, errors and weaknesses do need to be pointed out but should be balanced with some positive feedback as well.

You should think about how it would be best to deliver your feedback. Do you give the positive bits first and then the negative, or should you mix it all up in any order? The sandwich method of giving feedback is to talk about some positive things first, then some negative, and to finish with some more positive feedback. That way, you end on a high note. However, some people can get confused by this sandwich mixture and lose sight of what was positive and what was negative. Indeed, people have a tendency to focus on the negative and may 'forget' everything you said that was positive feedback.

An alternative method is to give all the positive feedback first and then all the negative. This method leaves little room for confusion, as there is a clear distinction between what went well and what could be improved upon.

Remember

Whichever method you choose to use, it is important to build on strengths and not to focus at length on mistakes or errors.

Only give as much feedback in terms of quantity that you feel the coachee can take on board. Too much will confuse and be over-powering and will make for a situation where the person is less likely to act upon what you have said.

Watch for any signs of strong negative feelings. Deal with them at the time by exploring and checking whether the person has understood what has been said. This checking of understanding is important, as your coachee needs to take action if your feedback session is to be of use. This is not likely to happen if he or she resents what he or she has heard, disagrees with it or simply doesn't understand you.

By the end of your feedback session you will be in a position to seek agreement to your coachee moving forward. This is rather like the 'do it now' stage of a coaching session, where you are seeking a commitment to what needs to be done. This may involve helping someone to complete a PDP or it may be a commitment to holding another coaching session based around a specific development need.

Remember

Feedback will be at its most effective if you secure an agreement to taking any action that might be required as a consequence of what has been discussed.

Feedback says as much about what makes *you* tick – your values, beliefs and opinions – as it does about the person you are giving feedback to. Use the occasions you give feedback to learn about yourself by becoming more aware of the manner in which you give feedback.

How to help colleagues respond positively to personal feedback

In this unit, we have discussed *receiving* feedback (in the context of you reviewing your own strengths and development needs) and *giving* feedback. If you put the two together, you will be well on the way to understanding how you can help colleagues to respond positively to your feedback.

You will need to be someone whom your colleagues trust and whose opinions they value – in other words, you must be a customer service role model. There is little point in coaching someone to improve his or her telephone handling skills if your own are dire. Some people, however, will need to be motivated to spend time listening to your feedback. This is a little unfortunate, but pointing out to someone the benefits of receiving feedback may well do the trick!

Active knowledge

Consider what the benefits are to you of receiving feedback on your performance. Now ask someone to whom you have given feedback to share with you how he or she benefited from receiving your feedback. Next, find out how giving and receiving feedback has benefited your customers and your organisation.

Use this information to update your personal development plan.

Some people tend to get defensive even when they are listening to positive feedback. This is even more the case when you give *negative* feedback.

Keys to good practice
Giving your coachee negative feedback

✓ As before, describe the actions you observed and their results.

✓ Ask your coachee if what you have just described as happening was his or her original intention. Usually you will get a 'no' answer.

✓ Ask him or her what he or she could have done differently.

✓ Help your coachee to identify any possible barriers to doing things differently (e.g. a lack of resources or basic skills).

✓ Discuss any alternative course of action.

✓ Agree what he or she would do next time in a similar sort of situation.

✓ Draw the feedback to an end by summarising the key points discussed and any actions that have been agreed.

Case study

Cathy works as a staff development officer for an airline and has been observing Emma at work on the check-in desk. Emma has been involved with check-in duties for 6 months now and has previously received coaching from Cathy regarding her lack of patience with customers who are slow to produce all their documentation at check-in.

Cathy's observations are that Emma shows her lack of patience and understanding only when queues start to form and when she cannot make herself understood with non-English speaking passengers. Cathy has observed Emma tapping the desk with a pen, frowning and calling out to customers in the queue that they are being held up because her customer cannot find his or her paperwork. She has also observed that Emma speaks in a monotone voice and at a rather hurried pace when asking the passengers the airline's baggage security questions.

Cathy is concerned Emma has not taken any notice of the coaching she has previously received as her behaviour with customers remains below the standards required by the airline.

1 At what point (and where) should Cathy give feedback to Emma?
2 How should Cathy describe what she has seen?
3 What possible options might there be to helping Emma reach the required standard?
4 What role could Cathy continue to play in the development of Emma's customer service skills?
5 What would you like to see written on Emma's PDP?

Being a customer service role model

Probably the most powerful tool you have in helping colleagues to respond positively to your feedback is to be so inspirational in what you do they aspire to be like you. This may sound corny, but can you think of someone you work with who is happy in what he or she does, whom customers seem to like and who is respected by his or her employers? What is it that makes this person special? Probably that this person goes out of his or her way to help customers just as much as you need to go out of your way to provide constructive feedback to your coachees.

Done the right way, you will find this a rewarding experience and, indeed, may soon be in demand for your ability to coach others in customer service.

Consolidation

This activity is best done 'for real' in your workplace. Imagine a colleague has asked you to help coach him or her to use personal development and action plans as he or she is having difficulty in drawing one up. How would you set about this?

Next, imagine that, two months later, you review progress with your colleague only to find that nothing has happened. What would you do?

End-of-unit test

1 What systems and procedures might an organisation have in place to develop the skills and knowledge of its employees?

2 What is a personal development and action plan?

3 Why is it a good idea to use a learning log?

4 How should the 'action' column on a learning log be completed?

5 List six customer service skills.

6 Where might you obtain information from on your own performance?

7 'Feedback can be obtained from anyone, but the best feedback is from someone whom I trust and respect.' True or false?

8 'The best way to coach someone to improve his or her performance is to ask questions and to listen, not just to tell him or her what to do'. True or false?

9 What is the point of asking questions in a coaching session?

10 How would you go about showing your coachee you are listening to what he or she is saying?

11 List some activities or options that might be available to help a colleague develop his or her customer service skills.

12 What sort of information would you include in a coaching plan?

13 What are the four steps you should follow when running a coaching session?

14 'When I need to coach someone by giving an explanation of what to do, I first explain, then I demonstrate, then they practise, I give feedback and we both then reflect on what has happened.' Is this a good structure to follow?

15 Name three top tips for giving feedback.

Organise and promote products or services to customers

Unit CL 7

In the *commercial* world we readily appreciate that, even though we might be offering a great customer service, if we can't *promote* sales our organisation will go out of business. But what about those organisations that are not in the commercial sector? Many non-commercial organisations promote things in addition to their key products or services. For example, people working in hospitals or the police service often have the opportunity (or even the *responsibility*) to promote *additional* services to their customers. While the economic well-being of their organisations may not be at the same risk as a commercial company, the quality of the service they provide could be considerably enhanced if they promoted these additional services.

There are some organisations, therefore, whose apparent role is to *reduce* the number of their customers as a consequence of the additional services they can promote. This can be regarded as the *creation of opposites,* and a few examples from the police service might serve to illustrate this.

Apparent role of the police service. To *reduce* the numbers of:

• criminals
• accident victims
• people parking illegally.

Creative role of the police service. To *increase* the numbers of:

• law-abiding citizens
• people who can anticipate and avoid accidents
• people who use revenue-generating car parks.

In non-commercial organisations, therefore, promoting services means getting your customers to make an informed decision to do something, to go somewhere, to change their habits, etc.

Whether in the commercial or non-commercial sector, to be genuinely good at promoting products or services to customers, you have to respond to their individual needs. This is based on what you know about the customer and on what the customer tells you he or she needs. This is the principle of *one-to-one promoting* and is basically very simple – you treat individual customers individually.

The elements for this unit are:

7.1 Offer additional products or services.

7.2 Organise customer support to promote use of additional products or services.

7.3 Monitor the promotion of additional products or services.

WHAT YOU NEED TO LEARN

- Offer relevant additional products or services to your customers.
- Identify the benefits of offering additional products or services for the customer and the organisation.
- Explain the benefits of additional products or services to your customers.
- Ensure that customers are given accurate information that is in accordance with their own needs.
- Identify ways of encouraging customers to ask about additional products or services.

Offer relevant additional products or services to your customers

For the additional products or services you offer to be *relevant*, you must know as much as possible about each individual customer. Your customers may be individual shoppers in a retail outlet, customers in a restaurant or clients in an advice centre. The principle remains the same. Let's look at a few examples. If you work:

- with customers who are making an expensive buying decision (e.g. about a car, holiday or a piece of electrical equipment), you may have the opportunity to sell insurance
- in a restaurant, you have the opportunity to suggest additional dishes, drinks and menu items
- in a drug abusers' counselling centre, you may find yourself promoting services designed to change your clients' whole lifestyle.

If you are dealing with major corporations, you need to apply the same principles: you need to know who is going to make the decision and what his or her preferences are in his or her role as representing that organisation.

Active knowledge

What sort of additional product or service offers can you make from the range currently available within your organisation?

If you work in an organisation where you want your customers to return on a regular basis, you should aim to make your customers more loyal and more rewarding by establishing a *learning relationship* with each one. A learning relationship is one that becomes more informed with every new meeting. The customer tells you what he or she needs and you organise your product or service to meet that need. Hence, with each contact you get better and better at fitting your product or service to this particular customer.

If your organisation isn't in the business of generating repeat visits, it is still in your interests to create a better relationship with your customers: you want your customers to recommend you to others. Hence you should aim to create a *promotional relationship* with your customers, where your customers become your champions. For example, if you worked in a local tourist information office, you are unlikely to develop a learning relationship with your clients because it may be some considerable time before they visit you again – perhaps even never! However, if your service is so good customers feel they have had a wonderful holiday, they will recommend your locality to their friends. More importantly, they will recommend their friends visit your tourist information centre.

Active knowledge

What kind of relationship with customers best suits *your* organisation – a learning relationship or a promotional relationship? Give the reasons for your answer.

Strategies for meeting your customers' needs
Know as much as you can about your customers

Finding out details about your customers means not just appropriate personal details such as names, addresses, telephone numbers, etc., but also details about their preferences and about what contacts they have with every part of your organisation. You need to know and remember each customer individually and to disseminate the information about that customer across your entire organisation.

Figure 7.1 is a checklist of questions you could ask yourself to gather this information.

Active knowledge

Draw up a list of questions similar to the ones given in Figure 7.1 to help you gather information about your own customers.

> *Individuals as customers*
>
> ✓ What do I know about this customer?
>
> ✓ Have I already got any information about him or her? Are there any notes or other information available about this customer in the organisation?
>
> ✓ Have I heard anything about him or her from anyone else? If so, what?
>
> ✓ Do I know anyone who has dealt with this customer previously?
>
> *Organisations as customers*
>
> ✓ What do I know about the customer's organisation?
>
> ✓ Who are *their* major customers?
>
> ✓ Who are my competitors for their business?
>
> ✓ Have they changed their business or management recently?
>
> ✓ How good or bad are their sales and profits (if relevant)?

Figure 7.1 Gathering information about customers: a checklist

Prioritise your customers in terms of their value and needs

Customers are different in two principal ways: they represent different levels of *value* (some are very valuable, some not so valuable) and they also have different *needs*. Your organisation will obviously gain the most by concentrating on the most valuable customers. Notice we have said *valuable* or *rewarding* – not simply *profitable*: commercial organisations usually find it simpler to relate

> ✓ How much does each customer spend (for commercial organisations)?
>
> ✓ How much income does each customer generate (for non-commercial organisations)?
>
> ✓ Which of these customers are potentially the most valuable to your organisation?
>
> ✓ What is the potential volume of business you could do with this customer?
>
> ✓ Does the customer currently use your products or services? If not, why not?
>
> ✓ If they do, what do they like/dislike about them?

Figure 7.2 Assessing your customers' needs and values

value to profitability, but non-commercial organisations will have their own measures of customer value.

The questions you need to ask yourself to assess your customers' needs and values are given in Figure 7.2. When you have answered these questions, you should be in a position to concentrate on those customers who are likely to be the most rewarding, and you should also be able to identify the additional products or services that match their individual needs.

Some government organisations may have to meet statutory requirements and may not, therefore, be able to differentiate between customers in this way. These organisations may either have to omit this step or determine their own ways of prioritising customers.

Interact with your customers to get as much information as you can

The next step is to interact as much as possible with your customers. To improve the effectiveness of each meeting, collect only *relevant* information and only when this is needed. This is to obtain a better grasp of the customer's individual needs or to quantify more accurately a customer's potential value.

Remember

You still need to do this even if you find it difficult to differentiate between your customers in terms of their value to your organisation.

In addition, every meeting with a customer should take place in the context of all previous meetings with that customer. The meeting should pick up where the last one left off. This means holding records for each customer and organisation.

Some organisations use computer software (called CRM systems) to manage their customer relationships. This software enables all staff to hold relevant information on all customers. With this information, the organisation can customise its approach to each client. Other organisations rely on card indexes or simple databases to record this information.

This approach, however, may be difficult in retailing, where customer contact is short and impersonal. It should, on the other hand, be possible to categorise customers by *groups* rather than as individuals (e.g. pensioners, school pupils, car drivers, etc.). You may similarly find you can organise your responses according to the day of the week or the time of day (e.g. mothers of school-age children who shop before collecting their children from school, family shopping on Sundays, etc.).

Active knowledge

Ask yourself the following questions for your own organisation:

- What information do I need to know about each individual customer or group of customers to promote additional products or services?

- Do we hold this information at the moment? If so, how can I access it? If not, how do we get hold of it?

- What additional products or services do I think our customers will be interested in?

Make an offer that meets individual or group needs

The final step is to make the offer. To do this you, will need to communicate directly with your customers. Of course, you will need to prepare yourself but, as you already know, you will be making an offer that is directly relevant to your customers' needs.

In planning your meeting, ask yourself the following questions:

- What is my objective (to arrange a demonstration, to present information, to set out options, etc.)? The clearer you are about your objective, the more successful you are likely to be.

- What objections might I encounter and how will I respond to these? It is helpful if you work out the possible objections *before* your

Objection	Response
The customer is used to dealing with one of our major competitors	We have a new and improved product, which is better
Our prices are higher than our competitors	We have an extremely low level of returned goods
We are further away from the customer than our competitors	We can deliver daily to any part of the country
The customer has very young children and finds it difficult to get to our office for regular meetings	We can make appointments fortnightly rather than weekly or can go to the customer's home
The customer doesn't like discussing personal matters in an open office	We have a private office for dealing with sensitive interviews
The customer doesn't like to queue for hours to talk to a member of staff	We now arrange staged appointment times, which reduces queuing

Figure 7.3 Working out how to respond to possible objections

meeting with the customer. To do this, you could use the format shown in Figure 7.3, listing the objection on the left and how you would respond on the right.

- What presentation equipment, etc., needs to be available? What do I need by way of flyers, catalogues, forms, etc.?

- Are there any similar situations I have dealt with recently which I could give as good examples of this additional product or service? (*Note*: be careful about using names, and don't share information that could be proprietary, sensitive or confidential.)

Case study

Helen is a stylist who works in a hairdressing salon with a number of other stylists, one of whom is the owner of the salon. Helen and the other stylists complete record cards for each of their clients so they have a clear history of all the appointments made and each client's hairdressing requirements. They also keep a note of all the additional products each client buys when they visit the salon.

Before each appointment, Helen spends a few minutes familiarising herself with the customer's background and preferences so she is able to suggest not only that the customer may need to replenish her normal purchases but that she could try some new or alternative products Helen thinks she might enjoy. Because Helen has a number of clients, she has a good knowledge of the salon's stock. So if someone is reluctant to try something new and needs assurance, Helen is able to say several other of her clients have used the product and are delighted with the results. She is also able to warn her clients about using products that seem to be damaging other of her clients' hair and to suggest better alternatives.

One day the owner of the salon decided to move the shop to the other side of the town to larger premises. While Helen and the other stylists were unsettled by the move because they thought they would lose a lot of their clients, the new salon had much more space and the owner wanted to be able to offer additional beauty treatments. The problem was – which ones?

1 What sort of a relationship had Helen built with her customers over the years?
2 What could the salon owner and Helen do to make sure as many of their existing customers as possible moved with them to the new premises?
3 How could they find out which additional beauty treatments they should offer?

Build learning relationships with your customers

Active knowledge

How do you find out if your additional products or services are relevant to your customers?

Identify the benefits of offering additional products or services for the customer and the organisation

As we have already pointed out, it isn't wise to try to promote your products or services during the information-gathering stage. Save most of the information about your additional product or service until all the facts and benefits for your customers have been identified.

Information-gathering

If a customer asks 'Tell me what you have to offer that I don't already know about', it is all right briefly to introduce your company, product or service, but it is very important to avoid a lengthy monologue. You should give a brief comment and then complete your response with: 'I could tell you about our products or services but my comments might not match your specific needs. You're a busy person, so I'd like to find out quickly the best way in which we can help you or your organisation. Perhaps if I could start by asking you a few questions? Is that all right?'

Active knowledge

Write a brief paragraph outlining how you would respond to a customer who has just said: 'Tell me about what you and your organisation have to offer.'

Only after you have an idea of your customer's needs can you tell how your additional products or services apply to his or her situation. The next step, therefore, is to match the customer's needs with the *features* and *benefits* of your additional products or services.

Facts and features

A *fact* is provable. A *feature* is a distinctive part of something.

In most situations, you can combine facts and features into a distinct parcel of information for your customers. You use facts and features to gain some credibility in your customer's eyes. Facts and figures prove you have done similar things in the past many times and with great success.

When quoting facts you must be sure they are quantifiable. If they aren't, you are using a *claim*. While there is nothing wrong in making a claim (e.g. 'We're the best'), by what standards are you to be *judged* the best? So you must, therefore, be prepared to back your statements with data if this is available. For example:

- In a recent survey by ... *Magazine*, we were voted the best value-for-money supplier in the business.

- In the recent publication on hospital waiting lists, this hospital is rated amongst the top 25% in the country.

- Our housing services have the shortest waiting lists in the North West.

If you haven't got any facts, you could use an *opinion* or quote *comments* from customers. For example:

- Many clients feel we are the best because of our quick delivery and high rate of success.

- Many patients choose to come to this day surgery because they like the idea it doesn't involve them in an overnight stay in the hospital.

- 'The best after-sales service I have ever received' (Mrs K, Holtwood Cottage).

Non-commercial

Many local authority and charitable advice centres now offer individual appointments as well as a 'drop-in' facility.

5 For security/peace of mind

One of our most fundamental needs is for safety and security – not just in the physical sense but also to protect our families, loved ones and possessions.

Commercial

- Insurance companies perpetually remind us of the need to protect ourselves.

- Financial advisers help customers feel secure when they know their money has been wisely invested.

- Mortgage providers absolutely insist we take out property insurance for the duration of the mortgage, not only for our peace of mind but also for their own.

Non-commercial

Staff working in housing departments, charities or voluntary sector bodies should remember this fundamental need when proposing measures to their clients that relate to their safety and security (e.g. when rehousing people or when advising elderly people about moving into sheltered accommodation).

6 For convenience/comfort

Convenience and comfort have always been very significant when emphasising the benefits of products and services.

Commercial

- Freephone or 0800 numbers provide a convenient access to organisations. If that same number is linked to a 24-hour help-line, order-line, etc., customers have a doubly convenient service.

- Internet shopping offers the convenience of checking the marketplace for competitive prices.

- Utility and other companies might be able to offer tightly defined appointment times for meter readings or repairs.

Non-commercial

It might be possible for the staff of, say, social security departments or charitable organisations to make appointments to see clients in their own homes rather than the clients having to go in to their offices.

7 For flexibility

Flexibility simply means being prepared to adjust your product or service in some way to meet your customer's requirements.

Commercial organisations can provide alternatives in the way their products or services are packaged or delivered, or can offer alternatives in the way their customers can pay their invoices.

Non-commercial organisations might be flexible in the way payments are received (e.g. paying off a debt through monthly instalments or by a series of post-dated cheques rather than in one lump sum).

8 For satisfaction/reliability/pleasure

All customers want to know they have made the right decision. They need reassurance that, after all their considerations, they have made very best decision. Organisations offer personal satisfaction if their products or services are perceived as being reliable, if they enable customers to improve their effectiveness and if customers obtain pleasure from acquiring them.

Commercial
- When buying personal computers, customers hope to achieve self-improvement or increased effectiveness, as well as gaining pleasure from the entertainment software.
- In the leisure industry, products may be linked directly to pleasurable sensations, such as skiing, boating, watching television or playing video games.

Non-commercial
Educational establishments can offer this reassurance by emphasising the satisfaction enhanced capabilities can bring, as well as by quoting figures about their exam successes. They can also reinforce their message by explaining how the experience of learning new skills can be both enjoyable and rewarding.

9 For status

Customers may want to be recognised as being part of a group – the more successful and, therefore, the more exclusive that group, the better. The key word in this context is *membership*.

Commercial
- Car manufacturers have recognised this by the various badges they put on their cars – Gti, XL, V8Turbo, etc.
- Clothing and footwear manufacturers' branded goods are often bought simply for the additional perceived status wearing these brand-named items brings.

Non-commercial
We all like to have some status within the context of where we live. Even if we are homeless, most of us would prefer to be accommodated in a hostel rather than sleep rough on the streets.
Staff dealing with homeless people will recognise the urgent, if

sometimes unmet, desire for such people to be recognised as part of a social unit.

10 For health and safety

In a *commercial* context, safety may include such additional products as burglar and fire alarms incorporated into, say, a new housing development. It may also relate to the safety aspects of a product – the safety zone of a car, for example. A service may similarly include safety inspections and advice, checking for adherence to fire and safety regulations or dealing with public health issues. In a *non-commercial* context it might mean the provision of a resident warden or a personal alarm system in a retirement home.

Health in a *commercial* setting may mean private medical insurance that will ensure your customers remain in the best of health with the minimum of disruption to their lifestyles. In a *non-commercial* setting it could mean a drug rehabilitation service with the ultimate aim of restoring clients to normal health or a medical practice with additional health-check screening.

Active knowledge

Look at the list of ten benefits. Choose the top *five* that are most relevant to your work. For each one, give the reasons for the benefit to your customers.

Explain the benefits of additional products or services to your customers

It would be wonderful if everyone jumped at the opportunity to place a large additional order with you or took advantage of every additional service you suggested. However, putting up resistance or objections to proposals is only human nature.

If your customer raises objections

If you have done your homework properly, you should be able to meet most of the objections voiced by your customers. There are some objections, however, that will need further work:

• the customer is not the decision-maker
• the customer does not like you personally
• there is no money.

Sometimes these can be smoke screens, so don't give up immediately. If they are true objections, you will need to do some more work. Try to put matters on hold until you can come up with an alternative solution. Then you should attend to the objections (see Figure 7.6).

Objection	Action
The customer is not the decision-maker	You should have found this out during your information-gathering phase! Ask the customer just who will make the decision. If you have presented your case well, this person could act as your ally when dealing with the real decision-maker
The customer does not like you personally	Face up to the reality of the situation and get someone else to take over this customer. Be positive about it – say something like 'I wonder if X can help you better than I can. He or she has had a great deal of experience with this kind of product/service'
There is no money or 'I can't afford it'	This is the time to remember the benefits of being flexible about payment arrangements. You may need to buy time to clear this with your manager.

Figure 7.6 Attending to objections

The worst objection you can encounter, however, is one that is not voiced. When a customer expresses a concern, he or she is giving you clues about a vital worry you must find out about before you can establish exactly what it is the customer actually wants or does not want.

If your customer cannot make up his or her mind

If the customer says 'I want to think about it' or 'I don't know', you must ask more questions to uncover the real objections behind his or her uncertainty. These types of objections are often termed 'hidden'. It may be the customer does not really know why he or she wants to delay matters (it could simply be he or she needs a little more time to rehearse the reasons for saying 'yes'). You need to be particularly sensitive to the customer's motivation at this point. If you push too hard you may cause a reaction that stops matters in their tracks; if you don't push at all, you will let the customer slip through your fingers. Use the mirroring techniques discussed in Unit 2 (page 71) to reinforce your relationship with your customer.

You could begin your questioning with a direct approach:

• What reservations do you have?
• What is causing you to hesitate?
• Do you mind my asking why you feel you need more time?

If you feel a direct approach is not appropriate or if your customer does not know the answers to those questions, you might prompt him or her for replies to direct questions about the benefits of the additional product or service:

- Is this service not going to save you enough time?
- Does it not meet your safety specifications fully?
- Is this model not sufficiently prestigious for you?

Active knowledge

Rehearse your response to customers who may have hidden objections to your additional products or services, using the most common benefits outlined earlier. You could do this as a role play.

Listen carefully to get clarification or specifics

It is vital you listen carefully to what your customer is telling you to understand fully his or her concerns. For example:

Customer: It's too expensive.

You: Could you tell me what 'too expensive' means to you?

Customer: I can't see how I need this additional service to help me with my current problems.

You: What sort of service would help you in your circumstances?

This is definitely the time to ask as many questions as you can because you need to know exactly what your customer thinks. After obtaining each objection, you should ask: 'Is there anything else about this point that concerns you?' Keep asking until you are sure you have all the information you need.

Connect with your customer's feelings

At this point your customer is probably thinking something like:

- I don't want to make a fool of myself by making the wrong decision.
- I'm not sure I have examined all the possible alternatives.
- I need to get clearance from my boss about this.

Here you can use a *cushion*:

- I understand why you might feel that way.
- I appreciate your concern.

Don't use the phrase 'I know how you feel' because this may lead people to respond silently 'You have no idea how I feel'. You now need to go back to how you linked features to benefits. Follow the cushion with such phrases as 'I felt that way at first' then add the *reassurance* your customer needs – 'So I researched why our prices were slightly higher than our competitors' and found we have far fewer rejects'. A typical reassurance may go something like Figure 7.7.

I understand how you could be concerned about our higher price (*cushion*). A number of our customers felt that way initially (*link*). But then they found that long-term benefits such as ... far outweigh the initial cost (*reassurance*).

or

I know you don't want to spend any more time than is necessary in this hospital ward (*cushion*). Most people, like you, usually want to get home as soon as possible (*link*). But if we can X-ray your chest now, as part of our general screening programme, we can save you time if you ever have to visit us in the future (*reassurance*).

Figure 7.7 A reassurance

Active knowledge

Rehearse a link for two situations that might arise in your own work, using the cushion and reassurance technique as outlined above.

Always check you are meeting your customer's needs

Always find out if your customer agrees with and understands your explanation. Do this by asking either a general or a particular question:

- Does this make sense?
- You do want maximum flexibility, don't you?
- It's important to you to have long-term credit arrangements, isn't it?

Never argue with customers, even if they give you an objection you suspect is untrue. So avoid beginning your response with 'Yes, but' because this writes off the customer's reasoning and is also argumentative.

You will often hear repeated an objection you have already covered. Be patient and explain it again because no one understands and remembers 100% of what has been said. Try to restate the information in a slightly different way.

Remember not to take rejection personally

Don't take rejection personally

You can't always get to 'yes' even though you have answered all the objections that have been voiced. 'No' is not a personal rejection – it's a business (or service) refusal.

Ensure that customers are given accurate information that is in accordance with their own needs

We have emphasised throughout this element the importance of finding out as much as you can about your customers. In doing this you put yourself in the unique position of being the one person (or one team) who knows more about satisfying your customers' needs than anyone else. This means you can suggest new and additional products and services to your customers that are *good* for them.

This type of promotion is nothing more than recommending specific extras and items that show your customers they are worth your time and effort. It is the process of building relationships with your customers that will provide them with a better service. And the less effort the customer has to make, the better he or she enjoys his or her overall experience and the more satisfied he or she is with the service received.

Promoting is not just taking orders

Your customers have already made, or have decided to make, a commitment, so they have decided to do something and not just to browse. You are therefore in the perfect position to give them additional information. If you do this, you are helping your customers to make decisions that are good for them. You have everything to gain and nothing to lose: what's the absolute worst that could happen if they say 'no'?

Know as much as you can about all your products or services

The customer service person who acts only as a vending machine or leaflet dispenser does so because he or she probably has little idea of what else he or she could suggest. If you really know your way around your products and services, you are ideally placed to make suggestions about additional services (see Figure 7.8).

In retailing, this is called *merchandising* (see also Element 7.2, page 290). Rather than put one item on display, organisations add related items to complement the original. The same concept applies to non-commercial organisations although, perhaps, merchandising may stretch your customers' imaginations more than they might have expected!

Remember

If you don't know all you should about your products or services, don't forget the basic rule: 'When in doubt, find out.'

If you work in a ...	and someone is already interested in ...	you could suggest as an addition ...
Food store	strawberries	cream
Clothes shop	a winter coat	scarf and gloves
Travel agency	a holiday	travel insurance
Utility company	gas/water/electricity	a service contract
Doctor's surgery	short-term inoculations	long-term inoculations available from the local hospital
Veterinary surgery	dealing with a dog that bites	local obedience classes
Hospital	surgical aids (i.e. crutches, etc.)	hire or loan facilities via the district nurse service

Figure 7.8 Making suggestions about additional products or services

Active knowledge

What aspects of your products or services could you merchandise?

Using the right words and gestures

When you are promoting a service, people remember the *first* and *last* things you say. So, for example, if you worked in a restaurant, selling the *second* bottle of wine to customers who have just finished the first one is easy if you say 'Shall I bring you another bottle now or when I bring your main course?' (as you pour the remainder of the first bottle into their glasses). If you had just said 'Do you want another bottle of wine?' you are inviting a choice of either 'yes' or 'no' – and so you have a 50% chance of getting 'no'. Suggesting 'now or when I bring your main course' requires your customers to make a positive decision to say 'no', but gives *two* easy opportunities to say 'yes'.

In a non-commercial environment you are likely to arouse suspicion and hostility if you use such a commercial approach. There is no

When promoting a service, what you say and when you say it may determine the customer's response

reason, however, why you should not use this same principle in the way you present additional products or services to your clients: 'While on the subject of keeping your teeth free of plaque, would you like me to book you extra appointments with the hygienist so we can keep your plaque level down?'

Maintaining eye contact with your customers is most effective when you combine it with the right words: slowly nod your head up and down as you make the suggestion. (Body language and communication skills are discussed in Unit 2.)

Active knowledge

Rehearse the ways you could promote your products or services using the techniques outlined in this section.

Identify ways of encouraging customers to ask about additional products or services

Customers are people

If you are going to read your customers accurately, you should always engage them in conversation first to establish *rapport* (see Unit 2, pages 70–72). Talk to them about the weather, compliment them on their appearance or comment on items they have with them – and ask them what they do or how they came to be at this meeting with you.

It is said people don't care *what* you know until they know you *care*. How do they know you care? They will know if you:

• look at them
• smile at them
• talk to them
• thank them.

This is a regime that can be hard to maintain with difficult customers (see Unit 2 for more information about dealing with difficult customers).

Active knowledge

Working with two colleagues (one acting as a customer and one as an observer), practise your abilities of looking at, smiling at, talking to and thanking your customers. Ask for feedback from the observer on how much you cared or how sincere you were.

Remember

We can usually all spot the customer service person who is not sincere from what he or she does and says.

Checking your customer's interest

Once you are in your stride, it's important to check your customer's interest by obtaining regular feedback. In a commercial environment this is sometimes called 'taking your customer's buying temperature' – because you are finding out whether your customer is still 'hot'. In a non-commercial environment it is equally important to check your customer's interest level. Some of the things you might say are as follows:

* How does that match your ideas?
* What do you think of this feature?
* What do you like most about what you've seen?
* How does this fit in with your objectives?
* If you decided to go ahead with this, how many items would you need on the first order?

You now have the chance to restate the features of your additional product or service if your customer needs further information. If your customer has positive feelings, you also have the opportunity to

Closing is all about obtaining a commitment from your customers

reinforce them and to give the customer the reassurances he or she needs.

Testing whether your customers are ready to commit themselves

How do you know when your customers are ready to sign up to your additional product or service? In commercial organisations, a good time would be when the customer asks about delivery or payment terms.

Remember

Closing is really just about obtaining a commitment. This may not actually mean getting a signed order: it could be a commitment to a demonstration or to a quotation.

Closes can take many forms and you should always be aware of the purchasing routines your customers may follow. If you are selling to a customer with very formal purchasing procedures, asking for a signature too early will annoy him or her because it will require the customer to abandon his or her normal routine. In non-commercial organisations, you need to aim for the same commitment and to remember that, although money may not be changing hands, you need to be aware who will be making the decision and under what terms.

This sense of *when* to close comes with experience, but salespeople are constantly looking for new ways of closing. If, however, you have done your required homework, closing should not be difficult.

Ways of closing

If everything has gone according to plan, you should *not* be in a position where you have to force your customer into a sale. Your closing should be a perfectly natural follow-on from all the work you have done. Figure 7.9 is a checklist of closing phrases you might like to adapt to your own situation.

✓ How would you prefer to pay – cash or credit card?

✓ Would you like me to add this to your other goods so they all go on one invoice?

✓ This is how it works. I'll need your signature today so we can send the information to the accounts department and simultaneously to despatch. You will then receive your first order within two days.

✓ Would you prefer to be invoiced on the 1st or on the 15th?

✓ Should we deliver this to your head office or to another site?

Figure 7.9 Closing phrases: a checklist

Active knowledge

Rehearse the closes you could use with a customer at the end of a typical transaction. Write down the four you consider to be the best.

Consolidation

You have been asked by your organisation to set up a new Customer Help Centre that includes a help desk and call centre. Your organisation wants to be able to promote as many services as possible via this centre. You have some information about customers but not as much as you would like. Staff from other parts of the organisation have been seconded to your team to help with the technical background of some of the services that you will be offering. What steps should you take in establishing this new centre (assume that all the physical and equipment needs are covered)? What benefits will you concentrate on? How will you ensure that customers get accurate information?

- shoe sales and chiropody services (chiropodists can recommend specific types of shoes based on their understanding of their patients' feet)
- social services staff and home aids for disabled people.

If your additional product or service belongs to this category, co-ordinating your activities with the other organisations will improve your relationships with your customers. You can also *broker* the awareness you have of your own customers' needs to other organisations. Similarly, your share of customers might increase without the need to open up new lines of activity because customers are recommended to you by other organisations.

Active knowledge

Does your organisation fall into either (or both) of these categories? If so, could you improve your links with other organisations to promote additional products or services? Give examples of how you might achieve this.

Organise the provision of products or services which are supplied from outside your own area

To organise products or services from other parts of your distribution channel, you need to know as much as you can about the role of your partners in the channel. Perhaps the best way of approaching this is to treat your partners in the same way as you should treat your customers. Your aim should be to make your partners more loyal and more rewarding to you by establishing a learning relationship with each of them. Then each time you and your partners revamp your products or services, you should get better and better at aligning your products or services with those of your partners. Even if you are not in the commercial sector, this same principle of a learning relationship will make your services progressively more valuable to your partners and, hence, to your customers.

Learning relationships with outside partners are likely to be most effective when the arrangements between the two organisations are formal. To achieve this, you will probably have to set up some form of contractual or written arrangement. On the other hand, a promotional relationship may suit your organisation better. Here, each organisation recommends its customers to the others as a way of providing a full solution to the customers' needs. However, you won't have the same amount of control in a promotional relationship as you would in a learning relationship.

You may be able to build learning relationships *within* your own organisation without having to resort to contractual arrangements. In

Invoicing

- Are invoices sent at the convenience of the customer or at your own convenience?

- Could you provide an itemised invoice (for example, could you divide it up in such a way that helps customers distribute their own costs)?

- Can you offer cash discounts, and how would you deal with these?

Payment terms

- Do your invoices offer favourable terms to customers if they settle promptly?

- Could you offer some customers smaller payment terms over a longer period of time?

- Could you offer to forestall initial payment but with higher payment at a later date?

Figure 7.12 Is your organisation learning together?

such case, strategic management decisions are likely to have the same effect as contractual obligations. For example, after-sales services might have a learning relationship with sales, and there might be a provision to follow up the outcomes of specific cases in, say, the work of social service departments or charitable organisations. Using the examples of invoicing and payment terms, Figure 7.12 lists some questions you could ask to make sure all the different parts of your organisation are *learning together* to provide your customers with the best possible service.

Active knowledge

How might your organisation use other companies or organisations to improve its promotion of additional products or services? Give examples of how this might be achieved.

Consolidation

Prepare a report for your own organisation – or your particular part of it – outlining new ways in which you might promote additional products or services to existing customers. Give at least two examples of the way in which you might contact your customers to promote these additional services. What key points must you concentrate on? What other departments would be affected by your proposals? What steps would you take to ensure matters run smoothly?

The basic purpose of monitoring is to enable you to:

- recognise and devise effective methods of informing decision-makers about your products or services

- gather essential data on the efficiency and effectiveness of your operations (e.g. the number of contacts with customers per hour or per day, the number of times meetings fall through, the best times to arrange contacts, etc.)

- compile and update a database of valuable information about each customer or client.

For example, customers may not take advantage of your offer of additional products or services for some very specific reasons: they may not have a need for that particular offer or it may not be a suitable time for them to respond. The fact they haven't taken advantage of your offer this time doesn't mean there won't be other times when your offer exactly meets their needs. Different offers suit different people at different times.

Remember

You need to keep on communicating *all* your offers to *all* your customers *all* the time.

WHAT YOU NEED TO LEARN

- Devise methods to inform customers about additional relevant products or services.

- Use different methods of informing customers and record successes and failures against each method.

- Use your record of successes and failures to identify the best approach for offering additional products or services.

- Share information with others regarding the best approach to take when offering additional products or services to your customers.

Devise methods to inform customers about additional relevant products or services

You need to examine which ways are the most effective in informing your customers about relevant additional products or services.

Meeting your customers directly

As we noted earlier, direct meetings with your customers can be the most productive way of promoting additional products or services but can also be the most expensive. You should ask the following questions:

- How often do you meet directly with your customers?
- How long is the average meeting?
- How useful are these meetings compared with other ways of contacting customers?
- What percentage of your total promotional activity is done this way?
- Could you get information to your customers more promptly or accurately using a different method?

If you consider this to be the best method, you need to establish a way of selecting and conducting customer meetings on a *priority* basis – who are most important, who the most valuable, the most time-consuming, etc.

Direct contact with customers can be valuable, but be aware that it can also be time-consuming

At the point of service

This is an ideal way for organisations to promote additional products or services to their customers:

- Can you use information collected at the point of sale to take advantage of the differences between customers and so to promote services to them individually or in groups?

- Can you give them something that would be useful to them (e.g. a hospital or medical centre could give patients a printed note of the time of their appointments and a confirmation of attendance)?

- Could you provide the same service but without your customers having to visit your premises the next time?

By post

Direct mail marketing is a very popular way of providing information to customers. Small firms, however, tend to be overwhelmed at the prospect of sending several thousand letters and meeting the response from within their own resources. It is possible, on the other hand, to outsource this service to a specialist bureau who can send a direct mail shot at a time that suits their customers.

You must find out what the response rate is to a direct mail shot to establish how useful this technique is. If you have a good response rate, you might consider using this technique in preference to others that are less effective.

The telephone

If your activities do not warrant the use of a call centre, some of the points you may want to consider for outgoing calls are as follows:

- How often do you use outgoing calls to contact your customers?

- How useful are these calls compared with other ways of contacting customers?

- What products or services do you promote in this way?

- What percentage of your total promotional activity is done this way?

- Who is going to make these calls, and how many people will be needed and for how long?

Using the telephone to promote additional products or services takes practice and, in the early stages, will probably require you to use a script to help you get your message across.

Faxes

The same principles we have outlined for the post can be applied to fax messages. The additional benefits of fax messages are, of course, their speed and immediate responsiveness. If you are able to send multiple copies of the same message overnight, not only will you have saved time and money but you will also have set up the possibility of receiving early replies.

The added benefit of fax messages is that they are printed, which implies full commitment from the sender.

E-mail
You can use the speed of e-mail to encourage 'online' ordering and to follow through with further suggestions. You can also use the flexibility of e-mail to forward information to your customers at times that take advantage of off-peak loads and prices.

Websites
If we take the example of selling books or CDs over the Internet, the new sites in this area demonstrate lessons that can be applied to many other organisations. When you make a book or CD selection, four or five other titles are automatically listed which fit in with your interests. Research suggests that up to 30% of customers decide to buy a second or third title because of the suggestions made. Most organisations would be very pleased if half that percentage of their customers decided to accept suggestions of additional products or services – by whatever method!

Active knowledge
How might your organisation use the methods outlined above to improve its promotion of additional products or services? Give examples of how this might be achieved.

Use different methods of informing customers and record successes and failures against each method
While you may not be able to choose between all the alternatives outlined in the last section, you should use as many different methods as are reasonable. When you come to recording your successes or failures, you will need not only to check on success from your organisation's point of view but also from your customers' point of view.

Customers
When you are checking with customers which of your methods is the most successful, you should first decide on the following:

• what you want to know and how you will report this
• whom you will be covering in the survey
• how your questions are going to cover the issues involved
• the method by which the data is to be collected
• the way in which the data will be analysed.

Figure 7.13 is a checklist for obtaining feedback from your customers through a survey on the effectiveness of your promotional techniques.

Whom and *what* are you going to ask?

- Who are the people who can answer your questions on an *informed* basis?
- How many of these people will it take to make your sample 'valid'?
- What are the major issues you need to cover?
- What sort of language is appropriate? Do you need to avoid or include jargon?
- How will you measure the variables (e.g. those things customers express an *opinion* on)?
- What sensitivities may people have to the issues you are raising?

Make sure the people you choose are:

✓ representative of the sort of people who use your products or services
✓ capable of answering the questions on an informed basis
✓ willing to answer the questions.

Remember that:

- the larger the sample, the more likely it is it will represent the views of the whole group
- the larger the sample, the more expensive it is to administer
- the larger the sample, the more likely that extremes in behaviour/attitude/opinion will cancel each other out
- practical considerations like time or money will limit the size of the samples
- for a sample to be random, the population from which it is chosen must be sufficiently large to represent all shades of opinion.

You must ask the right questions in the right way

Ensure that:

✓ if you use answer ranges (i.e. 1–5 or a–e), you keep the ranges the same to enable comparison of like with like
✓ you keep question types the same – don't collect one set of answers as numbers when a similar set in the previous survey were undertaken as a range.

Survey similar people to ensure the style and weighting of the answers are maintained.

Keep the questions:

✓ short and simple
✓ few in number
✓ jargon-free
✓ easy to understand.

Ask yourself:

✓ Are the questions unambiguous?
✓ Are the questions leading the respondent?
✓ Will the questions elicit the type of responses being looked for?

Make sure your respondents know what you want by making your intentions clear in your instructions

✓ by asking the questions clearly and concisely
✓ by giving the respondents the opportunity to reply in an appropriate manner.

Figure 7.13 Obtaining feedback from your customers via a survey

Five simple rules for ensuring your customers reply

Customers are not normally enthusiastic completers of this sort of form. Follow these simple tactics, however, and you'll get the feedback you need.

Keys to good practice

Designing customer surveys

✓ *Keep it to one page* Limit your survey to one side of an A4 page.

✓ *Limit the number of questions* No more than ten questions or items.

✓ *Minimise writing* Instead of asking customers to 'fill in the blanks', ask for a letter grade (i.e. a-e), a numeric rating (from one to ten) or give them a list of choices to check off. Make it easy!

✓ *Fax back* Include your fax number at the bottom of the page, and encourage your customer to fax it back to you. It's cheaper than enclosing an SAE, and you'll get a better response rate.

✓ *Reward them* Say 'thank you' to customers who respond by acknowledging their reply, entering them in a draw or by sending them a small gift (e.g. a voucher towards their next purchase). The best way to reward respondents, however, is to share the results of your survey. People are naturally curious about what others have said.

Figure 7.14 is an example of a customer survey designed to gather information about the effectiveness of promotional techniques.

Colleagues

When it comes to reviewing the success of the methods you have used with your colleagues, you could use one or more of the following.

Post-performance checklist

• What worked well?
• What didn't work?
• What should be different next time?

Measure the results Review what you've accomplished:

• Did you get what you expected from this campaign?
• Did you achieve your target number for contacts and discussions?
• How many new customers did you get to know?

Conduct a survey amongst your colleagues Choose about five questions, depending on your goals. Your questions could include the following:

PROMOTIONAL EFFECTIVENESS QUESTIONNAIRE

At Dingly Dangly Products we aim to provide our customers with accurate and up-to-date information about our products at times and in ways that suit our customers best. To help us continuously improve our service to you, would you please take just a few moments to complete this questionnaire and return it to us in the attached pre-paid envelope. As a thank you to all respondents we will send you a voucher giving you 25% discount on your next puchase from Dingly Dangly Products when we receive your completed questionnaire.

PLEASE TELL US SOMETHING ABOUT YOURSELF

Your Name
Your Address

Your telephone number (daytime)
Your e-mail address
Are you   Male   Female
How old are you?

WHAT SORT OF DINGLY DANGLY PRODUCTS HAVE YOU BOUGHT? (Please tick the appropriate boxes)

Product	How many times have you bought one?				For yourself or someone else?			
Automatic Bread Butterer	Once	❏	More than once	❏	Yourself	❏	Someone else	❏
Electric Tea Stirrer	Once	❏	More than once	❏	Yourself	❏	Someone else	❏
Water Diluter	Once	❏	More than once	❏	Yourself	❏	Someone else	❏
Ice Cream Melter	Once	❏	More than once	❏	Yourself	❏	Someone else	❏

HOW DID YOU FIND OUT ABOUT DINGLY DANGLY PRODUCTS? (Please tick as many boxes as necessary)

From Personal Recommendation   ❏   By E-mail?   ❏
From Newspaper Advertising   ❏   From a Retail Outlet?   ❏
From Television Advertising   ❏   By another method – please tell us   ❏
From Postal Delivery   ❏
From Our Web Site?   ❏   ....

IF YOU RESPONDED TO AN ADVERTISEMENT (Please tick just one box per question)

		Excellent	Good	Poor	Bad
Was the information in the advertisement	helpful?	❏	❏	❏	❏
	accurate?	❏	❏	❏	❏

IF YOU RESPONDED TO PUBLICITY AT HOME OR IN A SHOP (Please tick just one box per question)

		Excellent	Good	Poor	Bad
Was the information in the publicity	helpful?	❏	❏	❏	❏
	accurate?	❏	❏	❏	❏

IF YOU RESPONDED VIA OUR WEB SITE (Please tick just one box per question)

		Excellent	Good	Poor	Bad
Was the information on the web site	helpful?	❏	❏	❏	❏
	accurate?	❏	❏	❏	❏

WOULD YOU LIKE TO HEAR MORE ABOUT DINGLY DANGLY PRODUCTS IN THE FUTURE?

May we send you more information about our products in the future?   Yes   ❏   No   ❏
If you said yes, how would you like to receive the information?

                                                                                    Post   ❏   E-mail   ❏

Thank you for the time you have taken to complete this questionnaire, all the information you have provided will be treated with the utmost confidence. Dingly Dangly Products does not share or pass information about individual customers to any other party or organisation.

Figure 7.14 Customer survey: how effective are your promotional techniques?

- Which method of communication produced the most results? Ask your colleagues to give the actual *numbers* of contacts made (i.e. a quantitative measure).

- Did any one method stand out as the most successful? Ask them to rate each method in a *range* (i.e. a qualitative measure).

- Did some methods prove unsuccessful? (You can get this information from the answers to the question immediately above.)

- Was any one method easier than the others for: **a** the customers; and **b** the staff ? (Use ranges to get this information.)

- Was any one method more expensive or more time-consuming than the others?

Use your record of successes and failures to identify the best approach for offering additional products or services

Now you have information from both your customers and colleagues, you can analyse the results to produce a report. This report could contain statistics, graphs, charts and tables, and it could form the basis of a presentation you will have to make to your manager or colleagues. The important thing to remember is that you base your report on measurable facts rather than opinions.

An example of the sort of report you might prepare is given in Figure 7.15.

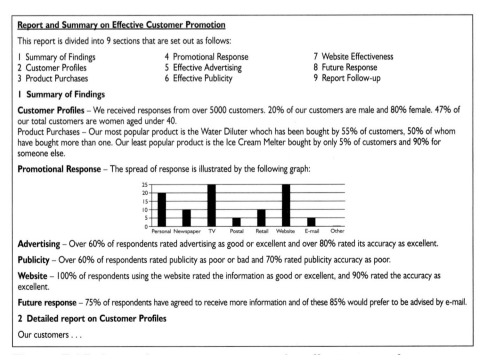

Figure 7.15 A sample report concerning the effectiveness of promotional techniques

Share information with others regarding the best approach to take when offering additional products or services to your customers

Your team or department shouldn't be the only ones working to promote additional products or services to your customers. To achieve a truly excellent service, the *whole* organisation must be involved. This suggests three fundamental needs. To:

1 share your approach with the rest of your organisation – and to reinforce this through discussions

2 ensure good internal communications so your organisation operates in a consistent, seamless way when viewed from the outside (i.e. by the customer)

3 make sure every member of staff supports this approach and that this fact is recognised throughout the entire organisation.

Sharing your approach

As a customer service 'champion', it is important you (either as an individual or as a team) encourage a positive attitude towards promoting additional products or services in your organisation. A good way to do this is to *network* with other members of staff (or even outside suppliers if you are a small organisation) to find out their views and ideas – and to make suggestions of your own. Draw up a chart of your organisation's structure and approach other departments to see how they can support your promotional activities. Also, make sure ideas to promote additional products or services are raised at internal meetings.

Internal communications

Co-operation between departments and sharing information are beneficial to the organisation as a whole as well to its customers. For example, if your department has agreed to supply additional products on credit terms for a particular customer but doesn't inform the accounts department, then payment may be demanded immediately – causing unnecessary annoyance to the customer and giving the impression the 'right hand doesn't know what the left hand is doing'. Any special arrangements negotiated with customers need to be communicated clearly to all other relevant departments.

Use every method at your disposal to disseminate information throughout your organisation about the best ways to promote additional products and services. You could use, for example, reports, newsletters, your organisation's intranet, etc.

In conclusion

Getting everyone involved in promoting additional products or services can be a major challenge. However, it will be easier to achieve if you establish clear goals for people to focus on and if you share information. Try hard to get senior management involved, as good attitudes towards this sort of activity must permeate from the top down to be sure of the greatest success.

Remember

✓ Your success rate will improve if everyone in your organisation is committed to championing additional services and shares information about this.

✓ Colleagues feel more motivated when they have a say in processes and systems.

✓ Targets help you and your colleagues to focus on the task in hand.

Active knowledge

What would be the most appropriate methods to use to keep other members of your organisation informed about the best approach to take when promoting additional products or services? Give the reasons for your decisions.

Consolidation

You have been asked to produce a report on the effectiveness of your organisation's efforts to promote additional services. What methods could have been used? How would you have obtained the information to demonstrate effectiveness? Produce a survey to use with your colleagues. How would you promote the information you have gathered amongst your colleagues?

End-of-unit test

1 What is a learning relationship? How does it differ from a promotional relationship? How do you set up these types of relationships with your customers?

2 What are the differences between facts, features and benefits?

3 Why should organisations pay special attention to the benefits of their products or services?

4 What are the ten most common benefits when buying a product or using a service?

5 What response should you make if your customer argues with you or if he or she eventually turns down your offer?

6 How does it benefit your customers if you have a full knowledge of all the products or services available from your organisation?

7 How can merchandising help you to promote additional products or services?

8 What are the alternatives you might consider when planning how you can promote your additional products or services?

9 What are the various methods you could use to contact your customers, and what should you consider when looking to improve those contacts?

10 What are distribution channels, and how can you make sure they work effectively both within and outside your organisation?

11 What methods might you use to keep on communicating effectively with all your customers?

12 Why is it important to monitor your successes and failures?

13 How can you ensure your customers reply to your requests for information?

14 What are the issues you must consider if you want to encourage your colleagues to promote additional products or services to your customers?

15 How can you make sure information concerning your approaches to promoting additional products or services is shared throughout your entire organisation?

Unit CL8

Lead the work of teams and individuals to improve customer service

Why do organisations use teams? To:

- benefit from the co-operation that develops when groups of people work closely together
- build on the sense of achievement every team member can feel
- increase their employees' commitment to large projects by using small-sized groupings of people
- develop people's problem-solving skills.

Thus by using teams organisations look to gain:

- improved decision-making
- increased productivity
- better-quality products or services
- improved awareness of customer needs
- better use of their employees' skills and abilities.

Remember

The important aspect of your job is to *deliver exceptional service to your customers.* How you lead your team or run your company is important, but your prime focus at all times must be the delivery of that service.

Stages of team development

You were introduced to the idea of the stages of development a team goes through in Unit 3. Here we will look at some of these stages in a little more detail. The classic theory on team development was introduced by Bruce Tuckman in 1955. As noted in Unit 3, he described the four stages of team development as *forming*, *storming*, *norming* and *performing*. Figure 8.1 summarises these stages.

What makes a team successful

We can all recognise the difference between a sports team that has trained together and one that has not. For a start, the former is far more likely to be successful than the latter. Similarly, if we went to a theatre to watch a production that had not been rehearsed, we would fairly quickly notice the poor quality of the product on offer.

Fortunately, we are all used to experiencing examples of extremely high-quality teamwork from the leisure, entertainment and broadcasting industries. These products are usually the result of the

---

Forming

- The 'honeymoon'.
- The team clarifies what it needs to do.
- Team members need to get to know each other before they can take any risks.
- The team looks for direction in virtually all matters (when and where to meet and what behaviour is appropriate).

↓

Storming

- Frustration and disagreement can set in.
- The demands of the tasks begin to bite and the team has to decide on the roles individuals are to play.
- There is often a great deal of discussion and argument (but a good team leader should *not* stifle this).

↓

Norming

- Reality strikes.
- Team norms, boundaries and other rules of behaviour are established.
- Competition between members ceases and trust and co-operation emerge.
- True strengths and weaknesses become clear.

↓

Performing

- Good interpersonal relationships have been formed.
- The team is ready to define and resolve problems.
- The team comes up with solutions, gets on with the job and starts to enjoy the experience.
- Goals are more related to tasks than relationships between team members.

Figure 8.1 The four stages of team development

people involved spending a great deal of time training, rehearsing and practising together.

If we look at the things successful teams do, we can see that:

- they have a clear idea of what they are going to achieve and that everyone in the team is committed to that goal
- they have organised themselves to take the best advantage of the individual skills team members bring with them
- they work together as a group in ways that bring out the best results for the team as a whole.

Active knowledge

Which of the four stages of development (as shown in Figure 8.1) is your team at? How will this affect what you plan to do with your team? Give the reasons for your answer.

The elements for this unit are:

8.1 Plan and organise the work of teams and individuals.

8.2 Provide support for team members and individuals.

8.3 Review performance of team members and individuals.

WHAT YOU NEED TO LEARN

- How to establish clear roles and responsibilities within your team.
- How to agree and set goals with team members.
- How to involve team members in planning and organising their work.
- How to allocate work to others to gain understanding and commitment.
- How to motivate team members to improve performance.

How to establish clear roles and responsibilities within your team

To run your team effectively you need to be clear about what you expect of yourself, of the organisation you work for and of the team you are leading. If your team is to thrive, you will need to create a culture where responsibility and authority are delegated to your members to produce the results you have agreed.

Remember

Your team is not just a group of people with specific job responsibilities; they are a mix of individuals each of whom needs to relate to all the others.

The knowledge and skills of the team members are usually complementary and the personal success of each member, as well as the team as a whole, is therefore dependent on each and every member of the team. It is vitally important, therefore, that each team member, and particularly the team leader, respects the input and efforts of all the individuals who make up the team.

Establish objectives

In setting objectives for the team, you must be clear about what you and your team want to achieve. This may seem very obvious, but we have all been to meetings where no one seemed to know what was happening or what to do.

Figure 8.2 is a checklist on how to establish your overall objectives.

> ✓ Always remember your targets: what you are setting your sights on and how you are going to achieve success.
>
> ✓ Some of the demands on your team will inevitably come from outside, particularly from the management of your organisation, who will have specific business objectives. Have you co-ordinated your team goals with your organisation's business objectives?
>
> ✓ Spend some considerable time talking regularly with your team to make sure they all continue to understand their objectives.
>
> ✓ In particular, you need to check how they are going to do things and how they are going to work together to achieve them.
>
> ✓ Make sure you have a periodic review of your team targets. Check the team achievement of your current objectives and whether you need to set new or redefined goals in the light of progress to date.

Figure 8.2 Establishing your overall objectives: a checklist

Active knowledge

- Have you set out your *own* overall target? (This may be through a company or departmental plan or through a mission statement; it may also not be written down but may be understood by all team members.)

- Have you discussed with your team how you are going to achieve that target?

- Have you worked out what approach you will take to achieve each of the subsidiary targets that will enable the team to reach their main target?

Recognising the contributions made by others

You and every other member of the team must be accountable to each other for the success of the whole team. In work situations, this can sometimes be a bit of a problem. Whilst we appear willing to put our fate in the hands of others as far as sports teams are concerned, it is much more difficult to do this with our jobs.

Respect is an important element of teamwork. If people deliver what they promise, the other members will feel they are reliable and can be trusted. A team that works for each other in this way is much more likely to overcome our natural resistance to allowing others to decide our fate for us.

The secret is to invest time and work into your team and its projects. All of us become more committed to something if we make this

Tasks should be delegated evenly to all members of the team

investment, and we will be more likely to trust and rely on each other if we make the investment *jointly*. The key issues are *reliability* in what we deliver to other members of the team and readiness to be *accountable* for our actions. This brings us back to the need to ensure we have set clear, achievable goals for the team, which the team believes they can deliver because they have confidence in each other.

Job descriptions

No team can function properly if its members do not have a clear idea of what is expected from them. As noted in Unit 3, if you work in a large organisation, you will probably have a job description that sets out your duties and responsibilities (see Figure 8.3). If you work in a smaller organisation, on the other hand, you may have had your duties explained to you verbally when you started your job. As a team leader you should ensure your team job descriptions – written or verbal – are reviewed regularly and kept up to date by reflecting any changes that have taken place since the last review.

Job descriptions are often supplemented with a person specification that is used during recruitment to match candidates with the preferred background of education, experience and personality needed for the job (see Figure 8.4). It is particularly important to use

JOB DESCRIPTION

1. **Job title:** Department: Reports to:

2. **Main function of job** (Note: In addition to these functions employees are
required to carry out such other duties as may reasonably be required)

Liability for cash/stock deficiencies:

3. **Location(s)**

4. **Supervisory responsibilities/position in structure**
(Attach outline organisation chart, if appropriate)

5. **Main duties**	% time spent	Level of Responsibility

6. **Responsibility for resources**

7. **Specific working conditions that may apply**

8. **Qualifications/education required**

    Experience required

    Specialist training required

    Any particular aptitude/skill required

Date of Description **Reviewed on:**

Figure 8.3 A sample job description

you can take ideas on board and react to them appropriately. You also need to develop your skills in communicating to your team members, which means using your face-to-face and written skills to their maximum effect.

Active knowledge

Using the qualities given in Figure 8.5, which do you consider to be your strengths, and *why*? Which do you consider you need more work on or experience of, and how are you going to achieve this? Give some evidence relating to your job in support of your claims.

How to agree and set goals with team members

What the team hopes to achieve

You may have been set up as a permanent part of your organisation to cover a specialist area or you may be leading a short-term or temporary team which has been set up to solve a particular problem. In all cases you, as team leader, must know exactly what it is your team is expected to achieve.

Don't underestimate the importance of everyone knowing what is expected of him or her

Who is going to do what in the team

You may be a team of two people working together, one of you the leader and the other one the subordinate. Even in this simplest of situations, you must both be clear who is going to be responsible for what. By contrast, you may be leading a large team of people. In this case the need to know who is going to do what becomes far more critical and demands much more attention to detail. You will need to have organisation charts, job descriptions and staffing schedules.

All members of the team know what is expected of them

It is reasonable that, if you have planned out individual roles and responsibilities for your team, you should pass these on to the staff expected to undertake the jobs. The best way to do this is to provide detailed written job descriptions, person specifications, policy statements and procedure guidelines. Many organisations find this a tiresome chore, but inevitably misuse time and resources sorting out the resulting confusion.

Set guidelines on costs, time frames and administration

These should be set out in procedure manuals or guidelines, but if you are a very small organisation you may find it simpler to make some notes and display these on a noticeboard. The important thing is that these guidelines exist and that all team members know how to access them.

How guidelines are to be monitored

It is very rare indeed to have designed a set of guidelines and to have found they have all been perfectly adequate for their job over a period of years. Change is a constant aspect of life. You must decide on a reasonably balanced review period that will enable you to keep your procedures and job descriptions active and up to date. Too often will result in little or no change; too infrequently will cause the resulting procedures to be ignored.

What your boundaries are going to be

As well as looking at the responsibilities within your team, you need to examine how your team fits in with other parts of your organisation. If each team has clear objectives that are linked to overall organisation objectives, this task will be made much easier. The points of transition between parts of an organisation are usually the points where things break down, so you must check to see whether you are doing too much or too little to ensure the seamless transfer of information and action throughout your organisation. This requires meetings with other teams, sections or departments to understand clearly who does what.

Whether the boundaries are set by your team itself or whether they will be imposed by others outside the team

If you are leading a team or a section within a well established organisation, it is likely the boundaries for your team will have been set by the senior management. In these circumstances you should always make sure you have the opportunity to review those boundaries on a regular basis. This means either waiting for such situations as your regular appraisal meeting or instigating discussions with those other team leaders in regular contact with your team. If you are setting up or running a temporary team you will certainly have to meet your fellow team leaders to review your boundaries.

Set SMART goals

Remember SMART from Unit 3 (pages 121–122): **S**pecific, **M**easurable, **A**chievable, **R**ealistic and **T**imebound? When you are setting goals for your team, these too should be SMART (see Figure 8.6).

Active knowledge

Practise writing some SMART objectives for these organisations:

- an electrical retailer has had a lot of problems with returns of faulty equipment but does not have enough replacement items. It is unable to pacify its customers

- a printing firm has as its goal: 'We are always customer-focused.'

Define success in 'hard' and 'soft' terms

The *hard* criteria for determining success are such *measurable* things as time, cost, resources and technical standards. The *soft* criteria are more about *how* the task was completed (the attitudes, skills and behaviours demonstrated by the team and its members). These also include such things as relationships with the customer and attitudes to things such as quality, reliability and attention to detail.

It is particularly important to recognise these soft criteria because your customers or clients often do not specifically mention them. Yet *reliability* is the single most important aspect of delivering outstanding customer service. How many times does a customer specify their needs by referring to your team's attitudes or reliability standards? It would be very rare indeed, but they will complain bitterly if your team falls below their perceived standards, despite the fact they have not specified them. Your job is to define and insist upon the maintenance of those standards on behalf of your customers and clients.

Specific goals spell out what your team wants to do and how it is going to do it:

We need to improve our responsiveness to customers, so therefore we are going to answer the telephone within three rings.

It is the addition of three rings which makes this a *specific* goal.

Measurable goals enable the organisation to check whether it has made any progress:

Cut response times by 50% over the next three months.

Measurement could be done by each individual – if the organisation has the technology to measure individual response times. It could also be measured across the whole team.

Achievable goals are focused on what needs to be achieved rather than on the method used:

We will ensure our customers are informed of changes at the earliest opportunity.

This goal should be enlarged to include an activity statement such as:

We will ensure that our customers are informed of changes by e-mail or telephone within twenty-four hours of the change taking place.

Realistic goals demand:

- your team has the necessary resources
- there are no circumstances preventing you from achieving your goals
- the resulting costs are not too high.

Unrealistic goals demotivate teams.

Timebound goals set a specific time frame for achieving goals, such as in the 'activity statement' example above.

Figure 8.6 Setting SMART goals for your team

Active knowledge

- What are your team's success criteria in *measurable* terms for the 'hard' aspects of its role?

- What are its 'soft' success criteria? Have you found out about any of these from complaints you have received regarding your team's performance?

- Have you written team goals to encompass the 'soft' criteria? Can those 'soft' criteria goals also be written in SMART terms?

How to involve team members in planning and organising their work

Good planning means involving team members as much as possible – keeping them in touch with the 'big picture'. Making sure everyone can see the 'big picture' puts the plan into its context, which is very important if your team is scattered over a wide area. Don't underestimate your team's capability to grasp the important aspects of your organisation's business: they will be quite able to organise themselves if they have a clear understanding of what is needed.

Case study

During and after the Falklands conflict, a UK company deployed teams to repair aircraft in dispersed locations on the Falkland Islands. The performance of the individuals in the teams rose by 100% without the need for team leaders to specify how things should be done. The reason was that each individual member of the team was on the spot, could see exactly what immediate response was needed and could see various ways of improving performance using his or her own initiative.

1 Why do you think the UK company decided to put its teams in dispersed locations on the Falkland Islands?
2 How do you think the team workers might have felt about this decision?
3 Why exactly did team performance improve?
4 Overall, what organisational targets were achieved?

Organising the flow of information in teams

If your team is reasonably small and based in one particular place, you could pass on information on noticeboards or have weekly 'information sharing' meetings. If your team is larger and more scattered, you could publish a newsletter or use e-mail to pass on the information. The most important thing is to pass on the information by the most convenient method. But there are, however, two points you need to remember. You need to:

1 work out the best way to record that each member of your team has received the information. Putting a small notice on a board in a corridor will not guarantee everyone will read it
2 make it easy for team members to give you their responses to the information. If they can't respond or if you have made replying too difficult, you will have wasted the exercise.

Active knowledge

In your own organisation, how is most information disseminated? For example, write down how people find out about:

- a change in work procedures
- if someone is leaving, retiring, getting married, etc.

Do the systems work well? If not, how would you improve them?

Why individual needs are important

Because it is important not only to achieve the tasks that have been set for the team but also to build up the relationships within the team, you need to take into account the things that motivate the individuals in your team.

Maslow developed a *hierarchy of needs*, which suggests that, as we get closer to achieving satisfaction at one level, so we move on to the next. These levels are shown in Figure 8.7. Whilst an organisation may not be able to do much about the first level of need (apart, from perhaps, giving its employees a pay rise), organisations can have an impact on the levels above this. For example, if people feel:

- afraid to speak in meetings, they will not have progressed beyond the second level of needs
- they are not welcome at meetings, they will not have progressed beyond the third level of needs
- their contributions are not appreciated, they will not have progressed beyond the fourth level of needs.

It is vitally important, therefore, each team member is given the opportunity to contribute to the team his or her own mix of skills and experience, and that he or she feels safe, has a sense of belonging and knows his or her contributions are appreciated.

So if you have someone in your team who is good at coming up with new ideas but is not given the opportunity to do so, you will have a very frustrated individual indeed. But how do you find out if someone has this capacity to generate new ideas? While there are psychometric tests people can take to assess their aptitudes and attitudes, these belong to the realm of the specialist practitioner. So instead the answer is you *talk*.

You make sure that when someone new joins your team you spend some considerable time finding out who he or she is, what he or she can do, what he or she likes and dislikes at work and what he or she aspires to in the future. You should make notes about your conversation to show it to the person involved, to obtain his or her

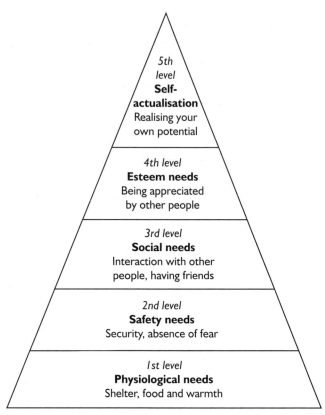

Figure 8.7 Maslow's hierarchy of needs

agreement to what has been said, and you should store these in his or her personal file. The notes can then be used in appraisal meetings with this person.

Matching tasks to personalities

From what each team member has told you, you should be able to match the right people to the right jobs. Common sense also comes into play here: you would not put a shy and introverted person in a front-line complaints section or an extrovert in a room of his or her own with only a photocopier for company. People do change, however, because we all have different experiences which colour our attitudes: the shy and introverted person you could not place in the complaints section five years ago may now be ready for a such an opportunity.

Charles Handy (in *Understanding Organisations*) says that, to get the best performance from your team members, you should bear in mind the following:

1 Criticism improves performance only when:
- it is given with a genuine liking for the other person
- it is related to specific instances
- the subordinate trusts and respects his or her superior.

2 Improved performance results when:

- goal-setting, not criticism, is used and the goals must be specific, jointly set and reasonable
- the superior is regarded as helpful, facilitating, receptive to ideas and able to plan
- performance evaluation has been initiated by subordinates as a prelude to further goal-setting, not appraisal.

If you are looking to improve someone's performance, use this approach and be prepared to be flexible and receptive to proposals. Whatever you agree, this should be written down because it is the fundamental description of what your team is going to achieve and how each individual is going to be involved in the process.

> 'People don't do the wrong thing because they *want* to do the wrong thing. They do the wrong thing because they are not clear what the right thing is' (Debra Dunn).

Case study

A company providing Modern Apprenticeship training in association with its local Training and Enterprise Council (TEC) introduced some new software to cope with the growth in the attendant paperwork. At first the manager alone used the financial planning module in the software and negotiated the subsequent payments from the TEC. After a few months, another member of staff took over the responsibility to free the manager for other tasks.

After some further months the information produced by the software had become unreliable and a new approach had to be considered because the TEC were refusing to pay. In reviewing the position jointly, the manager and member of staff discovered the root causes of the problem – lack of structured training on handover which led to wrongly entered data, and lack of guidance on the techniques for negotiating money from the TEC. They first called in the software engineers who were able to provide a simple solution to correct the inaccuracies in the data.

They then spent some time in reviewing how they would approach the TEC to recover money that had not been paid. With the secure knowledge that the information available was absolutely accurate, and with a briefing on the correct approach to take, the member of staff had no problems in agreeing a retrospective payment package with the staff from the TEC, and has continued to do so successfully from that point on. The previously reticent team member had been successfully coached into playing a significant negotiating role despite initial thoughts by the manager that no one else could do the job.

Use planning cycles to get feedback

You learnt in Unit 1 about the importance of obtaining feedback from your customers and colleagues (both those within and outside your organisation), as well as about the need to establish planning cycles. Figure 8.8 summarises this need to input feedback into your planning cycles.

This means frequent and relatively short periods of doing, followed by a period of reflection, sharing of knowledge gained and consolidation before the team moves forward again. Each cycle of planning and doing should, therefore, reduce the amount of uncertainties you may be facing. You overcome uncertainty and obtain feedback not simply from planning but by *doing*.

Remember

Understanding the results of your actions will enable you to revise your plans, both in the short and long term.

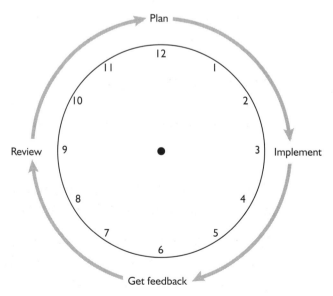

Figure 8.8 The planning cycle

You must determine the most appropriate time intervals for achieving targets or milestones. If you are dealing with relatively certain conditions, you can afford to have longer time intervals. Leaving the intervals too long, however, could mean you miss a target and are unable to catch up. The key is to set milestones that are always in sight because they will reinforce your team's need for regular progress and successes. They will also ensure the team never goes too far off track and are, therefore, an insurance policy against failure.

Active knowledge

- What are the time intervals of three team activities undertaken by your organisation?

- How regularly are these reviewed (there may be some where the current answer is 'never')?

- Are these reasonable time intervals?

- Could they be revised?

Setting up planning cycles

Every aspect of your team's work will be covered by planning of some sort (whether annually, monthly or even daily!). In each case, you need to follow the process of planning, implementing, getting feedback and reviewing. Getting the feedback will be the most time-consuming part – which is why so many people ignore this aspect of the cycle. However, if you begin to see a regular pattern appearing from your feedback, you may be able to increase the intervals between cycles.

Each time you hold a review meeting, you need to take an ordered approach to your planning. For example, you may want to structure your review for each of your agenda items in a particular way (see Figure 8.9).

Active knowledge

What types of planning cycles are used in your organisation? How does your planning involve the members of your team?

How to allocate work to others to gain understanding and commitment

The relationships your team will have with others, both inside and outside the organisation

As we have seen, successful teams have a strong sense of purpose and direction, and a realistic plan for turning their vision into reality.

> **Agenda item 1**
>
> *Planning* This item was planned for introduction in May in the South East of England at 20 branches, followed by other branches in October.
>
> *Implementation* Delivery was late and only 5 branches introduced the product in May, 10 in June and 5 in July.
>
> *Feedback* Customer reaction has been excellent and sales have exceeded expectations by 20% (Sales Dept information). Distribution, however, continues to be a problem although current levels can be maintained for three months (Production Dept information).
>
> *Review* Check delivery times and volumes. Can deliveries be increased after 3 months? Can the 20% increase be met and when? Who is responsible for finding this information?
>
> *Re-planning* Hold current levels and distribution where they are. Increase delivery to present 20 branches as soon as indicated. Postpone introduction to other branches to New Year. Check production figures for New Year. Next cycle meeting December.

Figure 8.9 An example agenda item

And we have also seen how good teams don't just happen: they have to be actively created and managed. Team leaders need to create an environment where people can give of their best. To be a good team leader, you also need to be aware of the relationships your team will have with others. These relationships will mainly be with two different sets of people:

The customers

- What sort of relationships do we have with our customers?
- How good are we at empathising with them?
- Who is going to handle the customers, how and when?

Your organisation

- What are our key relationships with others in our organisation?
- Who gains and loses as a result of our efforts?
- What means will we use to communicate our results with the organisation?

Active knowledge

What are the answers to the questions above for *your* team?

The answers to these questions will mean the team leader is able to develop a strategy for dealing with these relationships.

Create a sense of belonging

To help people feel a sense of belonging to your team, you should organise a well thought-out induction process. New staff joining your team should be given an explanation of:

• the 'big picture'
• their role and performance expectations
• some of the more important ground rules.

They should also be introduced to key contacts, both within and outside the organisation.

To help create a sense of joint identity, you should find ways of bringing your team together, not only at work but also at leisure. If the going has been tough for some time, it is important to have impromptu get-togethers.

Remember

Fun can become work and work can become fun.

Active knowledge

If you have induction sessions for new team members, what is included in these sessions? When was the last time your team had an informal get-together?

Maintain a flow of communication

Ensure constant communication

It is important you constantly monitor and facilitate the flow of information. For example:

- Who *has* this information and *who* needs it?
- What is the best way to stay in touch with each other and to keep ourselves updated?
- What *formal* methods do we use (reports, briefing groups, review meetings, etc.)?
- What *informal* methods do we use (impromptu meetings, social activities, etc.)?

Active knowledge

What are the answers to the above questions for your *own* team? Are there any areas of your current practice you could improve?

Present plans to gain commitment

You now need to present your plans to your team to gain all the team members' approval. If you have been using the planning cycle approach, you will have already obtained your feedback and amended your plans; if not, you will need to revisit that stage to make sure your plans will work.

We all recognise the fact that even 'the best laid plans of mice and men …' can fail so, to reduce the risk of failure, you must involve absolutely everyone in your team in responding to your plan. The two main reasons for this are:

1 it will ensure you review your plan from every perspective, not just from your own or from those people who work closest to you
2 you gain commitment from your team if they have an opportunity to say 'yes' or 'no' at the earliest stage.

Some people will be quite eloquent in their response whilst others may not feel confident enough to give you feedback, particularly if it is negative. You can reduce this problem by asking specific questions about the plan. The risk with this, however, is that you may not ask all the right questions and therefore miss some vital comments. To overcome this potential shortcoming, add two general questions:

1 What *positive* effects will this plan have on your job?
2 What *negative* effects will this plan have on your job?

How you gather the information will depend on your circumstances (see the section 'Organising the flow of information in teams' earlier in this element on page 322).

Case study

A domestic utilities servicing company has reorganised its way of working so the service engineers no longer report to the office each morning to collect their work schedule and supplies for the day. The engineers now work from home and use their mobile phones to contact the office. Their supplies are sent to them (or their customers) in advance by a parcel delivery service. Teams of staff in the office plan and organise the workload and the delivery of supplies, equipment and materials.

After a week of this new operation, the company is inundated with phone calls from angry customers and, later, from angry service engineers. The problems include non-arrival of supplies, the separate arrivals of engineers and supplies, and the inaccurate allocation of time for jobs (which means customers are waiting around unnecessarily for engineers to arrive or, worse, that appointments have to be cancelled).

1 If you were the team leader, what would you have done to prevent these circumstances from arising?
2 What should the engineers themselves have done about this situation?
3 Do you think the team at the company responsible for the new arrangements had done sufficient planning? Give reasons for your answer.

Active knowledge

Write an account of a team meeting you ran in your own organisation to plan and implement some changes:

- Did it go well?
- Did you feel your team understood and responded to your plans?
- How did you obtain their commitment to the changes?

How to motivate team members to improve performance

Facts and myths about motivation

The subject of motivation is very complex. However, we outlined some of the basic principles of motivation theory earlier in this element, particularly Maslow's hierarchy of needs. You now need to consider some of the ideas of Herzberg, who developed a theory of 'hygiene factors'. His premise was that people are not motivated to give their best performance until some of the fundamental basics of their jobs are satisfied. For example, people might feel dissatisfied by their working conditions or salaries, or they might not like their supervisors or the others they work with. These factors might make people very dissatisfied but they do *not* do the opposite – make people feel motivated to work hard and to give their best. So giving someone a pay increase does not necessarily make him or her work harder; it only stops him or her from being dissatisfied until the next time.

This is not to say that payments cannot help to improve performance, but they must be geared to the results you want your team to achieve. This way payments act as rewards for achieving team or personal targets. Money alone, however, will not motivate *all* people to achieve your team's targets. Most people also need *job satisfaction* and *personal fulfilment* and, although these things do not always produce better results (often they do), they should result in lower absenteeism and staff turnover.

Tiffin and McCormick (in *Industrial Psychology*) adapted Herzberg's work to demonstrate people's positive and negative attitudes about those things that are supposed to motivate them at work (see Figure 8.10).

Figure 8.10 Positive and negative attitudes to motivation factors at work

Active knowledge

What positively motivates the members of your team? Does motivation change with a person's seniority in the organisation?

Always aim for success

The driving force behind successful teams is the motivation that comes from being successful. Such teams exude the energy, excitement and commitment that being successful releases. They also thrive on the recognition that success brings.

Remember

The old adage 'Nothing breeds success like success' is quite true: the best motivator of all is for the team leader to create a well organised, well managed and successful team.

Keys to good practice

Creating a positive climate

✓ Put forward your vision of what the team is going to achieve. Use this process as an opportunity to enthuse your team members on the benefits of sharing that vision.

✓ Spend a lot of your time talking to the team about what sort of climate and which ways of working together are likely to contribute to the team's success.

✓ Choose your team carefully to include those people who are 'turned on' by this shared vision.

✓ Agree arrangements with your customers and clients so your team has a clear definition of its limits.

✓ Create the climate you want within your team by displaying it in your own behaviour and attitudes (i.e. be a good role model).

✓ Establish and maintain good systems, procedures, etc., for planning and staff appraisal.

✓ Make sure you always give praise and recognition whenever they are due.

Ensure your team is action and performance orientated

If your team is very positively orientated, the natural outcome will be that they will have no problems in getting on with their tasks.

Successful teams respond quickly and positively to problems and opportunities and they are optimistic – even when the going gets tough. Do not fall into the trap, however, of thinking that all you have to do to get results is just to tell people what needs doing. Sometimes 'success criteria' will not be heard by, recorded or communicated to your team. In particular, technical specialists often find it difficult to relate to the 'soft' criteria that may or may not be specified by your customers. Remember the points we made earlier in this element about defining success in terms of 'hard' and 'soft' criteria, and of your role as guardian of the 'soft' criteria.

Your role, therefore, is to translate your overall success criteria into individual successes. So you need to give your team members specific objectives that must be completed within specific time frames. You will also need to agree both the hard and soft criteria of your team members' performances and how these will be judged.

Active knowledge

Note down an example from your own team of when you needed to introduce some soft criteria in response to outside pressures.

Commit your team to quality

Throughout this element and, indeed, throughout this book, we have emphasised that the single most important aspect of giving great customer service is *reliability*. To make sure your team delivers a reliable service, you must examine your quality standards very carefully.

Figure 8.11 Achieving quality

Quality in customer service can be defined as 'the satisfaction of agreed customer requirements'. *Total* quality is 'the mobilisation of the whole organisation to achieve quality, continuously and economically' (Neil Huxtable – *Small Business Quality*). If you concentrate on the customer satisfaction part only, you may find that ever-increasing demands increase your costs, reduce your profits and even result in a loss. Using *total quality management* (TQM) techniques ensures your improvements in customer service are matched by improved efficiency and doing things right the first time.

TQM emphasises the idea of *internal* customer satisfaction, whereby each individual employee within the organisation is a customer in his or her own right, with needs and expectations to be met (see Figure 8.11). You must demonstrate your commitment to TQM if you want your team to be successful. Many organisations make the mistake of handing all quality matters over to a specialist department or treat it as an add-on to other initiatives. If this is the case, your team will see quality as a secondary issue, to be taken up only when other priorities have been dealt with.

Case study

A large multinational computer company received a call for help from one of its clients. One of the client's PCs had gone down and it needed to be repaired urgently. The client company asked if an engineer could add their repair to the top of his list of visits. Although it was usual to take a kit of spare parts so engineers would have everything they needed when they went out, stores did not have the time to do this for the engineer. The engineer knew he had some common spares in his van and, with luck, he wouldn't need the specialised kit of parts. Unfortunately, however, his preliminary diagnostic check showed he did indeed need the kit of parts. The PC needed a new printed circuit board.

Somewhat embarrassed, he ordered a new kit using his mobile phone. Some time later the courier arrived with the package and the engineer quickly got to work, but had to give up because the circuit board had not been included in the delivery. He reordered the kit with special instructions to check the circuit board had been included. Six hours after placing their call for assistance, the client's office was still not up and running again.

A second courier brought the right spares and, in just a few minutes, the engineer succeeded in replacing the old board. Annoyingly, the system crashed and, after the tenth crash, the engineer gave up. A senior engineer would have to sort this one out tomorrow. The next day the senior engineer reported to the first engineer: 'No problem, sorted it out in five minutes. You were loading an old version of the software – everyone's on version 2 these days.'

1 What is lacking in this company's approach to TQM?
2 What would have prevented the first engineer from omitting to take right kit with him?
3 What effect would this incident have on the client company's relationship with the computer company?

Active knowledge

- What TQM systems do your organisation and your team have in place?
- Do you build quality into all your team meetings?
- What aspects of your team management still need quality-orientated action?

Anticipate the future

Successful teams value leaders who maintain the team's direction, energy and commitment. They expect the leader (with their help) to fight for support and resources from key figures within their organisation. To achieve this, you need to take two, almost opposite, approaches which you need to balance very carefully:

- first, you must rise above day-to-day events and pressures to take a broader and more objective view of what is going on *now* and what is *likely* to happen

- secondly, you need to 'get up close and personal' to agree individual objectives and to obtain the resources that are needed in the short term.

If you make sure you continuously communicate the 'big picture' to your team, you will overcome their natural antipathy to activities that do not immediately involve them. Also, if you translate the big picture into revised milestones for each team member, you will demonstrate to them how their roles fit in to the whole and how they integrate with each other.

This approach is particularly important if your team is scattered over a wide area because it is so easy for staff in remote locations to feel out of touch and neglected. In such cases it is vitally important you use face-to-face methods to involve all team members. You should consider holding team meetings lasting at least two days so members can meet together socially and can forge a common sense of identity.

How to influence your team members' performance
To achieve all this you need to know how you can influence other people. Some of the methods you could use are shown in Figure 8.12. However, these are not really recommended, for the reasons given in the figure. Influencing people, therefore, is not perhaps as easy as it seems. You could, on the other hand, adopt the approaches as shown in Figure 8.13 to help you, and these are to be preferred to the tactics shown in Figure 8.12.

Active knowledge
Write down details of an instance when you have had to influence other members of your team:

• What method did you use?

• Was it successful?

• Why was it successful or *not* successful?

Create systems that are staff friendly
We all have a mix of skills we can call upon, and you should make sure your team has the right mix of technical, problem-solving and decision-making skills. If not, you will have to train existing staff to meet the shortfall or, alternatively, buy in additional expertise. Equally importantly, you must ensure you have team members who have (or who are ready to develop) good interpersonal skills.

If you ask yourself why people work and thrive under considerable pressure and for long hours, the answer will probably that these people are getting the satisfaction they are looking for. As a team leader, therefore, it is important you set out the soft criteria you require – the personal commitment of time, skills and emotional energy – along with the opportunities, satisfaction and rewards that are available to your team members. You also need to check whether your vision is sufficiently challenging and whether planned milestones or targets will act as positive motivators to your team.

Active knowledge
• How would you handle the situation when some people are temporarily under- or overworked?

• How will you reward and celebrate success?

• What are the incentives you give to people to perform outstandingly?

Reward staff

You do something for me and I will reward you with (e.g. some time off or a pay rise).

Remember the person doing something for reward only is unlikely to change his or her attitude or behaviour over a longer period of time.

Be an expert

You do what I say because I have the right sort of knowledge, skill or experience (and you don't).

This can backfire because people will do the exact opposite if they think you are using your expertise for yourself only and not for the team.

Use your contacts

I am influential because of who I am and whom I know.

But can you be sure this sort of influence will motivate staff in the right direction? You may find you have influenced staff in a way you had not planned.

Change the environment

I can modify the environment in which you work in a way that requires you to act differently.

This is fine with the people who are happy with the change, but what about those who aren't? If this tactic does not work, there are other methods you could fall back on but this would really be an admission of failure.

Use your job title

I am the boss and you have to listen to me.

This tactic comes straight from your organisation's structure. If you can't get support by this means, you should start to worry!

Threaten them

You will be punished if you don't do what I want (e.g. be demoted or lose your job).

How is this likely to motivate someone to give his or her best performance?

Figure 8.12 How to influence team members' performance: doubtful tactics

- *What are you actually capable of doing in the situation?* You could hardly use the expertise approach if you are not an expert, so you need to look at the resources you have available (e.g. rewards, information, time or skill).

- *What kind of behaviour will the other person welcome most?* If someone is not used to making his or her own decisions, putting that person into a role which demands decision-making skills is not going to please him or her or fill him or her with confidence.

- *What approach will the other person least likely oppose?* If you are offering something that is likely to be well received, you can present it in a way that gives the team members more control over what they do. But you might have to promise more resources if you are asking them to do something they may oppose.

- *What are they least likely to resist?* If you are not clear enough in your explanations, people will resist you. So take care with the way you say things. If what you want them to do will cause an increased workload, you should provide such support as additional training or coaching.

Figure 8.13 How to influence team members' performance: preferred tactics

Consolidation

You have been appointed to a new job in a new company that has never employed anyone with your skills before. The management of the company have asked you to build a team around you to deliver outstanding service both internally and externally. Your first six months have been very successful and you have experienced continuing growth in your part of the business. Your Senior Manager now wants a report from you explaining the team's excellent performance. What did you have to do to ensure your success? What steps did you take to integrate your team into the successful one it now is? How did you allocate work to new and untried staff, and how have you motivated them to give their best? How did you define success for your team?

WHAT YOU NEED TO LEARN

- How to give support and direction when team members need help.
- How to encourage team members to work together.
- How to check that team members understand what they are required to do.

How to give support and direction when team members need help

Getting people to follow you is what leadership is about, and the most important part of gaining followers is that people must have confidence in you. But how do you gain that confidence?

Some people say that, as a team leader, you need to sell yourself to your team. You need to persuade them as to the value of your ideas and you must follow through by delivering the goods. These are undoubtedly important elements of leadership; but 'delivering the goods' not only means getting the job done but also building your team's confidence.

Good team leadership

Jon Katzenbach and Douglas Smith (in *The Wisdom of Teams*) believe there are seven necessary elements to good team leadership:

1 keep the purpose, goals and approach relevant and meaningful
2 build commitment and confidence
3 strengthen the mix and level of skills
4 manage relationships with outsiders, including removing obstacles
5 create opportunities for others
6 do real work
7 neither blame nor allow specific individuals to fail, and never excuse away shortfalls in your team's performance.

Styles of team leadership

Most teams are *functional* in that they are assembled by a leader who runs most meetings and sets (or at least approves) most agenda items and decisions. The leadership skills required for this kind of team management are to:

- maintain control
- focus and direct team members' activities
- accept responsibility for final decisions

There are many positive styles of management that won't leave team members feeling dictated to

- set and enforce work and quality standards
- distribute rewards and sanctions according to the team members' performance
- motivate team members.

This set of leadership skills is well suited for many business situations and purposes, at least for attaining short-term organisational goals. There are, however, other styles you could adopt (see Figure 8.14). It may be appropriate for you to choose one of these other styles rather than the more traditional functional style.

Active knowledge

- What leadership style do you use?
- Did you choose this style deliberately, or did the circumstances within your organisation determine your choice?
- Are there any situations where you could use a different style but on a temporary basis?

Making leadership work

Whatever your style, if you want to make sure you get the best from your team members you need to:

- trust them to use their judgement in doing the work they are accountable for

Style of leadership	Example
Delegated	The delegation of a limited part of the team's leadership or of selected leadership tasks to team members
Elected	The team leader could let the team select leaders itself. This could be the election of one leader for a lengthy period of time or a series of leaders for shorter periods of time
Shared	The leader shares the task of leadership with others in the team. The extent of sharing may depend on a number of factors (duties, length of time, etc.)
Empowering	This approach leads to self-directing teams where all decisions are taken by team members with no one member being a leader at any point in time

Figure 8.14 Leadership styles

- evaluate and develop their individual capabilities
- make sure no one is either 'under' or overwhelmed by the challenges of his or her work.

To ensure things keep working in the face of change and uncertainty, you also need to make sure that:

- the work assigned is still relevant – this is especially important in rapidly changing circumstances
- you monitor processes and systems so that resources are used properly
- you communicate a sense of purpose and relevance so your team have a context for their work and their judgements
- you agree procedures beforehand for use in cases of unresolved differences.

Active knowledge

- Does your choice of leadership style allow you to follow these guidelines?
- Could you make any changes to improve the way you do things?
- If so, what would they be?

Decision-making

Decision-making is one of the core processes of working with a team and, to capitalise on opportunities, it's important you recognise there are different levels of participation in decision-making. Each level is appropriate at certain times and in certain situations. SMART leaders know which to go for.

Style	Situation
Level 1 – Tell (directive) You tell them what you have decided	When you are under pressure in a crisis situation or if you have the knowledge and expertise no one else has
Level 2 – Sell (input) You ask for input before making a decision. You listen to comments and then decide	When the team is unsure, this is a good time to 'sell' your decision to everyone else
Level 3 – Consult (dialogue) You discuss the issue fully before you decide. Everybody goes along with your decision	Team members have particular specialist knowledge or expertise to contribute
Level 4 – Participation (ownership, consensus) You reach a decision everyone buys into and takes responsibility for	If you're working on a complex or highly pressured project, you'll probably need the input of specialists
Level 5 – Delegate You ask them to decide. They take control	When the plan/project is too large or complex to manage on your own, or when you have good sub-leaders and specialists

Figure 8.15 Levels of decision-making

There are five well-known levels of decision-making, most of which are modelled after Tannenbaum, Schmidt and Zoll (see Figure 8.15). These are just guidelines to help you see when it might be appropriate to use a *different* style. You have to judge and know your team well enough to know which is appropriate at which times.

Active knowledge

Read these two situations and decide which leadership style might work best. Give your reasons.

1 A call-handling team in a dedicated call-handling centre. The team is large, newly formed and inexperienced. Staff turnover is high. The centre manages calls from four different mail-order companies.
2 The three-person customer service team for a specialist book-publishing company. The team have worked together for five years and each member has a high level of product knowledge.

How to encourage team members to work together

Working together inevitably means holding meetings and, once you've determined that a meeting is the most effective way of dealing with the issues in hand, you need to examine the value and limitations of meetings as a way of exchanging information and making decisions.

Managing meetings

Good meetings don't just happen: they have to be worked at. You need to use a number of strategies to make sure you make the best use of this investment of your team's time. You need, for example, to schedule milestone meetings to review your progress and future actions, and you also need to schedule meetings to communicate information, to solve problems and to make decisions.

You will need meetings to help you with your hard criteria and these are, in the main, straightforward meetings to organise, but you should also remember that you can arrange meetings for other purposes as well (see Figure 8.16).

There are a number of basic rules to abide by if you and your team are going to work well together. You can, however, do a lot before a meeting to make sure it's a success:

1 *Preparation* Circulate an agenda (see Figure 8.17) and relevant papers well in advance so team members have time to read them and prepare a response. They, in turn, should do some preparation and have noted the main points they want to discuss.
2 *Objectives* Think about what you want from the meeting before it starts. Encourage everyone to put his or her objectives on the table as the meeting starts and, if necessary, amend the agenda as a result of this process. Make sure everyone is quite clear why he or she is there.

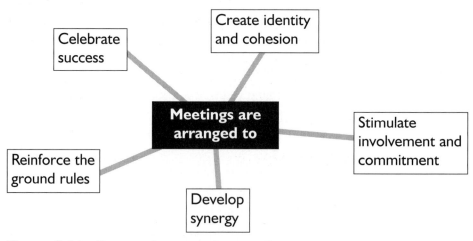

Figure 8.16 Reasons for arranging meetings

3 *Agenda management* To achieve the most you can in the time you have available, once you have agreed on the objectives, structure the time to make sure you have allocated sufficient space for each issue.

Active knowledge

- What procedures do you have to prepare for meetings?
- How long before the meeting do you circulate the agenda?
- Do you allocate specific times for agenda items?

Review of Customer Feedback Meeting	10/05/01 9:55 AM to 11:55 AM Room 101 Head Office Building

Meeting called by:	Customer Services Dept	Type of meeting: Fully Minuted
Facilitator:	Customer Services Manager	Note taker: Department Administrator
Timekeeper:	Department Administrator	

Attendees:	CS Manager; Administrator; Area Reps
Please read:	Previous minutes, Recent Board Report
Please bring:	Area CS Feedback Information

Agenda

1.	Matters Arising from previous Meeting	Chair	10
2.	Feedback Information from South-East	London representative	5
3.	Feedback Information from South-West	Bristol representative	5
4.	Feedback Information from North-East	Leeds representative	5
5.	Feedback Information from North-West	Manchester representative	5
6.	Feedback Information from Scotland	Glasgow representative	5
7.	Feedback Information from Wales	Cardiff representative	5
8.	Response to Feedback Information	Customer Services Manager	20
9.	Quality Issues Arising	All members	15
10.	Identification of Revised Targets	Chair	20
11.	Resource Implications	All members	20
12.	Any Other Urgent Business	Chair	5

Additional Information

Observers: Finance Dept Rep for Revised Targets item
Resources required: Laptop, Projector & Screen
Special notes: Lunch provided after meeting

Figure 8.17 An example of a good agenda

Once the meeting has started, there are various techniques you can use to make sure everyone's time is well used (see Figure 8.18).

Dealing with conflict

You are bound to encounter conflict in your meetings from time to time. Look on this as an opportunity to reach a constructive understanding amongst the team members. Figure 8.19 gives some examples of how you can overcome conflict.

Review and react

At the end of every meeting, spend some time with the team members reviewing how the meeting went. Check the hard criteria to see they have been covered fully. Equally importantly, however, review your soft criteria (such as your ground rules) to make sure they are still appropriate and working properly.

Remember

Make sure you allow adequate time for this activity in your agenda.

Always summarise the actions that have been agreed, identify the individuals responsible for these actions and agree a deadline for completion. Decide on the date of the next meeting and circulate the minutes or summary as soon as possible.

✓ *Communication and understanding* Make sure that two-way communication is happening between all members of the team (see Unit 2).

✓ *Stay focused* Do not allow meetings to wander off the subject. You may find that while discussing one agenda item the discussion moves on to another. You can overcome this by making sure you summarise each agenda item and agree action points as a conclusion (see the final point below).

✓ *Encourage participation* Encourage the active participation of all team members during the meeting. Make a particular point of asking reticent members for their views and opinions if necessary.

✓ *Check for agreement* Make sure you get a positive declaration of agreement when you ask for commitment from the meeting – don't take silence as meaning assent. This is particularly important if you need widespread commitment from all team members.

Figure 8.18 Managing time in a meeting effectively: a checklist

Arguments where members are not willing to contribute positively

✓ Stress the importance of working together.

✓ Ask the whole meeting to help.

✓ Point out the benefits of meeting as a team.

✓ Emphasise the importance of the agenda item.

People will not focus and are taking too long without getting to a solution

✓ Summarise the differences and agreements.

✓ Emphasise the deadlines and time limits.

✓ Arrange new tasks to overcome the differences.

✓ If necessary, defer the rest of the agenda to another meeting.

Team members are disruptive

✓ Listen to their concerns and deal with them or schedule them for the next meeting.

✓ Remind them of the agenda and meeting objectives.

✓ After the meeting arrange to remind them of the rules for your meetings and get their agreement to use them in future.

People do not participate

✓ Become more active and ask them more questions.

✓ For the next meeting, assign agenda items to individual team members.

✓ Encourage presenters to use more visual aids.

People do not follow up on agreed actions

✓ Ask for reasons and listen carefully to the answers.

✓ Emphasise the importance of teamwork and deadlines.

✓ Remind them that agreement is always sought when identifying actions.

✓ Reset or reallocate the actions.

People become confrontational

✓ Do not respond to the confrontation.

✓ Listen without commenting.

✓ Express understanding for the issues.

✓ Remind the whole meeting everyone is always learning new skills.

✓ Promise to address the issues.

Figure 8.19 Overcoming conflict in a meeting: a checklist

Active knowledge

You are chairing a meeting that looks as if it will run badly over time and fail to reach any agreement. Two senior staff members are dominating the discussion but are talking about inconsequential aspects of the meeting business and are not concentrating on the agenda items at all. In response to this, two other members of the meeting have withdrawn entirely from participating in the discussions and are visibly upset at what they regard as time wasting. Another member is angrily arguing against each and every point that is being made by the two dominant members. The remaining members of the meeting are bemused by events but make no attempt to help rectify matters. You need to get this meeting back on track and produce results, whilst ensuring that everyone remains at the meeting – what do you do?

How to check that team members understand what they are required to do

When you are checking your team understands what it has to do, you need to have in mind the following:

- What do they expect from you as their team leader?
- What is the team's progress so far?
- Under what circumstances should you review progress?

What teams expect of their leaders

Whether a team leader is appointed by the organisation's management or elected from the team itself, the members of the team will have expectations about the leader's personal qualities and professional skills. In 1994, *Best Practice* magazine summed up seven years of surveys reporting the expectations of team members. Figure 8.20 summarises what team members expected their leaders to be.

> - Honest (87%)
> - Competent (74%)
> - Forward-looking (67%)
> - Inspiring (61%)
> - Intelligent (46%)
> - Fair-minded (42%)
> - Broad-minded (38%)
> - Courageous (35%)
> - Straightforward (33%)
> - Imaginative (32%)
> - Dependable (31%)

Figure 8.20 Team members' expectations of their leaders

Note that the highest ratings are given for telling the truth, knowing the business and anticipating change. These are the principles upon which you should base your *own* approach to reviewing progress and instituting change.

Active knowledge

Using the characteristics of good team leaders given in Figure 8.20, ask members of your team to rate these in the order of their preference. Check their combined responses against the percentages given in the figure. If there are significant discrepancies in the order of preference (not the actual percentages), can you explain why?

Review your team's progress

Reviewing your team's progress is invaluable because it gives you a chance to think about what has happened, how you've worked together and whether you could make any improvements in the future. Replaying experiences and looking back at them not only helps you to determine what progress you've made but can also help you to:

- identify the strengths of individuals or the team itself
- recognise the weaknesses of individuals in the team, which can lead to developing plans to improve performance
- improve quality and build confidence
- look at priorities and how these compare to what you are actually doing
- ask yourself the important question 'why are we doing this?' so you can put things into the bigger picture.

Team reviews, therefore, may be used for a number of different reasons (see Figure 8.21).

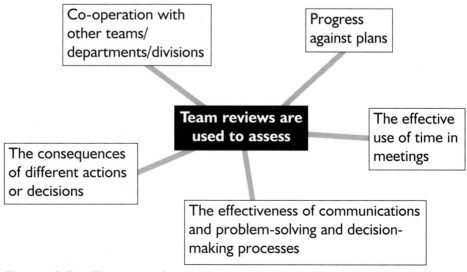

Figure 8.21 The uses of team reviews

As you can see, there are lots of opportunities to apply review techniques to improve your own and your team's performance. There are four main areas to focus on (see Figure 8.22).

Remember

Don't forget the information given earlier in this element on planning cycles. Your review process is only part of your planning cycle.

Timing your review

Don't assume that the only time for review is at the end of a project. Reviews can take place at different times: at the start of a project,

> ✓ *Task* Focus on the specific objectives for your team. Establish whether your tasks have been completed or how far from completion you are.
>
> ✓ *Content* Focus on the specific learning, knowledge or principles that can be drawn from the project. Note what works and what doesn't and how these might be applied next time.
>
> ✓ *Process* Pay attention to the attitudes, behaviours and dynamics of the team and of individual contributions. The purpose of this is to raise awareness of these issues and to improve relationships that may be interfering with performance.
>
> ✓ *Application* Look at future actions and ways forward. You may be setting new targets or objectives and deciding who is responsible and accountable for them.

Figure 8.22 Review techniques to improve team performance

```
┌─────────────────────────────────────────┐
│            At the start                   │
│ Gives you the opportunity to apply        │
│ learning and conclusions from earlier     │
│ activities and/or to focus on what you    │
│ want to achieve. Basically it focuses on  │
│ the planning phase of an activity.        │
└─────────────────────────────────────────┘
                    │
                    ▼
┌─────────────────────────────────────────┐
│          At regular intervals             │
│ Used at pre-planned times or at fixed     │
│ milestones. It gives the team the         │
│ opportunity to stand back and check on    │
│ progress.                                 │
└─────────────────────────────────────────┘
                    │
                    ▼
┌─────────────────────────────────────────┐
│            Spontaneously                  │
│ When you're just not sure if things are   │
│ right or not and you need to stop the     │
│ action to check it.                       │
└─────────────────────────────────────────┘
                    │
                    ▼
┌─────────────────────────────────────────┐
│            On completion                  │
│ This is an opportunity to reflect on the  │
│ outcome of the work you've just done and  │
│ what helped or hindered its progress. It's│
│ also a good time to summarise and to plan │
│ for improvement.                          │
└─────────────────────────────────────────┘
```

Figure 8.23 Timing the reviews

periodically or at regular intervals, spontaneously (but, hopefully, not in a panic) or on the completion of the project (see Figure 8.23).

Supporting your team

Supporting your team will take various forms, many of which will be difficult to anticipate. The are three areas you should concentrate on and prepare for:

1 solving problems
2 training and coaching
3 setting up a 'safe' environment for taking risks.

Solving problems

You should help your team members to solve their *own* problems so you do not have to solve problems for them. Figure 8.24 gives a checklist of how you can do this.

> ✓ *Identify the problem* What is the problem? What is causing it? If the problem were solved, what would happen? What are we trying to achieve?
>
> ✓ *Generate initial alternative solutions* What are the possible alternative solutions? If we had no restraints, what would we do?
>
> ✓ *Establish the criteria for successful solutions* What SMART criteria must the solution meet?
>
> ✓ *Decide on a solution that best fits these criteria* How does each alternative fit against the SMART criteria?
>
> ✓ *Take action with your chosen solution* Who needs to do what? What needs to be done by when?
>
> ✓ *Evaluate your solution* How effective was the solution to the problem? Will it suffice in the future?

Figure 8.24 Solving problems: a checklist

Active knowledge

Think of a situation when you had to solve a problem with members of your team. Did you use a structured problem-solving approach? Write up a case study (using the headings given in Figure 8.24) to demonstrate how the decision was made and evaluated.

Training and coaching

You may need to bring your team members up to speed not only in their technical skills but also in a broad range of interpersonal skills, abilities and attitudes. There are three particular areas of teamwork training/coaching you may need to concentrate on (coaching is covered in deail in Unit 6).

1 Acquiring new administrative responsibilities

Your team members will probably have little experience in dealing with the administrative aspects of their work (matters such as budgets, staffing and performance evaluation are often considered to be the team leader's responsibility). You may, therefore, have to teach your team members not only how to stay within a budget but also how to create one, how to negotiate for resources, how to recruit and select colleagues and how to monitor their performance.

Active knowledge

For some of the examples just noted, you may need to set up a training programme to address the necessary shortfalls. Choose one particular area and write down what training you would implement to make your team competent in this area.

Diversity is a positive aspect of teamwork

2 Setting targets for themselves and for the team

Employees have traditionally been trained to take direction from the team leader, not to act on their own. Even if people have already had some experience of teams, they may still know only a little about establishing goals and devising mission statements. If this is the case, you will have to change your team members' assumptions about the nature of their work.

Remember

Your targets and goals should be SMART.

Active knowledge

How can you train your team members to set SMART targets? What sort of coaching sessions would you need to devise to achieve this?

3 Utilising the talents of other team members

Most people like to work with colleagues they know in work everyone understands, but new technology (in particular) may bring together team members who have no concept of what some of their colleagues are doing. You must convince team members that diversity is a *positive* aspect of teamwork. By making all team members aware of the contributions all the other team members can make, you will enable them to appreciate the 'big picture' and how exactly everyone fits in to this.

Active knowledge

How could you arrange for your team members to shadow or at least spend some time with others to observe them in their roles?

Set up a 'safe' environment for taking risks

We emphasised in Element 8.1 that a team leader should never contemplate failure. It is unlikely, however, that all the members of your team will be able to adopt the same ultra-positive approach. To combat this feeling of insecurity, you need to ensure a safe environment that allows for the possibility of failure (and the learning that comes from it), as well as for a degree of risk-taking.

Team members who have been empowered to use their own judgement in decision-making must be allowed to survive the results of those decisions, good or bad. No one is guaranteed to be successful every time, and team members must be reassured that their high-risk efforts are supported by you and by the organisation as a whole.

However, if your organisation has a culture of 'time is money' and approves only of traditionally structured working days, you may need to set aside a certain breathing space to coach staff to take risks and to make their own decisions.

Active knowledge

How can you make sure your team can take decisions in a blame-free environment?

Consolidation

It is time for your annual review and this year you have been asked to concentrate on your leadership style and successes. Your review starts with a detailed self-assessment on these issues. Prepare this self-assessment, including detailed examples to support your claims. Give examples of your leadership style in normal circumstances and of the techniques you have used in making decisions. Show how you have encouraged people to work together and how you have checked that they understood what they were supposed to do. Include in your self-assessment details of any team review that you may have undertaken for whatever reason.

- How to evaluate the performance of teams and individuals.
- How to provide sensitive feedback.
- How to encourage team members to discuss their performance.
- How to introduce improvements and change.

How to evaluate the performance of teams and individuals

As we saw in the previous element, teams that perform well often review their performance and provide feedback to one another and the team as a whole. They congratulate themselves on their successes and treat failures as opportunities for improvement. Individual members actively seek feedback, accept it positively and provide feedback to others in non-threatening ways.

Fair performance review procedures

It is important your review procedures are seen to be fair, and you need to decide the basis for your performance review system. Ask yourself the following questions:

- Will team members evaluate one another?
- Will the success or failure of the team's efforts determine the performance evaluations of all its members?
- Will the team leader (i.e. *you*) try to evaluate the work of each individual team member independently?

You should consider the following four approaches to developing fair performance evaluation procedures.

Team objectives

Use this method of evaluation to negotiate agreed-upon goals with the team as a whole. Team members understand that they swim or sink together. Becoming a member of the team means, in this case, linking your evaluation to the performance of *all* team members.

Team consensus

Ask the team to come up with its own ways of evaluating the performance of its members (some teams may assign this responsibility to the team leader). Other teams use a consensus or voting system to give their members 'exceptional,' 'good,' 'adequate' and 'inadequate' ratings.

Self-evaluation

Team members can be asked to write up a self-evaluation of their work, perhaps following categories provided on a standard evaluation form (see below). Under this system, members must usually give specific examples of their contributions to support their assertions.

External evaluator

An evaluator from outside the team can conduct performance evaluations by confidential interviews with individual team members. Under this method, team members meet one at a time with an evaluator to discuss not only their own work but also that of others. After talking to all the members, the evaluator has a good general picture of who did what in the team.

You will have to decide with your team what *attributes* you will use when appraising individual performance. Figure 8.25 shows some of the more traditional attributes that are often appraised under performance review systems. However, only you, your organisation and your team can decide on which characteristics will provide a fair basis for reviewing performance.

Having decided on which qualities you will use, you need to decide on the *method* you are going to use. This can be very complex indeed, but two simpler methods are as follows. Using a system of *rating scales,* each person is rated as 'exceptional', 'good', 'average', 'unsatisfactory', etc., for each of the attributes. A *forced distribution* method is often used in larger departments. Team leaders must rank team members in order, with 10% of the names in the highest box, 20% in the next highest, 40% in the middle, 20% in the next lowest and 10% in the lowest. This exercise is repeated for each attribute.

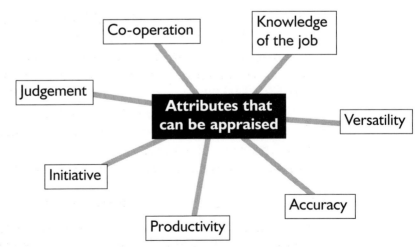

Figure 8.25 Team members' attributes that can be appraised

Beyond these formal evaluation procedures, your team must develop mechanisms for obtaining frequent feedback:

- Who will deliver praise or blame to the team, and on what evidence?
- To whom should the team turn for advice and guidance?
- How are these sources of feedback linked to the formal performance evaluation system?

Some organisations have resolved the feedback dilemma by having teams report regularly on their work to the organisation's senior management. This is often known as a 'no surprises' system of evaluation.

Active knowledge

Have you a performance appraisal system you use? Try using the simplest system (the rating scales above), with a few of the attributes suggested, on some members of your team:

- Does it work well for you as team leader?
- Could you use it with each team member rating every other member?
- Could you use it for self-ev`luation?

Confidentiality: who should receive which pieces of information

The effectiveness of your feedback to team members could be severely compromised if you have not agreed and made clear to everyone just who will retain the information and who will have access to it. While few people would object to information on their successes being made known to a wider audience, practically no one would be happy to allow information on his or her failures to receive the same publicity.

The most fundamental principle of information retention is that the person to whom the information refers must have ready access to it. If you work in an organisation large enough to have a human resources or personnel department, these people will have guidelines they could give you on the confidentiality of documents. If you do not have access to such resources, you need to agree the guidelines with your management, team and staff. There is also a growing number of statutes that govern the way in which we hold information on people (see Unit 1, Element 1.3).

How to provide sensitive feedback

Teams expect their leaders to have honesty, competence and forward-thinking. You will, therefore, always be expected to give honest direct feedback to another person, especially when the other person's behaviour is inappropriate to the situation.

Remember

It is equally important to give positive feedback when praise is due.

Basic principles of giving feedback

Feedback is not something everyone likes because often it feels like negative remarks wrapped up in a positive way; but quality feedback doesn't have to be a difficult experience. To produce quality feedback, you must follow some of the well rehearsed principles of giving feedback.

Keys to good practice

Giving feedback

✓ Comment on the behaviour, not the person.

✓ Be specific and unambiguous in your comments.

✓ Give feedback that is non-judgmental about the other person. The feedback should simply concern behaviour that affects you.

✓ Take responsibility for your thoughts, feelings and opinions by making 'I' statements (rather than 'you' statements, which implicitly blame the other person).

✓ Speak directly to the other person (rather than talking about him or her to others).

✓ Conclude by telling the other person the behaviour you would prefer.

For example, you are giving someone feedback about problems with his or her communication style: 'I was concerned that a couple of times during our last meeting you interrupted me mid-sentence.' Not: 'You don't know how to listen, are rude when you interrupt people and you have no manners.' The latter is insulting and you can see why someone wouldn't want to get that kind of feedback. The former focuses on specific behaviour and on something the person may not be aware he or she is doing.

You might similarly start your comments to a member of your team like this:

Quality feedback doesn't have to be a difficult experience

'I need to talk to you about the way you spoke to your last customer. On that occasion I thought you sounded aggressive when he complained about the time it had taken to serve him. I believe your response annoyed the customer and he left the company disappointed with our service. Next time I would like you to take a few moments before you launch into disputing with the customer and remember the training we used which set out our procedures in these circumstances …'

(You would then repeat your procedures for dealing with angry customers.)

Following these principles will certainly mean your feedback is likely to be fair and accurate. To make sure your feedback is effective, you need to manage the timing and the environment so your comments are properly received.

Encouraging the recipient of your feedback to check it with other people is important. It means that, while you can give someone feedback, in the end it's your particular perception of the situation, and it would be useful for the person receiving the feedback to check if other people see the same thing. Once you start hearing a number of people telling you the same thing, it becomes harder to ignore.

Keys to good practice

Giving feedback: at the right time and in the right place

✓ Make it clear your intention is to be helpful.

✓ Meeting on a one-to-one basis is best unless the recipient requests otherwise.

✓ If someone hasn't asked for feedback, first check to be sure he or she is open to receiving it.

✓ Time your meeting correctly. For example, if it's over a heated issue, don't do it 'in the heat of the moment'; give everyone time to cool down and think things out.

✓ At the end of the meeting, check to be sure the recipient understood your feedback in the way you intended it.

✓ Encourage the recipient to check the feedback with other people.

Active knowledge

Try this role play in pairs. A is the team manager, B is the team worker. B has just had a very rude and unreasonable customer on the phone. After listening for several minutes, B loses patience and says to the customer: 'If you could just be quiet for a minute and listen, then I could explain.' A overhears B and decides to give feedback. B still feels the answer he or she gave the customer was justified.

Evaluate your role play:

• Did it work well?

• Did B feel the feedback was positive?

Receiving feedback

When you are receiving feedback from others, whether criticism or praise, do not let your feelings get in the way of using the important information that is being offered you.

One final point. It can be useful at times to have an independent and objective person in a feedback session. If you feel the need for this, you must agree it with the recipient beforehand and you must ensure the chosen person is seen to be independent by both parties.

Keys to good practice

Receiving feedback

- Listen without commenting until the other person has finished speaking – don't interrupt. You will have time to give an explanation or a defence later in the meeting.

- Ask for comments on your behaviour rather than on your personality.

- If the feedback is too generalised for you to be able to comment, ask the speaker to be more specific: 'What exactly was it about my approach to the situation which you liked/disliked?'

- If the feedback is personalised or aggressive, do not immediately become defensive. Express your feelings by saying: 'I felt angry/upset/confused when you said that.'

- Do not accept criticism without justifying it first. Look for feedback from a number of people. If you find a consistent theme then you may accept it. Take responsibility for aspects of the feedback you will act on – it is your decision how you will change your behaviour.

- Ask the speaker how he or she would expect you to behave in the future.

- Accept compliments positively – be aware of your own strengths.

The importance of agreeing a course of action

You will, of course, waste all your efforts in preparing and delivering feedback if you fail to agree a course of action resulting from your meeting. The whole principle of success stemming from constructive feedback is based on things happening as a result of the discussion. Remember the planning cycle we introduced earlier in this unit? Feedback is a reflective part of this cycle.

Agreeing a course of action is also essential because it demands you deal not only with an immediate problem but also with the underlying causes. If problems come back to haunt you again and again, you can agree procedures that prevent them from re-emerging.

Not agreeing a course of action merely silences the argument and gets the team back to work while underlying issues remain unresolved. In contrast, action plan strategies solve the immediate problem and deal with the underlying issues through effective feedback. As a result, the team can get back to work without standing guard over the (possibly nasty) interaction between the two members.

Evaluating the effectiveness of your actions is vital. You know a review has been effective when it fulfils the *purpose* of reviewing and you can:

- observe new behaviour in the people involved and
- see learning put into action.

Active knowledge

Note down a personal example of when you used review feedback to ensure some action was taken:

- Did you observe new behaviour from the person involved?
- What learning took place as a result?

How to encourage team members to discuss their performance

To encourage team members to discuss their performance, you will have to introduce some means of *measuring* their performance. But first, however, you will have to decide *what* to measure. The obvious choice is to track your progress against your business targets, but you may also choose to look at shorter-term objectives, such as the introduction of new procedures. Don't make the mistake of waiting until the end of a year to go through this process because it may be very discouraging for team members to find that misunderstandings have existed for all that time.

Keys to good practice

Measuring performance

✓ Introduce an agreed means of measuring performance.

✓ Make sure you are measuring the right things, simply and regularly.

✓ Involve everyone, make your findings understandable, and publish them.

✓ Discuss and evaluate your findings and take action on them.

✓ Recognise your team's successes.

Introduce an agreed means of measuring team performance

Begin with something simple or something internal to the team. For example, start with a 10-item point-of-service survey rather than in-depth interviews with 20 critical customers. Keep your means of measurement straightforward; it is a means to an end not an end in itself.

A team success survey is an example of a tool that incorporates a breadth of information in one survey (see Figure 8.26). Depending on the needs of the team, other tools may focus on just one aspect of the team's success.

TEAM SUCCESS SURVEY

Name:.. Team:.. Date:................................

Please circle the number on each scale you feel is most descriptive of your view, as it relates to each item.

1 Clearly states its mission and goals

| 1 | 2 | 3 | 4 | 5 | 6 | 7 |

Activities demonstrate a lack of understanding of goals

Activities demonstrate a clear focus and understanding of goals

2 Operates creatively

| 1 | 2 | 3 | 4 | 5 | 6 | 7 |

Unwilling to experiment with new ideas

Team takes on new ideas and demonstrates a creative approach

3 Focuses on results

| 1 | 2 | 3 | 4 | 5 | 6 | 7 |

Does not reach objectives on budget, schedule or quality

Accomplishes objectives within budget, on schedule/quality

4 Clarifies roles and responsibilities

| 1 | 2 | 3 | 4 | 5 | 6 | 7 |

Roles and responsibilities are uncertain

Each team member understands what is expected of him or her

5 Is well organised

| 1 | 2 | 3 | 4 | 5 | 6 | 7 |

Structure and procedures are disorganised

Structure and procedures supported by team members

6 Builds upon individual strengths

| 1 | 2 | 3 | 4 | 5 | 6 | 7 |

Knowledge, skills and talents of members under-utilised

Knowledge, skills and talents of members put to good use

7 Supports leadership and each other

| 1 | 2 | 3 | 4 | 5 | 6 | 7 |

Leadership role always in the hands of one or two people

Leadership role shared among team members

8 Develops team climate

| 1 | 2 | 3 | 4 | 5 | 6 | 7 |

Team feel they would be better off working individually

Team works with energy, involvement and team spirit

9 Resolves disagreements

| 1 | 2 | 3 | 4 | 5 | 6 | 7 |

Disagreements interfere with productive work

Members deal openly and constructively with disagreement

Figure 8.26 A team success survey

10 Communicates openly

| 1 | 2 | 3 | 4 | 5 | 6 | 7 |

Day-to-day communication is limited and guarded

Communication is frequent, honest and direct

11 Makes objective decisions

| 1 | 2 | 3 | 4 | 5 | 6 | 7 |

Someone solves problems and makes decisions for the team

Team identifies and solves own problems through consensus

12 Evaluates its own effectiveness

| 1 | 2 | 3 | 4 | 5 | 6 | 7 |

Team does not evaluate its own effectiveness

Team continuously evaluates effectiveness and performance

Figure 8.26 (Continued)

Active knowledge

Use the team success questionnaire with your team:

• Did you find it relevant and/or useful?

• What lessons have you learnt from using the questionnaire?

• How might you use the questionnaire to set or review targets?

Measure the right things simply and regularly

You need to know both where you're going and how you're going to get there. The right things to measure are the milestones and results that deal with your team's business objective.

One way of doing this is to use a meeting effectiveness questionnaire after the meeting (see Figure 8.27). Comment on improvements and changes in meeting productivity at *every* meeting. Merely asking members to complete the questionnaire once every six months would not result in more effective team meetings.

Active knowledge

Use this meeting effectiveness questionnaire with your team:

• Did you find it relevant and/or useful?

• What lessons have you learnt from using the questionnaire?

• Will those lessons change if you use the questionnaire several times?

Ultimately, you could set up an agreement with your team that might include the following items.

• What you are measuring (i.e. tracking business goals, improving effectiveness and motivation or evaluating performance).

MEETING EFFECTIVENESS SURVEY

Name:.. Team:.. Date:..............................

Please circle the number on each scale you feel is most descriptive of your view, as it relates to each item.

1 Did participants receive sufficient notice to prepare for this meeting?

0	1	2
No time	Some time	Sufficient time

2 Did the meeting notice include the purpose and objectives of the meeting?

0	1	2
Not indicated	Stated but unclear	Clearly stated

3 Did the meeting begin within three minutes of its scheduled start time?

0	1	2
No	Yes, but we had to re-start for late arrivals	Yes

4 Was an agenda prepared in advance or developed at the start of the meeting?

0	1	2
No agenda or objectives	Vague agenda and objectives	Specific agenda and clear objectives

5 At the beginning of the meeting, were the agenda or objectives reviewed by the meeting leader?

0	1	2
No	Yes, but not covered adequately	Yes

6 Were participants prepared for this meeting?

0	1	2
Not at all prepared	Somewhat prepared	As prepared as possible

7 Were action items and responsibilities clearly defined and summarised?

0	1	2
Not at all	Some were, others not	Yes

8 I would rate the quality of the group's interaction and member participation as:

0	1	2
Having very little value	Fair	Very good/effective contribution

9 Did the meeting follow the agenda and achieve its intended purpose?

0	1	2
Did not follow agenda	Followed agenda somewhat	Followed agenda productively

10 Did the meeting end on time, or sooner if business was completed?

0	1	2
No	No, but within a reasonable time frame	Yes

11 Overall, how did you feel about your investment of time in this meeting?

0	1	2
Not at all satisfied/frustrated	Somewhat satisfied	Completely satisfied/good use of my time

Figure 8.27 A meeting effectiveness survey

- How often you are going to measure (e.g. daily, weekly, monthly or yearly).
- What tools you are going to use (e.g. survey, existing data, observation, interviews, etc.).
- What questions you will ask in the survey, interview or observation.
- What administrative details are needed (confidentiality, scoring, distribution of results, etc.).
- How you are going to review the data to study the results, note improvements, analyse the causes of performance shortfalls and take corrective action.

Members need to reach consensus on the measurement plan and be assured everyone on the team can live with the decisions.

Involve everyone, make your findings understandable, and publish them

The development, administration and interpretation of team surveys require a clear sense of purpose, some common sense, the ability to organise information and reasonably good communication skills. These skills exist in most teams, so involve everyone in your team in some way, however small.

Visual tools such as bar charts, summary tables, diagrams and pie charts are generally more effective than words alone. Figure 8.28 is an example taken from responses to questions 4-6 of the team success survey. But you could also show the same information diagrammatically (see Figure 8.29).

- What does this information tell you about questions 4-6?
- In your opinion, is this team functioning well?
- What future team development could be planned as result of these answers?

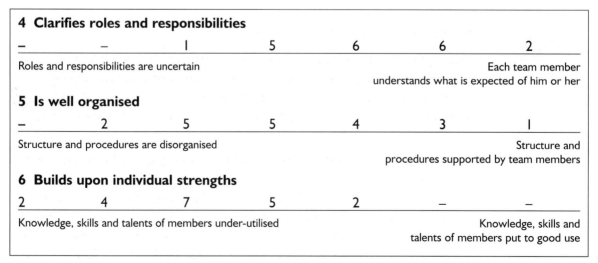

4 Clarifies roles and responsibilities						
–	–	1	5	6	6	2

Roles and responsibilities are uncertain — Each team member understands what is expected of him or her

5 Is well organised						
–	2	5	5	4	3	1

Structure and procedures are disorganised — Structure and procedures supported by team members

6 Builds upon individual strengths						
2	4	7	5	2	–	–

Knowledge, skills and talents of members under-utilised — Knowledge, skills and talents of members put to good use

Figure 8.28 Publishing your findings: the numbers

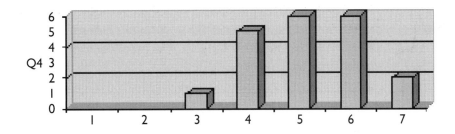

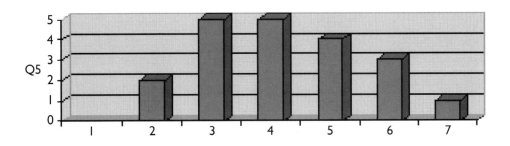

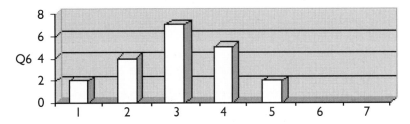

Figure 8.29 Publishing your findings: diagrammatically

• Which method of presenting this information (in numbers or in bar chart form) works best for you? Give your reasons.

Active knowledge

Use one of the surveys with your team. Produce the results in straightforward number format and also make charts of the same information. Which approach do the members of your team find easier to assimilate? If it is via the diagrams, are the results worth the extra effort?

Discuss and evaluate your findings and take action on them

It is often difficult for a team to evaluate its own work – even more to ask others to provide feedback about it. However, this evaluation becomes easier if you link it regularly to performance measurement information. When reviewing the results, discuss the purpose and use of the data. Take time to establish priorities, to define actions, to set time frames and to select assignments.

When something positive and constructive happens as a result of a performance survey, people notice. Action, especially improvement, helps people feel good about the measurement process and motivates them to continue it.

Key to good practice

Recognising team performance

Inside your team

✓ Free the team to establish its own work hours and patterns.

✓ Ask the team to coach a less successful team.

✓ Make available to the team new technology or other special resources not generally available in the workplace.

✓ Let team members know why they were chosen for the team and the high expectations top management has for the team's work.

From outside the team

✓ Compliment the work of the team in a report to top management.

✓ Invite a senior manager to attend a team meeting with the purpose of praising the team.

✓ Create social occasions where the team is honoured informally.

✓ Ask a newsletter writer in the organisation to write an article about the team's work.

✓ Seek out opportunities where your team can present aspects of its work to others in your industry.

✓ Nominate the team for competitions and awards within your industry.

Appraisal and pay

You will note that we have not discussed any aspect of financial rewards for your team. This subject is large and complex. If your organisation has a human resources or personnel department, they should be able to give you specialist advice on this topic. If you do not have such a department, the Chartered Institute of Personnel and Development is the key organisation for information in this field.

How to introduce improvements and change

Continuously improving customer service demands particular attitudes from all team members. Sometimes this means changes to systems and procedures. As a team leader, however, you should be aware of the need to manage the change and improvement process carefully and sensitively.

We all accept that some change is inevitable in most things, but we all have a natural resistance to change for some of the reasons shown in Figure 8.30.

Introducing change

So how do you, as team leader, organise improvements and, therefore, changes, to the way your team does things?

The 'big picture'

Provide the 'big picture' of the proposed changes and show how changes will fit in to the organisation as a whole. Communicate clearly what you propose to change by identifying the differences between the way things used to be done and the way they will be done as a result of the changes. If necessary, break the overall change into smaller digestible changes which can be introduced in a sequence, and allow time for information on the changes to be taken in before you start to implement them. Set out the benefits and the problems the changes may bring for the team and help your team understand the reasons for the changes.

Provide information

Make sure you provide information to your team members about the change before the effects are felt. Consult all those who will be affected and discuss the prospect of new roles, responsibilities and relationships. Involve your team members in planning for any anticipated changes. Survey them and ask for input at every stage. Listen to all the concerns and objections that are expressed and, wherever possible, let team members organise themselves in adapting for the change. Stay flexible on detail by providing guidelines which can be adjusted by the team.

Figure 8.30 People's natural resistance to change

New standards

If the changes demand new performance standards, set those new standards down before people have a chance to make mistakes. Set up coaching programmes so your team has every opportunity to be successful. Check you have the necessary resources and assistance and develop a method of monitoring the impact and effectiveness of the change.

Take practical steps to deal with reluctant team members

Remember

We mentioned earlier that team members expect their team leaders to be honest with them. When people in your team are affected negatively by change, you as team leader will need to remember this.

Help your team members in real, practical terms to adjust to the new arrangements. Sit down with them to understand their objections to the changes. If they have proposals that could be used as a compromise, take a careful and detailed look at them and, if necessary, set up a further meeting to give them a considered response.

If you are unable to agree any further compromise, look at alternative possibilities for the member of your team if he or she really can't cope with the new arrangements. Agree a short period during which he or she will give the new arrangements a try. At the end of that period arrange for further review and, in the interim, see if you can make any changes that will not impose on other members of the team. At this further meeting, agree with your team member whether he or she is now able to accept the changes, or whether he or she is still not able to accept them. If the team member is unable to do so, decide whether you have reached the level of your own responsibility and whether the matter now needs to be referred to your manager.

Don't just ignore the problem people and hope they will eventually leave. How you treat these people sends messages to other team members about what can expected from your organisation. If you let matters slide, the other members of your team will think that, in similar circumstances, they too will be ignored. They will all be asking the question – 'What's in it for me?'

Case study

With hard work and effort, a particular team introduced a whole set of new working procedures and received a special bonus. Later, they realised that one member of the five-person team performed very little actual work during the changeover and was not pulling his or her weight now. The team members grew increasingly resentful and the atmosphere in the team became quite intolerable. As time went on, the team's performance began to suffer.

1 Why do you think the team's performance began to suffer?
2 What should the team leader do?

Find out what support services exist inside or outside the organisation

Sometimes change can mean that some staff have no role in the new arrangements. In these circumstances, it is vitally important to utilise whatever other resources are available elsewhere in your organisation or outside. If your organisation is large, you will have a personnel or human resources department that employs specialists in this area. They may have redundancy and relocation policies that could help you deal with immediate issues.

If your organisation is too small to have this support, you can take a number of routes. If you have the necessary resources you could buy in help – the Chartered Institute of Personnel and Development (CIPD) has local branches throughout the UK and can recommend independent contractors. There are also a number of handbooks and guides that set out employers' and supervisors' responsibilities. The Library Service at CIPD can give you details of these handbooks.

You can also contact the Employment Service of the DFEE who have specialist advisers, or the Citizens Advice Bureau who will have a list of local contacts.

Consolidation

Your team is about to take on a significant new project that will severely test the skills and abilities of all its members. You need to guarantee your Senior Management that your team will be capable of meeting this new challenge. Unfortunately some members are unlikely to be able to meet the demands of the new project whilst others will need significant amounts of re-training. You will have to accept full personal responsibility for introducing the changes and dealing with those people who will not be part of the new team. Set out your detailed plans for the introduction of this project to your team.

Unfortunately, two members of your team who will not be going to the new project are very angry at this outcome, blaming you for lack of training in the past and threatening to take their case to the highest possible level. You have a good knowledge of their background and capabilities. What planning would you do before you meet them to resolve their complaints?

End-of-unit test

1 What are the four stages of team development? What do successful teams have in common? What are the two aspects of team leadership that apply in each type of team?

2 What do you expect has to be done to develop team-working skills?

3 What are the critical skills needed in order to be a good team leader?

4 What needs to be done to agree and set goals with team members?

5 What do you understand by the phrase 'Define success in hard and soft terms'?

6 How do you involve your team in your plans? Why are individual needs important when working in teams?

7 What considerations would you take into account when matching team tasks to personalities?

8 How do you use planning cycles to get feedback? How do you set up planning cycles?

9 What do you have to consider when you allocate work to others in order to gain their understanding and commitment?

10 What aspects do you have to consider in order to motivate team members and to raise their customer service performance?

11 What are the major aspects that you must consider when you need to influence the performance of fellow team members?

12 What are the seven necessary elements of good team leadership?

13 What are the various levels of decision making and under what situations are each most appropriate?

14 What strategies do you need to use in order to get the best use of time in your team meetings? How do you deal with any conflict that may arise?

15 What do teams expect of their leaders? How do you review your team's progress? How do you organise the timing of your review?

16 What areas of team training might you concentrate on and what aspects of each should you emphasise?

17 What are the basic principles of giving and receiving feedback? Why is it important to agree a course of action?

18 What are the keys to good practice when encouraging team members to discuss their performance?

19 What aspects would you have to consider if you wanted to introduce a means of measuring your team's performance? What would be on your checklist of good practice?

20 How do you, as the team leader, organise improvements, and therefore changes, to the way your team does things?

Useful addresses

Commission for Racial Equality
Elliot House
10-12 Allington Street
London
SW1E 5EH
www.cre.gov.uk

Copyright Licensing Agency
90 Tottenham Court Road
London
W1T 4LP
www.cla.co.uk

Customer Contact Point
Equal Opportunities Commission
Arndale House
Arndale Centre
Manchester
M4 3EQ
www.eoc.org.uk

Data Protection Commissioner
Wycliffe House
Water Lane
Wilmslow
Cheshire
SK9 5AF
www.dataprotection.gov.uk

DDA Information Line
FREEPOST MID02164
Stratford-upon-Avon
CV37 9BR
www.disability.gov.uk

DTI Enquiry Unit
1 Victoria Street
London
SW1H 0ET
www.dti.gov.uk

Health & Safety Executive
Health & Safety Laboratory
Broad Lane
Sheffield
S3 7HQ
www.hse.gov.uk

The Home Office
Human Rights Unit
50 Queen Anne's Gate
London SW1H 9AT
www.homeoffice.gov.uk

Institute of Customer Service
2 Castle Court
St Peter's Street
Colchester
CO1 1EW
www.ics-nto.com

The Office of Fair Trading
Fleetbank House
2-6 Salisbury Square
London
EC4Y 8JX
www.oft.gov.uk

Index